CAREER
RENEWAL

....

Tools for Scientists and
Technical Professionals

An expert is an addict.
>   —John Le Carre,
>   *The Russia House*

"Few ever see what is not already
  inside their heads."
>   —Susan Sontag
>   *The Volcano Lover*

"I cannot, said the fool
  and that is why he could not."
>   —Proverb

In my room, the world is
  beyond my understanding;
But when I walk I see that it
  consists of three or four hills
    and a cloud.
>   —Wallace Stevens
>   *Of the Surface of Things*

"I've got all the money I'll ever need
  if I die by four o'clock today."
>   —Henny Youngman

CAREER RENEWAL

....

Tools for Scientists and
Technical Professionals

Stephen Rosen
and Celia Paul

ACADEMIC PRESS

San Diego   London   Boston   New York   Sydney   Tokyo   Toronto

Cover image:
M. C. Escher's "Sky and Water I" © 1997 Cordon Art-Baarn-Holland. All rights reserved.

This book is printed on acid-free paper. ∞

ACADEMIC PRESS
525 B St. Suite 1900, San Diego, California 92101-4495, USA
1300 Boylston Street, Chestnut Hill, MA 02167, USA
http://www.apnet.com

Academic Press Limited
24–28 Oval Road, London NW1 7DX, UK
http://www.hbuk.co.uk/ap/

Library of Congress Cataloging-in-Publication Data
Rosen, Stephen
    Career renewal : tools for scientists and technical professionals / Stephen Rosen and Celia Paul.
        p.   cm.
    Includes bibliographical references and index.
    ISBN 0-12-597060-9 (alk. paper)
    1. Scientists—Vocational guidance—United States—Handbooks, manuals, etc.
    2. Engineers—Vocational guidance—United States—Handbooks, manuals, etc.
    I. Paul, Celia. II. Title.
    Q149.U5R67   1997
001′.02373—dc21   97-29068
                                                                        CIP

Printed in the United States of America
98 99 00 01 00   IP   9 8 7 6 5 4 3 2

CONTENTS

....

PREFACE

....

OUR PURPOSE AND INTENDED AUDIENCE

This book is intended to serve the career-choice and job-search needs of advanced undergraduates, graduate students, postdocs, "post-postdocs," "ex-postdocs," professionals who need guidance in determining their career directions, and individuals suffering career dissatisfaction or regret.

Is This Book for You?

Our primary target audiences are science and engineering professionals, holders of advanced degrees, and graduate students in behavioral and social sciences; biological, medical, health-care, and life sciences; chemistry; ecology and environmental sciences; mathematics; and physical sciences, as well as all technical and engineering specialties, such as mechanical, electrical/electronic, civil, architectural, computer, and software engineering. A number of attorneys have also found our career methods useful.

What's Inside?

Among the key features of this book, and their benefits to you, are:

1. A "Career Well-Being Inventory," based on the career strategies of "career-transition champions," that measures (a) your readiness to change jobs or careers and (b) progressive improvement in your ability to do so before and after trying the book's "career calisthenics."

2. First-person and case-history vignettes of real scientists, engineers, and physicians who morphed into new satisfying and successful careers (both within and outside of their original specialties). This allows you to see what career-transition practices worked (and what didn't) so that you can "cut to the chase"!

3. Career exercises, questionnaires, inventories, and "calisthenics", designed to boost your "career-transition ability," your career fitness, your career resilience, and your readiness to morph careers

4. Tips on how to present and market yourself in new career directions—with integrity, dignity, and wisdom! This feature helps you build or restore your self-confidence and renews your energy and optimism (which most employers look for!) in job interviews, even if they are KGB-type interrogations.

5. Systematic and complete tools to assess who you are—your favored skills, basic values, keenest interests, and fullest career preferences. This paves the way for you to explore and pursue a wide range of career options fully appropriate to "who you are."

6. Logical (no-psychobabble, no-nonsense) strategies—field- and battle-tested by actual scientists, engineers, and physicians—presented step by knowledgeable step. These tried-and-true techniques are tailor-made for technical professionals, holders of advanced degrees, and preprofessionals.

7. Your "Declaration of Career Independence" helps you to convert any past unproductive career-decision-making patterns into win-win career choices, strategies, and goals—what we call "theories of career victory."

How to Use This Book

This book may be used as a self-directed guide, or to supplement the career counseling group process, to accompany individual counseling, and to teach career-versatility planning to human resource and outplacement professionals dealing with credentialed professional populations. As Tobias, Chubin, and Aylesworth[1] point out, "Nowadays mentors must also be willing to chart a course for their charges even if there is no accurate road map." This book is designed to chart courses, provide road maps (and spare tires), and supply compasses to navigate necessary career transitions.

Redefining Yourself

You are about to embark on an exciting and challenging process—that of redefining yourself and changing your job or career. Perhaps how you can redefine and renew yourself is unclear to you now, but this is precisely the purpose of this book. You will discover that you have significant career assets and personal resources that you can draw upon in making your career transition (please see chapter 1, "Career Transformations").

But how have you managed your career up until now?

1. Did you watch things happen?
2. Did you make things happen?
3. Did you wonder what happened?

Ideal Outcomes

The ideal outcome of your career-management process (whether self-guided, directed, or a combination) is for you to look backward from a soon-to-be-present vantage point of a satisfying, fulfilling career choice and feel that your career choice was "inevitable." In retrospect, of course, this is easier said than done. The issue is: From the vantage point of a less-than-ideal present, looking forward, what do you do now to approximate or create such an ideal outcome?

Our Central Message

Our central message in this book is that you can measure and improve your "career well-being," just as you can measure and improve your personal health. Health is a condition of soundness or well-being and efficient functioning. Career health involves your career elasticity, your buoyancy, your latent powers of recovery, and your resilience in the face of your need or willingness to change.

THE BOOK'S ORIGINS

This book originated in reflections upon some disturbing statistics and trends concerning the career problems of scientists (see Chapter 1). It draws upon our close observations of career changers and career regretters: It includes career-transition narratives and case-study materials culled from our Scientific Career Transition Program alumni and others, woven into the text as techniques and examples of the program's most effective methods. Some "career-transition champions" have executed remarkable career transitions by drawing upon their impressive personal resources.

As a Yiddish folk saying states, "for example" is not proof, but enough practical techniques can be useful, and examples can be persuasive.

Occupational Mobility Lubricates the Economy

Over the next few years, some 12 million adults will change occupations *each year*. The U.S. Department of Labor[2] estimates that the overall career mobility rate for all ages is about 10 percent per year.

Turnover rates may be higher than average among those in the physical, mathematical, engineering, computer, social and behavioral, and economic sciences and the mechanical/electrical/electronic/civil engineering fields who are young or in mid-career. People with advanced degrees are in oversupply in a dwindling market for their services.[3]

We believe that portions of the U.S. education and training of Ph.D.s is outdated and fails to prepare them for flexible and full participation in a fluid economy, the scientific enterprise, and the technology marketplace of the 1990's.

The lengthy gestation periods for the production of science and engineering Ph.D.s are incompatible with planning—and thus inherently unresponsive to—the short, rapidly changing cycles of supply and demand for technical labor in the U.S. economy.

Doctoral Surplus, Confusion, and Ill-Preparedness

Advanced education gives new degree holders little or no preparation for the job market inside and outside their technical specialty, and especially outside the academia. "Versatility" in careers and doctoral education has been recommended[4] as a worthy goal, but no one seems able to evaluate or measure it. Consequently, many holders of Ph.D. degrees find themselves ill-prepared to face the current and near-term job market even in their own specialty, and this and other circumstances force many to ponder the job market outside their specialty (and the academia), without the know-how that might make a difference.

"Supply and demand do not work in the usual way to regulate the employment market [for science and engineering doctorates]," according to the recent study by the Rand Corporation and Stanford University's Institute for Higher Education Research.[5] Doctoral admissions are driven not by the economy's needs for holders of doctorate degrees, but by the academic science and engineering departments' and faculties' own needs for teaching and research assistants (inexpensive labor), and for intellectual replenishment. It's as if the tail is wagging the dog.

"The only way to solve the long-term underemployment and oversupply of doctoral degree-holders in science and engineering is for academic departments either to reduce the number of doctoral students they admit, or to convince more potential Ph.D. candidates not to seek the degree . . . but both are difficult to do," according to Massey.

Another Solution: Career Morphing

But another solution is to train scientists, engineers, physicians, and other credentialed professionals (our readers) to transform or morph themselves into other careers, like the fish morphing into birds on our cover.

Each of us has latent skills and talents. If we can uncover our hidden potentialities, we can behave differently—under the proper circumstances. Our assignment is to know our preferred skills and interests, and to find the appropriate venue in which to exercise them.[6]

THE SHORT VERSIONS OF THIS BOOK

The *shortest* version is: Recall the best things you've done, and then locate the opportunity and venue to do them again. A slightly longer version of what you will do to develop your career well-being and your own theory of career victory is: (1) You will answer the cosmic question "who are you?" in microscopic detail, then (2) based upon your detailed answers to this question, you will undertake a systematic and thorough exploration of your career options, and finally, (3) emerging from these two activities and fully compatible with them will be an organized development of strategies to get where you wish to be in your career.

Isn't this what everyone knows about careers? That would make this the end of the book, not its beginning. The trouble with "what everyone knows" is that not enough people know it with enough enthusiasm, conviction, and focus, and in sufficient detail to act upon it—which is our immediate goal. Short versions and what everyone knows have their limitations, as the following story illustrates.

But Short Is Incomplete

An astrophysicist finds himself seated next to a rabbi on an airplane about to take off. "Tell me, Rabbi . . . is it true that all of Jewish wisdom, moral and ethical behavior, and social intelligence can be summed up by saying, 'Treat others as you'd like to be treated'?" The rabbi strokes his beard, thinks a few moments, and says, "Let me answer your question with a question" (a well known Talmudic gambit). The rabbi says, "Is it true that all of astrophysics—supernova explosions, black holes, white dwarfs, cosmic radiation [author Stephen Rosen's scientific specialty], the Big Bang—can be summarized by saying, 'Twinkle, twinkle, little star'?"

A BRIEF MORPHO-GENESIS

We began by helping émigré scientists and engineers. We had government and foundation support. When the cold war ended, millions of refugees fled religious persecution and an expiring political system in the former Soviet Union. They were extremely challenging to work with, especially because of the attitudes and behaviors instilled in them by a dictatorial system of altruism. This was a system that inspired Soviet proverbs like "We pretend to work and they pretend to pay us" or "Say one thing, think a second thing, and do a third thing." Those who lived under this system believed that it was impertinent to make eye contact with someone they considered their superior. (We're not making this up; it happened over and over, and was highly counterproductive in career terms.) This is relevant to U.S. scientists and engineers, since they often maintain attitudes and present behaviors that are counterproductive to their career transitions.

The first refugee whose career we helped change told his refugee friends in Brighton Beach (Little Odessa), who told their refugee friends in Bay Ridge and Crown Heights, who told their refugee friends in Rego Park, who told their refugee friends in the Bronx that they could get "free advice" from an astrophysicist-turned-market-research-consultant (Stephen Rosen) and a career management expert specializing in the career problems of credentialed professionals (co-author Celia Paul, also Stephen's wife and partner, who still treats him as if he were her equal.)

Free Advice

"Free advice" was available only because we were able to incorporate as a nonprofit and to raise money from foundations and some wealthy individuals, and thus create a program. This was the genesis of Scientific Career Transitions (the program) for highly credentialed émigré professionals, scientists, and engineers. Their specialties ranged from A to Z—agriculture to mathematics to theoretical physics and on to zoology and beyond. This led inevitably to U.S. scientists.

The Program participants met in a donated facility, twice a week for three hours each session, in a six-week cycle. Several dozen volunteers contributed their time and experience. Over five hundred émigré scientists, engineers, physicians, and others became alumni of the Program. Many transformed themselves and succeeded beyond their wildest dreams in adapting to the oftentimes harsh and increasingly Darwinian U.S. job market. Many still share their lives and stories with us. Many are friends.

INSTITUTIONAL METAMORPHOSIS: OUR CAREER TRANSITION

A *New York Times* reporter observed us in action and wrote a story about these courageous and ambitious participants, and incidentally about our Program. Publicity helped us to grow and attract donors, job offers from employers, volunteers, and of course more participants and observers. Some were card-carrying members of the New York career-counseling establishment. Michael Teitelbaum of the Alfred P. Sloan Foundation visited, and suggested that we write a brief proposal on how to provide these services to far-flung U.S. scientists and engineers with advanced degrees in a dozen or so disciplines who were experiencing rude career awakenings and job shock. In retrospect, it appears inevitable that this led us to U.S. science and technology professionals.

We were introduced to Kevin Aylesworth, a young physicist and founder of the Young Scientists' Network (YSN), who helped us create our web. It's purpose was to reach geographically dispersed, Net-literate young and mid-career technically trained holders of advanced-degrees and to pass along the lessons we have learned from the Program. This nonprofit on-line operation is called Scientific Career Transitions Online. We launched our online version with an announcement on the Young Scientists' Network, which brought a bushel basket of inquiries from disaffected, disgruntled postdocs.

A Guide to the Career-Perplexed

Our idea was to deliver an on-line electronic "guide to the career-perplexed." (Articles about the on-line program also appeared in *Science* magazine, *The Scientist*, and other publications.) We were able to assess candidates' values, interests, and skills using the paper-and-pencil exercises that appear in this book, communicated asynchronously by e-mail, snail mail, and fax. We set up telephone appointments and chat groups to provide real-time, synchronous career advice, interview practice, résumé development, and career-research services. The electronic version is a work in progress, an experiment in remote education that attempts to substitute telephone, fax, chat groups, and e-mail for face-to-face contact.

The commission to write this book arrived (fittingly by e-mail) about a year after our on-line service began.

ENDNOTES

1. Sheila Tobias, Daryl E. Chubin, and Kevin Aylesworth, *Rethinking Science as a Career*, Research Corporation, (Tuscon: 1995).
2. J. P. Markey and W. Parks, "Occupational Change: Pursuing a Different Kind of Work," *Monthly Labor Review*, 112, no. 9 (1989); J. Meisenheimer, U.S. Bureau of Labor Statistics, 1996 (private communication). These are available on-line via Alta Vista and Young Scientists Network. Also, M. E. Watanabe, "Pressures Wearing Down Researchers," *The Scientist* April 18, 1996.
3. W. Massey, and C. Goldman, "Production and Utilization of Science and Engineering Doctorates in the U.S.," Stanford Institute for Higher Education, April 1995; later corrections issued by J. D. Ullman and R. W. Ritchie, July 28, 1995, and by W. Baker, May 10, 1995; J. W. Ausubel, "Malthus and the Graduate Student," *The Scientist* 10, no. 3, (1996):11.
4. NAS/NAE COSEPUP Report, April 1995.
5. See note 3.
6. Each of us is a sum of potential future states (somewhat like a state vector or quantum-mechanical wave function), so that when we are trained for a specialty (transformed by a "training" operation), we can "morph" into a state of job readiness (produce an eigenvalue) for one or more jobs or careers. How we get to those jobs is one purpose of this book, and it may require a transformation (other operations) to do so. But if we need to go through this same process all over again for an entirely new specialty, instead of drawing upon the often-hidden potential future states already resident within us, we are not using the most efficient career-transformation methods. Another purpose of this book is to explain how others have made efficient career transitions, and to show how you can make this transition from where you are now to where you'd like to be.

1

·············

CAREER TRANSFORMATIONS

·····················

HEAVY WEATHER FOR RESEARCH (AND NAPOLEON)

The research environment these days appears increasingly inhospitable to the virtual army of scientists, engineers, and technology and medical professionals that the United States has overproduced. The drying up of academic research funds has intensified the competition for always-scarce resources; it has increased career disaffection and perplexity among the foot soldiers of science; and it has brought heavy weather to sectors of our science and technology enterprise.

But consider Napoleon's army during his ill-fated Moscow maneuvers. In Napoleon's Russian campaign of 1812, his army suffered devastating losses during its retreat from Moscow. The "Carte Figurative" found nearby is a reproduction of a data and time-series chart drawn in 1861 by Charles Joseph Minard, a French engineer. This map seems, as E. J. Marey described it, "to defy the pen of the historian by its brutal eloquence."[1]

Edward Tufte, in his exceptional study of this chart, remarks:

⋮ *Beginning at the left on the Polish-Russian border near the Niemen River,*
⋮ *the thick band shows the size of the army (422,000 men) as it invaded*

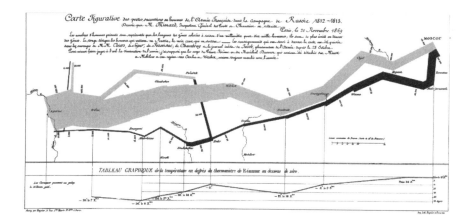

Russia in June 1812. . . . In September, the army reached Moscow, which was by then sacked and deserted, with 100,000 men. . . . It was a bitterly cold winter, and many froze on the march out of Russia. As the graphic shows, the crossing of the Berezina River was a disaster, and the army finally struggled back into Poland with only 10,000 men remaining. . . . Six variables are plotted: the size of the army, its location on a two-dimensional surface, direction of the army's movement, and temperature on various dates during the retreat from Moscow. It may well be the best statistical graphic ever drawn.

Chilly Funding Climate

Compare Napoleon's army, in its retreat and retrenchment, with the dwindling army of science and technology workers in the United States. It is not entirely an accident or mere exaggeration that journalists speak of the "war" against scientific ignorance and disease. Compare the icy winter of Napoleon's attrition with the current economic climate faced by our army of science and technology workers.

Would that the plight of the science and technology "army" and the "chilling" effects of diminished public funding of research in the closing decades of our millennium were depicted so vividly and with such "brutal eloquence." Compare the dramatic, brilliant multivariate clarity of this chart with the somewhat fuzzy, muddy statistics presented to the voting public on the ebb and flow of the U.S. technical labor market. Perhaps the public might be more sympathetic to our science and technology enterprise if we could present our case as clearly and powerfully as Minard made his.

Napoleon once said that soldiers of a conquering army do not call in sick. If we as scientists, engineers, physicians, and other advanced degree-holders are to conquer an inhospitable environment, we cannot "call in sick." We may have to consider alternatives, redirecting ourselves into new careers.

INVOLUNTARY CAREER CHANGES

Almost everyone will experience new careers, not as guaranteed employment, but as a provisional occupation. Welcome to the era of "contingency workers" who have to validate their job performance daily, who must prove that they generate more in revenues than their employer pays them.

If support for academic and institutional research continues to decline, as many anticipate, the science and technology careers of many professionals will be at risk. Working in a "comfort zone" or where you are now will be replaced by involuntary career changes.

These changes are inevitable, as Peter Fiske[2] says, and employment crises favor those who understand such crises and themselves, who know how the world outside their specialty works, who continue to explore new opportunities, who continuously refresh their career options, and who see connections and bridges to other careers.

Many of us are good at what we already do, yet this is a trap. According to Marvin Minsky, "If there's something you like [to do] very much, then you should regard this [not] as . . . feeling good, but as a kind of brain cancer because it means that some small part of your brain has figured out how to turn off all other things."[3]

Among the demons that we as scientists encounter are fear of mediocrity, fear of insignificance, fear of losing priority, and fear of being wrong, according to interviews conducted by Carl Sendermann.[4] He found that scientists often experience the "belated recognition" that they must have "a well-thought out career development plan."

WEBS AND BRANCHES

Metaphors shape our expectations, and *career* suggests a curvilinear path—unlike career mobility, resilience, and versatility, which suggest webs, branches, and fractals. "Work today is about expanding your web by working more connections (knowing more people) and spinning stronger strands (gaining more experiences and skills). A web is flexible, expandable, and you can always tear it down and build a new one elsewhere."[5]

But even the web metaphor is too limiting. A better metaphor would be a tree, which has roots, a trunk, limbs, and successive levels of branches and branching points.

Movement along the career web or tree calls for agile communication skills; strong relationships with mentors, colleagues, and contacts; and overlapping circles of influence, or webs of acquaintances.

Webs and trees are powerful metaphors for the way we make transitions from one level of thinking to the next. The scientific capacities and thoughtful independence that we possess as professionals, scientists, engineers, or physicians may not be able to solve our career problems. What are the other levels of thinking that can help us move in new career directions?

A simple answer is to look at seasoned professionals, scientists, engineers, and physicians who say that they are fulfilled or satisfied in their current careers, and have also experienced career satisfaction or fulfillment in virtually all prior careers. They are examples of flexible, resilient, and versatile career-transition problem solvers. They have discovered those levels of thinking or modes of action by which they can intuitively solve significant career problems: "social competence" and "emotional intelligence," which can be defined as the ability to know what's on other people's minds and the ability to make other people feel good.

"THE BUTTERFLY EFFECT": CAREER CHAOS AND COMPLEXITY

Edward Lorenz, a meteorologist at MIT and one of the pioneers of chaoplexity, has described "the butterfly effect." In principle, a butterfly flapping its wings in Iowa could put in motion a set of hydrodynamic events in our atmosphere that would culminate in a monsoon in Indonesia. Your career may now resemble a monsoon triggered by an earlier "butterfly effect" career decision, or career-decision pattern.

Careers people have, or the people having the careers, are not deterministic, Newtonian, or linear phenomena. The interaction cannot be understood simply by examining its component parts, since the whole is more complex than the sum of its complex parts.

Our career–person trajectories are unpredictable and nonlinear. The state of our current career may be the result of a complex superposition of our earlier educational states and preferences, our postdoctoral and post-postdoctoral positions—operated upon by real-world events like the economy and the market demand for scientists, engineers, academics.[6]

For most people, wisdom concerning the world's ways and the self-knowledge needed to make a career choice seem to come later in life than the need to make career decisions. Early small decisions that we must make despite our imperfect knowledge or lack of information can result in large career errors later.

Nevertheless, we do know from earlier studies that people whose professors in graduate school identified them as "outstanding" and who continued on in the physical sciences, the social sciences, law, medicine, engineering, architecture, and the humanities, have entered the highest ranks of their profession, their technical specialty, or management, and have emerged as satisfied and successful career transitioners.[7]

CASE VIGNETTES AND CAREER CHANGE NARRATIVES

Later in the book you will visit "career-transition champions," real scientists, engineers, and medical professionals. Many are personal contacts of the authors, sometimes out to the third or fourth generation of contacts. Some come from our pool of hundreds who have succeeded in making career transitions. They present convincing examples of how difficult and stressful career struggles can be. You will see the variety of circumstances under which others can change, and you will come to know the difference between the person and the change. Their comments are flagged by shaded text to differentiate their narratives from the rest of the text.

CAREER WELL-BEING AND HEALTH

Twenty-five centuries ago, Hippocrates said that it is less important to know what *disease* the person has than to know what *person* has the disease.

After helping thousands of individuals deal with their career problems one by one, and after reflecting on the career trajectories of career-change champions, we have discovered that it is not as important to know what career the person has as it is to know what person has the career.

Hippocrates' remark has inspired our exploration and celebration of the metaphor of "career well-being and health." What is the "career health" of the person having the career? We believe we can measure your career health using a simple paper-and-pencil inventory. You will find the "Career Well-Being Inventory" in Section 2.01. Since you can use this instrument to measure your own career well-being, you can measure your career well-being and fitness before you go through the self-assessment exercises in Chapter 3, then measure your progress and improvement after the exercises.

Parallels

We suggest that there are strong intuitive parallels between physical fitness and career fitness, between physical exercise and career-transition calisthenics, between predispositions to physical ailments and predispositions to career ailments, between career diagnostics and medical diagnostics, between preventive medicine and avoidance of career maladies. Addiction to toxic substances resembles addiction to career-destructive habits like sending out vast numbers of résumés. Muscle strength or atrophy has parallels in career terms. Career policy and health policy have much in common. These parallels are one premise of this book. We suggest that your career conditions and your physical conditions call for diagnostic procedures, preventive medicine, muscle flexing and exercise, and regular—even annual—checkups. Treat the *person*, not the disease!

Healthy athletes can teach us physical performance techniques they have perfected by "practice, practice, practice"[8]: exercises, living the wholesome life of a disciplined mind and body, healthy diet, learned and earned resilience, versatility, and mobility. So too can career-change champions teach us about career performance, career calisthenics, career practices, and career well-being.

WHO ARE YOU?

You are going to develop an in-depth profile of the one person responsible for your career health and career change (Sections 3.01 to 3.05). What is the career equivalent of your medical condition? What is valuable in your life? Where do your interests lie? What are your strengths? If you have not had opportunities for self-examination, you will want to invest considerable time in completing these inventories, profiles, and exercises in the greatest possible detail. The result will be an organized and useful interpretation of what you know about yourself.

The inventories, questionnaires, and exercises in this book are designed to help you determine (1) your career well-being and how you can improve it, (2) what you want out of work, and (3) what you can bring to your work. As you progress through the career-transition process, you will use your self-profile as a standard to determine which alternative career or job choices will best "fit" you, i.e., what will bring you greatest satisfaction.

Small Errors Amplify

Choosing your next professional position without first developing a self-profile can result in an occupational move that will not suit you—and you may not know this until after you've started the job (the butterfly effect). Poor career choices in the past may have resulted from not spending enough time on both self-examination and collection of job information—the equivalent of poor physical health, or making a small error in your initial condition that results in large or even catastrophic errors in your current condition. You can begin to break these counterproductive old patterns, old job-search habits, and self-damaging old career-transition themes by developing a rational and systematic career plan—your theory of career victory—that begins with the detailed self-profile questions contained in this volume.

Turning-Point Patterns

You will do a powerful exercise that systematically examines patterns in your previous career turning points (see Sections 3.01 to 3.04). Think about those times, both recently and in the distant past, when you have enjoyed an activity. Keep your mind open to all career possibilities, even if they are not yet practical for you. If you can, allow yourself to imagine and to dream of what you would love to do. These reflections will help you to choose a new career that will be based on what you do best—*and* what you enjoy. Often, initial career choices that seem impractical will ultimately lead you to other, more realistic choices. Jonas Salk said, "Do what makes your heart leap." A good place to begin thinking about what makes your heart leap is here, and now.

Finally, you will face some serious struggles and risks as you contemplate career and job change. While compromises are necessary, these exercises will define you and obstacles to your change. These exercises will also define what you are willing to invest (or sacrifice) in order to gain career fulfillment. Risk taking can result in enhanced self-esteem—which is an integral component of increased job satisfaction.

Max Weber said, "Each of us must find and obey the demon that holds the very fiber of our being." Think of the process of career change as a rich opportunity to discover and define yourself, and to fulfill your truest self, your truest career, your truest dreams—the truest fiber of your being.

SCRUTINIZING YOUR OPTIONS

Upon completion of this book, you will have a clear sense of who you are—your values, your skills, the skills you most enjoy using, and your interests. We call these your *preferences*. As you will see from our career-transition champions, those who work within their preferences tend to work with considerable satisfaction, comfort, pleasure, energetic activity, optimism, excitement, and collegiality. Those who work within their preferences also report that they view their career as "an activity embedded within the flow of life," "a useful pursuit of admirable goals," "a worthy expression of my life," "a bonding with reality," and "an opportunity to make others feel good."

Focusing on your preferences and related aspects of yourself will give you confidence, self-knowledge, and forward momentum toward realistic career fulfillment and practical career fitness. Eventually, you will be able to reflect upon and answer the following questions: What type of work environment is most suitable for me? What type of day-to-day work activities will give me the greatest satisfaction? How can I use these reflections to evaluate my scientific, engineering, technical, medical, or professional career? Flowing from these answers, what is my next career move?

If You Are Unsure

Some readers will be able to select and plan their next career move after completing this book. However, (1) if you were able to complete this book, yet were unsure of your next steps, or (2) if there are sections of this book that you are unable to complete, please do not be discouraged. These are signs that you may need additional help with your career planning, and the nature of your unanswered questions or uncompleted exercises will indicate the type of help that will be most useful to you. If you are tempted to gloss over these uncertainties, remember the butterfly effect! Small errors in your early career choices can be magnified or amplified over time, yielding an unsatisfactory career condition sooner or later.

In order to reveal your uncertainties and clarify your career objectives, you may wish to seek the guidance of a professional career counselor. Career counseling and detailed career testing can help you to generate job or career options, and to develop a job search or career-change plan—a "theory of victory" for your career. (See the material on career counselors in Section 3.11.)

Do It Yourself

However, it is our opinion that most people are able to change careers themselves, without career counseling, by learning to exercise their career-transition assets and tools (see the list later in this chapter), honing their social competencies, and using or developing their emotional intelligence.[9] You will see how the career-change champions have done it on their own. Of course, no one does it in a vacuum. We all need contacts and colleagues that we respect for reality checks, information, and support.[10]

WHAT TO EXPECT IF YOU DECIDE TO CHANGE CAREERS

You will be going through a period of change—extraordinary, often confusing, and yet exciting. For most people, it can be a period of struggle, filled with distress, and even sustained episodes of despair and dejection.

Like all change, your career transition will be accompanied by positive and negative concomitants and byproducts. You will become an expert on both aspects only to the degree that you experience the process fully, directly, personally, and deeply. And you will have to make adjustments and adaptations. You will have to flex cognitive abilities and "skill muscles" that may have atrophied or that you have never used. And it may be the atrophied muscles that the marketplace demands now.

It is important for you to know that this sort of change is normal and that the personal stress that accompanies it is also somewhat predictable. Indeed, if you felt no distress during this period of adjustment, that would be unusual. You must know that others who have gone through this process—who have experienced the ups and downs, been both elated and depressed, and alternated between high and low energy—not only survived but flourished, thrived, and rose to the challenges.

To chart these changes, examine the nearby graph, "What to Expect: Future Pacing, Adaptation, and Adjustment Cycles." This graph shows the normal reactions of most job hunters to the stress of adaptation and adjustment during their job search. If you know that periods of excitement and high energy will be followed by periods of discouragement, emotional letdown, and low energy, you can take comfort in the fact that others before you have surmounted these obstacles to the job search.

Do not schedule a job interview during a period of pessimism, depression, or low energy, because this mood will be apparent to anyone interviewing you (job interview) or anyone you interview (contact interview), and will probably be misinterpreted. Verve, energy, and enthusiasm are among the salient qualities employers look for. Because it is hard to hide our mood during an interview (even on the telephone or on-line—see "Face-to-Face, Voice-Only, or On-line" in Section 3.11), it may be advisable to schedule job interviews for a time when you are energetic, optimistic, and positive (see "What's Bad About Optimism? What's Good About Pessimism?" in Section 3.02).

There is no formula, no magical cure, no antidote for these changes. But they are natural and human reactions, and anticipation will help you to cope with such normal swings of the mood pendulum. If you are not being rejected, you are not fully engaged in your job search. In order to win, you have to risk some losses along the way.

FAILURE IS A JUDGMENT ABOUT EVENTS

"Success is a lousy teacher. It seduces smart people into thinking they can't lose," according to Bill Gates. Yet, smart people do fail, says Carole Hyatt,[11] because they have "poor interpersonal skills," were in the wrong environment with the wrong value system, are poor at self-management or are self-destructive, and are unfocused. Smart people who focus entirely upon their specialty resemble addicts who need their "hit."

Involuntary career change may become an opportunity to change ourselves; "failure gives us new options and a unique opportunity to learn." The stages following what is perceived as a career failure include a period of mourning, well described by Kubler-Ross: shock, fear, anger and blame, shame, and despair. When Churchill was forced out of the Admiralty in 1915, he took up painting. "A man can wear out a particular part of his mind by continually using it and tiring it. . . . The tired parts of the mind can be rested and strengthened . . . by using other parts. . . . When new cells are called into activity . . . relief, repose, refreshment are afforded."

WHAT TO EXPECT
FUTURE PACING: ADAPTION AND ADJUSTMENT CYCLES

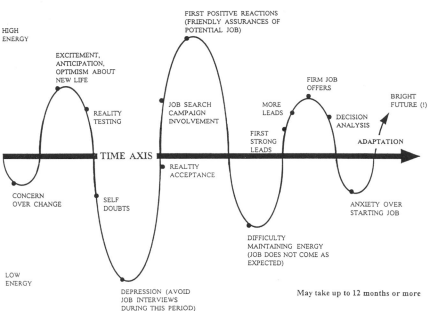

"Failure," Hyatt says, "is a judgement about events. . . . If you are the judge, then you also have the power to alter your judgements." A career transition requires a willingness to close the past chapter, to establish a support system, to ask for help (often very difficult for many of us), and to credit yourself for incremental successes that are the stepping-stones from one career to the next.

The next job or career does not have to be what you will do for the rest of your life. In fact, if you try to place too many constraints or specifications on your transition, the fit will be overdetermined. Worse still, you will be overwhelmed.

MATCHING YOURSELF WITH A CAREER CHOICE

What you need to do here is take what you know about yourself and match it as well as you can with what you know about particular careers. "In nearly all important transactions of life . . . which have a relation to the future, we have to take a leap in the dark," said the distinguished nineteenth-century jurist James Fitzjames Stephens. "We have to act for the best, and in nearly every case to act upon very imperfect evidence." He continues: "The one talent which is worth all other talents put together in human affairs is the talent of judging right upon imperfect materials . . . to see things as they are . . . opening our eyes and looking with whatever power we may have."

What are these imperfect materials? They are who you are and what's out there. Put another way, they are the information you have about yourself—your imperfect materials are your preferences, temperament, genetic predispositions, attitudes, beliefs, behaviors, habits, training, education, experience, and so on. Information about the marketplace for your skills is another set of imperfect materials—rapid changes in supply and demand for goods and services, and the sudden opening of new (and closing of old) technological niches. You seek a set of intersections, multiple coincidences, and overlaps of these two sets of imperfect information, suspecting that something resembling chaos, complexity, and emergent phenomena is at work here.[12]

CHANCE FAVORS A (SOON-TO-BE) PREPARED MIND: PLANNED SERENDIPITY

To unravel these chaotic and complex matters, we first look at those who have made career transitions with what they say are satisfying results. What these people offer are subjective observations and assertions about their own career turning points and metamorphoses. Taken together, their career-transition case histories suggest a way to measure career well-being (see the inventory in Section 2.01).

Second, we examine briefly the economic environment in which these changes are to take place, and the nature of the struggle this environment and your preferences require if you are to undergo those metamorphoses.

Third, we look at the systematic processes and logical progression of steps that we have found important and useful in attaining "career renewal." These are based upon our experience working directly with thousands of scientists, engineers, physicians, and attorneys, from the United States and overseas.

On a scale of career well-being or career fitness (as near as we can measure it), most of us are in the center of a normal distribution of Ph.D.s, scientists, engineers, technical, medical, and health-care professionals. Most of us do the mundane work required to get the job done and keep the enterprise going. Most of us neither win Nobel Prizes nor change careers happily and successfully five times. In plain English, that is, most of us are, or should consider ourselves, not race horses but plow horses. With hard, focused effort, our career transitions will be successful.

HALLMARKS OF CAREER WELL-BEING DURING CAREER TRANSITIONS

We selected over sixty junior and senior professionals in the science, engineering, and health professions who navigated their career turning points with varying degrees of grace under pressure; many interviews exemplify their resourcefulness, career resilience, career versatility, emotional flexibility, practical common sense, and insightfulness. These people's competence and well-being may hide the labyrinthine complexity of the intense struggle they experienced.

Here are some excerpted assertions, distilled from interviews with those who have made career metamorphoses and arrived at career satisfaction and fulfillment. See how many you agree with, keeping in mind that it's not the career the person has, but the person who has the career.

Hallmarks of Career Well-Being: Assertions of Career-Change Champions

"My work is a worthy expression of my life."

"I know who I am."

"I think about how my career changes me as a person."

"I lead a balanced life."

"I have a sense of my intellectual capacity."

"Logical, systematic scientific thinking is useful in many careers and venues."

"I am uncomfortable if large aspects of myself are undeveloped."

"I do whatever has the most positive impact, given my abilities."

"I pursue knowledge for the sake of knowledge."

"I believe in action rather than drift."

"I am intense about my family, my friends, and my work."

"I can communicate my virtues clearly."

"I work well independently."

"I take life as it comes."

"I feel satisfaction when I help others."

"Being right is the scientists' disease."

"My career is filled with fortuitous events and serendipity."

"I am composed in difficult situations."

"I learn by imitating my betters."

"Most of my jobs came to me."

"I solve my boss's problems."

"I shrug off adversity with ease and good humor."

"I have had many good mentors."

"I know what's important to me."

"I view my career as an activity embedded within the flow of life."

"My intelligence is a way to make others feel good."

Each assertion is an example of an attitude, belief, or behavior (taken from a long narration). Taken together, these assertions begin to suggest a pattern of career-transition strategies that lead to career satisfaction and a theory of victory for others. You have career-transition assets and tools that you may have overlooked.

YOUR CAREER-TRANSITION ASSETS AND TOOLS

1. You have a bushel basket of fundamental and exotic skills, of intelligence and curiosity, of other valuable attributes—many of them "bankable," coin of the realm, and reusable in other occupations or careers, or in completely different contexts.

2. You have friends and colleagues who know you, what you like to do, and what you are good at doing; these friends and colleagues are likely to know about career or job opportunities—or to know of others who know of such opportunities—that are unknown to you, but that are potential matches for you. Intelligence is also the ability to make others feel good. If you make others feel good, they may help you.

3. You have access to reservoirs of forbearance and patience, and in the fulness of time and in the course of living a disciplined life, a stream of opportunities will present themselves.[13]

4. You have the ability to recognize opportunities when they appear serendipitously, or to make them appear, and you are able to determine their "goodness of fit" with who you are.

5. You can "try on" the new opportunities as if they were new apparel; if they don't fit; don't wear them.

6. You can move in small steps: The first new job or career may be merely a temporary or provisional stepping-stone or an interim engagement en route to a later better position. Each job or job interview is practice for the next.

7. You have acquired self-discipline and learned how to learn by studying a technical specialty, and you can invest these assets in many other fields.

8. You have built upon old skills before; you can build on new skills again in future careers.

9. You have, or can acquire through the exercises and inventories in this book (or elsewhere), a deep knowledge of the decision patterns in your past career turning points. If these patterns are helpful, they give you confidence in your decision making; if they are not, you can change them.

10. You have taken risks before, and you can do it again; you can take action even with incomplete information. "Imperfect movement is better than perfect paralysis."

11. You are in control of your career—not your mentors or superiors, not a bad work experience or a previous career disaster, but *you.*

12. Science has identified more than one million animal species. Each fits and evolves into a niche in the food chain. So can you.

13. You have the diligence to discover the intelligence that resides in the marketplace—facts, data, wisdom, and knowledge—that can guide you to a niche that is just right for you.

14. You can take heart from the fact that scientists, engineers, and inventors are notable for their broad interests and abilities, and multiple careers. A list[14] of five hundred familiar ones reveals that second careers are common and widely varied; these people became painters, sculptors, architects, musicians, composers, poets, dramatists, and politicians.

15. Optimism is one of the best predictors of success. Optimists get to goals, and if one goal fades, they aim for another. Optimists break formidable tasks into discrete specific elements. Optimists see setbacks not as failure, but as challenges.[15]

The harder you work, the luckier you get. That is, chance favors the prepared mind, and luck has very little to do with realizing your career transitions.

COUNTERPRODUCTIVE CAREER STRATEGIES, DANGEROUS TO SMART PEOPLE

1. Working at changing your job or career only when you are unhappy.
2. Waiting, especially for opportunities to fall into your lap.
3. Deferring decisions until you are fired or burned out.

4. Intellectualizing about where to go and how to get there.

5. Hoping to fall into something by being a generalist.

6. Allowing negative prophecies and despondency to overwhelm your career decisions (the "nocebo" effect, the negative counterpart of the placebo).

7. Coming to conclusions prematurely, without reflection ("Chicken Little syndrome").

8. Imagining that you can read other people's minds without supporting evidence and corroboration.

9. Taking everything personally, which makes you feel angry, guilty, or depressed.

10. Believing that success in one area automatically translates to success in every area without the need for the same effort that led to the first success.

11. Making assumptions, without debate or doubt, about what your critics are saying about you, without bothering to determine the validity of these assumptions.

12. Aspiring to be perfect in all things, especially when you set your standards unattainably high.

13. Comparing yourself to others and accepting a negative and discouraging contrast (who can walk in the seven-league boots of genius?).

14. Worrying about what you can't change instead of coping with what you can.

15. Focusing on what you should have done in the past to the exclusion of what you can do in the future ("shoulda, woulda, coulda").

16. Responding "yes, but" to every positive thought, intention, or bit of good advice; dreaming up improbable rationales to excuse obvious negatives.

17. Deciding you must earn the same money or maintain the same level of status, responsibility, or prestige in your next career or job.

18. Believing you'll be hired to do only something for which you have been formally trained.

19. Getting another degree when it isn't a requirement for work you'd like to do.

20. Keeping your feelings of dissatisfaction to yourself, or dumping them on your family or friends, or in angry correspondence.

21. Expecting your work life to bring you complete personal fulfillment.

22. Burning your bridges behind you.

23. Postponing gratification in your work.

24. Holding onto an irrational belief that you owe a lifestyle commitment to your current employer or career, your next job or career, or your expertise (habituation or addiction).

25. Staying where you are for fear of failing elsewhere.

Many of these self-defeating career strategies are avoidable or alterable. Deborah Arron,[16] who mentions some of the ones above, suggests that you must know yourself, narrow your market, and then persist until you achieve your career goal. In addition, we suggest the following:

- You can do damage control by reminding yourself of your career-transition assets. You can check off the items on this list that remind you of your own thought patterns and label your mistakes. You can "objectify" your transition strategies by frequent reality checks, as Chapter 3 recommends.

- You can change faulty thinking into reinterpretations of events.[17]

- You can take a "Mistake-Makers Quiz" and examine ways to interpret events, reformulate your ideas, and learn to recognize these patterns.[18]

- You can interrupt a self-defeating strategy by naming it, then "recapacitating" and energizing yourself by concentrating on your career-transition assets. You can allow into your consciousness only those thoughts that reinforce your assets. Without denying reality, you can affirm your positive transition assets, and you can repeat these affirmations as often as necessary.

NOTES

1. Edward R. Tufte, *The Visual Display of Quantitative Information* (Cheshire, Conn.: Graphics Press, 1983).
2. Peter Fiske, *To Boldly Go: A Practical Guide for Scientists* (Washington, D.C.: American Geophysical Union, 1996).
3. Quoted in John Horgan, *The End of Science* (Reading, Mass.: Addison-Wesley, 1996), p. 158.
4. Carl Sendermann, *Survival Strategies for New Scientists* (New York: Plenum Press, 1987).
5. Anne Fisher, "Six Ways to Supercharge Your Career," *Fortune*, January 13, 1997, p. 46.
6. It may be possible to develop a model using linear vector spaces to characterize quantum mechanical "career operators," operating on our complex "career wave function," a superposition of our earlier preferences and career states, to produce our "career eigenvalue," or current career.
7. Eli Ginzberg and John Herma, *Talent and Performance* (New York: Columbia University Press, 1964).
8. This is the answer to the question, "How do you get to Carnegie Hall?"
9. Daniel Goleman, *Emotional Intelligence* (New York: Bantam Books, 1995).
10. Feel free to write to us directly by e-mail (srosenc@ix.netcom.com, cpaul001 @counsel.com) or by snail mail (Scientific Career Transitions, 1776 Broadway, Suite 1806, New York, NY 10019-2002; Telephone: (212) 397-1021; Fax: (212) 397-1022), or access our website at www.toa-services.net/sct001.html
11. Carole Hyatt and Linda Gottlieb, *When Smart People Fail* (New York: Simon and Schuster, 1987).
12. *A twelve-pound cannonball is dropped over the side of a ship directly above the deepest point in the Pacific Ocean, the Mariana Trench. How long will it take for the cannonball to reach the ocean floor?* Attempt an answer; pay close attention to how you arrive at your solution. Here is another: *How many piano tuners are there in the city of Chicago?* Scientists call these problems "Fermi problems," after Enrico Fermi, the Nobel Prize–winning physicist. Fermi, or "guesstimate," problems do not contain all the pertinent information necessary to reach a plausible solution. These problems are designed to teach people how to think for themselves. By dividing the questions into more feasible questions, some guesses can be made. Many people make arbitrary guesses because they reason that if they can't be completely correct, why attempt to be partially correct? The truth of the matter is that you are habitually required to make decisions based on incomplete data. Oftentimes, your best guess is your best answer. In case you still find the guesstimate problems perplexing, the Mariana Trench is approximately six nautical miles deep, and a cannonball drops at a rate of ten feet per second. It would take the cannonball about an hour to reach the ocean floor. Solving the piano tuner question involves breaking the question into several parts, including: How many people reside in Chicago? How many pianos are there? How many pianos can be tuned in a year? How often do you tune a piano? So, there are approximately 50 piano tuners in the Windy City.

13. God says to the guy praying to win the lottery, "You have to buy a lottery ticket to win!"

14. Robert Scott, Root-Bernstein, *Discovering* (Cambridge, Mass.: Harvard University Press, 1989).

15. Charles R. Snyder, *New York Times,* December 24, 1991.

16. Deborah Arron, *What Can You Do with a Law Degree?* (Seattle: Niche Press, 1997).

17. Jane Brody, "Changing Thinking," *New York Times,* August 21, 1996; Herbert Benson, *Timeless Healing* (New York: Scribner, 1996).

18. Arthur Freeman and Rose DeWolf, *The 10 Dumbest Mistakes Smart People Make and How to Avoid Them* (New York: HarperCollins, 1983).

2

············

CAREER WELL-BEING

························

2.01 YOUR CAREER HEALTH

What is your level of career health and career well-being, and how do you improve it? This is the subtext of your career transition.

Knowledge of your ignorance of your own career well-being is a form of wisdom, and annual career checkups are a form of preventive medicine.

Preventive medicine is the specialty of health care that scrutinizes the individuals to look for early warnings of health problems. Its purpose is to protect us, to promote and maintain our health and well-being, and to prevent disability, disease, and premature death. It aspires to be an objective science and medical specialty.

Is It the Transition the Person Makes, or the Person Who Makes the Transition?

Annual *career* checkups are preventive medicine applied objectively to our careers. But what do we check? Is it the ailment the person has, or the person who has the ailment? Is it the career transition the person makes, or the person who makes the career transition? It's the *person* who makes the *transition*.

How can we measure that person's career health? The narratives of healthy and ailing careers reveal where each narrator appears on a continuum of career wellness.

One constellation of career attitudes, career beliefs, and career behaviors appears consistently in the narratives of those credentialed professionals in this book who say that they are *satisfied* and *fulfilled* with their careers and career transitions. This is the career wellness syndrome.

Relative absence of these career attitudes, career beliefs, and career behaviors appears consistently among those who say that they are *disappointed* or *distressed* by their careers and career transitions. This is the career ailment syndrome.

These syndromes make sense if they are interpreted as two ends of a continuum of career health, from high career health among those satisfied with their careers to low career health among the career dysfunctional, distressed, or disappointed.

We have developed an original instrument that lets you measure your career health by finding where you are on the continuum between these two syndromes. The instrument is called the "Career Well-Being Inventory." It reflects career attitudes, behaviors, and beliefs that epitomize career well-being. The statements made by credentialed individuals whose successful and satisfied career transition stories are presented in this book represent the raw data of career well-being.

To determine your level of career well-being, ask yourself how frequently you concur with each statement, from "never" to "always." The statements are not meant to be absolutes (there are no "right answers"), but are intended to elicit the degree to which they apply to you. They are subjective self-assessments that we can interpret statistically as well as individually.

*H*allmarks of Career Well-Being and Career Resilience

Step 1   Estimate your overall career well-being, on a scale of 0 to 10.   _____

Step 2   Estimate your overall "career resilience," on a scale of 0 to 10.   _____

Step 3   Estimate your overall career versatility, on a scale of 0 to 10.   _____

Step 4   Now consider how frequently each statement below applies to you, on a numerical scale of 1 to 5.

Frequency: 0 = never, 1 = rarely, 2 = sometimes, 3 = frequently, 4 = mostly, 5 = always

Check the appropriate column next to each statement, and follow the directions below to find your score.

The Career Well-Being Inventory	Frequency:	0	1	2	3	4	5
1. I like the kinds of people who are attracted to my field. (3.01)							
2. I am honest and accurate in assessing my skills. (3.04)							
3. I am honest and accurate in assessing my interests. (3.07)							
4. I am honest and accurate in assessing my values. (3.03)							
5. These assessments confirm my career or job choices. (3.02, 3.05, 308)							
6. Decisions I made at important turning points in my career were beneficial to my career. (3.02)							
7. In retrospect, these decisions seemed inevitable. (3.05, 308)							
8. I am energetic and optimistic about my career and my life. (3.01)							
9. Professional colleagues, mentors, advisors, and role models were important in my life. (3.11)							
10. These people have been helpful in my career. (3.11)							
11. Excellent job opportunities and offers well suited to me have come my way as if by chance or serendipity. (3.12)							
12. In my professional and social life, I present my truest and best self. (3.13, 3.14)							
13. I'm honest and positive in assertions about myself and others. (3.04, 3.06)							
14. I strive to lead a balanced life. (3.01, 3.03, 3.17)							
15. "I work hard and play hard." (3.01, 3.02, 3.03, 3.04, 3.05, 3.07)							
16. I don't mind (I even enjoy) necessary drudgery in my job or career. (3.03)							
17. My work and I seem uniquely suited or well matched to each other. (3.02, 3.03, 3.04, 3.05, 3.06, 3.08)							
18. During career transitions, "imperfect movement is better than perfect paralysis." (3.14, 3.15)							
19. I am well regarded professionally. (3.11)							
20. I am well regarded socially. (3.11)							
21. I intuitively develop abiding relationships with my friends and colleagues. (3.11)							

The Career Well-Being Inventory *Frequency:*	0	1	2	3	4	5
22. These later on prove to be helpful in my career. (3.11, 3.14, 3.15)						
23. I seem to have many social and professional acquaintances and contacts who keep me up to date on what's happening. (3.11, 3.14, 3.15)						
24. I gain energy, pleasure, and renewal from my work or career. (3.01, 3.02, 3.03)						
25. I have a realistic view of trends in my field and how they fit into the larger picture. (3.08)						
26. I know what I can change, what I can't change, and the difference between them. (3.08, 3.09)						
27. "I can't control the wind, but I can adjust the sails." (3.08, 3.09)						
28. I make things happen because I work hard. (3.05)						
29. The harder I work, the luckier I get. (3.05)						
30. When I add valuable contributions to my field, I feel personal satisfaction. (3.03)						
31. No matter what work I do, I am fully and constantly aware of the fact that I must generate more income or value than I receive. (3.01, 3.08)						
32. Logical, systematic, scientific thinking is useful in many venues. (3.01, 3.02, 3.03, 3.04)						
33. I redirect my energies, instincts, and desires into useful pursuits. (3.08, 3.09)						
34. I defer pleasures and problem solving. (3.03, 3.04)						
35. I strive to be self-reliant. (3.05, 3.07, 3.08, 3.09)						
36. When I help others, I feel satisfaction. (3.03)						
37. In order to achieve my goals and avoid pitfalls, I plan systematically. (3.17)						
38. The people I work with are people I like or admire. (3.01, 3.02)						
39. I respect my colleagues at work. (3.01, 3.03, 3.04)						
40. I try to maximize my utility and usefulness in my work. (3.01, 3.03, 3.05)						

The Career Well-Being Inventory Frequency:	0	1	2	3	4	5
41. I am intense about my work, my family, and my friends. (3.03, 3.05, 3.07)						
42. I try to be adaptable and to accept compromise. (3.05, 3.06, 3.08)						
43. I have no career regrets. (3.02)						
44. Life is full of random events that I attempt to convert to adventures. (3.12)						
45. Humility is a great virtue. (3.03)						
46. I believe in action rather than drift. (3.17)						
47. I take things as they come, with equanimity and humor. (3.03)						
48. TOTAL NUMBER OF MARKS IN EACH COLUMN						
49. MULTIPLY ENTRIES IN ROW 48 BY NUMBER AT COLUMN'S HEAD						

TOTAL OF ALL ENTRIES IN ROW 49 = _____

RAW SCORE; DIVIDED BY 235 = _____

Step 5   To calculate your score, multiply the number of marks you made in each column by the number at the head of each column. Add these numbers and divide by the maximum score possible (235). Convert this into a percentage and compare it with the estimates (made on a scale of 1 to 10) of your career well-being that you made earlier.

Step 6   We are eager to have your input and results to increase our sample size and to compare with the career health of different populations. We invite you to send us your completed inventory. We offer you the opportunity to see where your results fall statistically in comparison with those of other readers and specific academic or industrial populations. Please add personal information in confidence: your age, your choice of careers, career changes, comments about the items above; your name and phone number if you wish to have an evaluation.

Step 7   To help you interpret and improve your own career health and well-being, please see Chapter 3 of this book. The numbers in parentheses refer to the sections that address the adjacent statement, so that you can exercise and improve that component of your career well-being.

Parallels Between Career Health and Physical Health

We suggest that career health has many parallels to physical health:

A. Some portion of our health is hereditary or a predisposition. In medical health terms, our physique and temperament contribute to our predisposition to ailments. In career health terms, personality, behavior, and attitudes contribute to our career trajectories.

B. Some portion of our health is under our direct control and amenable to improvement through prescriptive measures. In medical health terms, this corresponds to diet, exercise, and avoiding drug addiction or accident. In career health terms, career-transition methods, techniques, tactics, strategies, and practical courses of action influence career results. (See Chapter 3.)

C. Some portion of our medical health status is attributable to our physical environment, such as pathogens, air quality, climate, weather, humidity, and temperature. In career health terms, the economy, the values and "culture" that prevail within our specialty, our professional associations or professional associates, the "atmospherics" and conditions at our place of work or employment, and the degree to which we are compatible with these environments all contribute to adaptation.

Career health is measurable. Career-change champions seem to possess identifiable inner resources that enable them to cope well (often extremely well) with the cards they are dealt: resilience, versatility, the ability to recognize and exploit serendipity. Some of us seem to acquire good cards later.

There are common themes in the career-change narratives of many stellar scientists, engineers, and physicians. But we also find similar themes in the narratives of those of us who are in the center of a normal distribution of doctoral-level individuals.

We believe we have identified many, if not most, of these themes. Please feel free to contact us with your own suggestions: what does your observations or experience tell you are the key ingredients or hallmarks of career well-being? We welcome your recommendations for additions to or deletions from the "Career Well-Being Inventory."

Here is how David Z. Robinson, a person with an abundance of career transitions (including presidential science advisor and foundation executive) and career well-being, views his transition history: "If there were any patterns to these semichance events and career turning points, perhaps it is that I do a good job at everything I do. I have many outside interests and activities—tennis, bridge, poker, music, ACLU, ADA. I also enjoy working with other people very much. Being part of a group and serving or contributing to a cause is very satisfying for me."

He did not attribute his successful career transitions entirely to his contacts and accomplished friends, but it is clear that they were important. His comment that many of the smooth transitions he experienced were "semichance events" betrays his abundant modesty. Yet he has both authentic and deep self-confidence and a no-nonsense "can do" style that is extremely appealing to his colleagues and many loyal friends—all of whom he has maintained contact with. He is dedicated to "getting the job done" with minimal distraction, and his advice is sought by Nobel laureates and nonprofit organizations, on whose boards of directors he is pleased to serve. He exemplifies career well-being, and his score on the "Career Well-Being Inventory" surpassed 90 percent—one of the highest among the career-transition champions you will meet in these pages. Most of their scores averaged about 70 to 80 percent.

2.02 INTERNAL HINDRANCES TO CAREER TRANSITIONS

What is it about some of us as scientists and engineers that makes it difficult for us to change careers?

One explanation is that our expertise is a form of addiction. We purposefully narrow our focus to exclude extraneous observations. We strengthen other parts of ourselves. But this generalization is merely anecdotal, and perhaps abrasive and offensive.

Social scientists have observed and collected what they call statistical data about us.

Among sociologists who study the personality of scientists and those in related occupations,[1] there is consensus that we tend to be

Adventurous

Risk takers

Independent

Self-sufficient

Autonomous

Enthusiastic for work

Dominant

Sensitive

Very consistent findings[2] also show that we tend to exhibit an interest in things rather than in people or personal relationships; "somewhat loose controls" in behavior; an acceptance of challenge; unusual drive and commitment to tasks; and high aspirations, confidence, and self-esteem. But see the exceptions among our career narrators.

We have all met warm, emotionally competent, socially intelligent, extroverted, agreeable scientists, engineers, and technical and medical professionals.

However, "there is some evidence that the orientation which adult scientists display is observable during adolescence and leads to unusual dedication and commitment to intellectual activities *at the expense of other pursuits* . . . and an aversion to social, repetitive and persuasive activities."[3]

The investigative personality, whether from heredity, experience, training, or some combination, appears to preselect us for science careers or predispose us to patterns of preferences, competencies, activities, and cognitive tendencies, such as

Intellectual self-confidence

Mathematical/scientific ability

Complex, abstract, independent, original worldview

Able to integrate diverse stimuli

Susceptible to abstract, theoretical, analytic influences

Relatively insensitive to material and social influences

Prefers occupations and roles that facilitate preferred activities

Prefers roles and work that minimize aversions and incompetencies

Avoids enterprising occupations and persuasive roles

Characterized as analytical, rational, independent, radical, introverted, curious, critical, observational, symbolic, scholarly

In earlier decades,[4] the occupational mobility of scientists seemed to be determined by regional factors and the prestige of the Ph.D.-granting institution.

David McClelland[5] has made some generalizations (but see our narratives below) about scientists, based upon many assessment instruments. Scientists tend to "avoid interpersonal contact . . . ; avoid and are disturbed by complex human emotions . . . ; be unusually hardworking to the extent of appearing almost obsessed with their work."

Other proclivities of scientists[6] include the "achievement of recognition," working within a community of "great" men and women, and often the "feeling of comparative failure as scientists."

Many of these qualities have high survival value in an expanding universe of science and technology. And certain niches expand while others contract. However, some of these attributes also act as obstacles to the career change and the job search—in either an expanding or a contracting universe. They represent opportunities to stretch our behaviors and exercise those parts of our personalities that will support our quest for suitable occupations.

Here is Carole Urich, whose transition from bench chemist at Polaroid led her to be senior executive vice president. She converted her internal hindrances into assets by simply reframing them in a useful way.

CAROLE URICH

••••••••••••••••••••••

Transition from Chemist to Polaroid Senior Executive Vice President

I have a sense of my intellectual capability. I always watched others at work. I realized that if they could do what they were doing so well—science or management—so could I. My mentor was the guy who offered me the job as plant manager. He knew I could and should do it, and so I did. If I had invested in a Ph.D. in chemistry, I would have stayed with technology work, and because of that I probably would not have become a manager of people. I would still be at the bench.

I have had a lot of mentors, but I never consciously thought about it; it just happened. I would try to open up my mind and their minds. Unconsciously, perhaps. But also, I always seemed to be at the right time and place to move ahead.

I know I always established a basis of conversation with a wide variety of people. With all my bosses, I always tried to solve *their* problems. I never brought them *my* problems. I would never wait for them to ask me to solve their problems; I would go to them and say, "May I help you?" I anticipated their problems *before* they would ask.

But I worked at the bench with "reclusive scientists," who always seemed to *wait* to be asked to solve technical problems. These were academic folks—always reading and thinking. They rarely showed interactive behavior. They called that "playing politics," putting a negative spin on it.

I found, on the contrary, that if I wanted to change my work environment, I had to do what the recluses called playing politics. I practiced "relationship development." I formulated it (maybe unconsciously) in the affirmative. I guess I wasn't smart enough to recognize that I was getting so many mentors.

I was surprised that I was getting so many mentors because I was a shy and introverted child who spent most of my childhood hiding under my mom's kitchen table. I didn't overcome this quickly or easily. Once you train yourself to solve technical problems, you gain enough confidence to solve other people's problems and management problems as well.

I have a large population that reports to me now. But some people think that schooling is designed to help them find situations where they are comfortable rather than to change themselves. I did not get where I am today by being the same person I was a long time ago, hiding under the table.

For example, I learned I could always win technical arguments. Scientists love debates. I loved it as an intellectual exercise. But that's not winning (in management terms, that's losing). The person who is "the rightest" is usually the wrongest for a large organization that has to get people to cooperate on common goals.

Education, especially graduate school, trains people to think within a discipline. It doesn't teach people how to work collaboratively, how to think about work. Some of us are coachable, with a mind-set to make our boss or team look good. I found that whenever someone gave a good speech or behaved well with colleagues, I would make myself learn what that person did and copy it. I always tried to imitate my betters.

2.03 TRAINED INCAPACITY AMONG SCIENCE AND TECHNOLOGY PROFESSIONALS

Necessarily narrow modern specialties change now with such alacrity that formal schooling can barely begin to address and absorb rapid advances found in the field.

Yet almost a century ago, Thorstein Veblen, in his book *Theory of the Leisure Class* (1899), diagnosed another serious problem among educated populations. He noticed that the more formal training, schooling, and advanced education each of us receives, the more we are unable to achieve practical results in mundane but necessary economic pursuits, and the less versatile we tend to become.

The result is a pervasive decline of broad-band competencies, and their replacement by extreme technical competence in very narrow fields of expertise: scientists, engineers, physicians, and attorneys present vivid examples daily in our professional career management practice.

In effect, by strengthening one "muscle," or set of skills, at the expense of other needed muscles or skills, we become muscle-bound in one set of skills and enfeebled or atrophied in other (often more practical or street-smart) skills. Thus, exercising a favorite muscle, like an addiction to one's specialty, may not have great survival value if the market doesn't need it, especially if we neglect others that are needed to get the job done.

Veblen called this phenomenon *trained incapacity*.

We need to understand the anatomy of the atrophied muscles.

We scientists and engineers are now educated with such narrow and deep specializations that we are educated beyond our abilities—especially our abilities to market ourselves or make career transitions. We are, in ef-

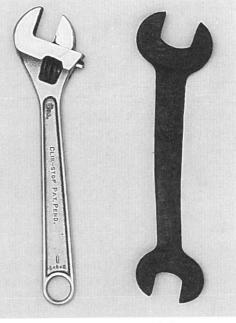

"Are You Adaptable"

fect, trained to be market-unready and thereby economically incapacitated by career immobility, and emotionally incapacitated by our expertise.

"Science casts such a narrow and brilliant beam of light on a part of our experience with such glaring intensity," physicist Victor Weisskopf said, "that the rest remains in even deeper darkness."

Here is Randy Krauss, a microbiology Ph.D. (1992) who began his post-doc in molecular medicine at the University of Massachusetts Medical Center, a very intense, competitive, and visible molecular biology laboratory. His energy and enthusiasm for bench science dwindled during this three-year fellowship. He explains how he faced up to his struggle to change career directions, and how he flexed new muscles and overcame trained incapacity. He also shows how difficult such a transition is.

Transition from Lab Bench to Education Coordinator

I was still enthusiastic about science, but the ups and downs that we all go through at the bench were beginning to get to me. It was becoming clear to me from looking at the progress of my research, as well as the ability of my colleagues to find permanent positions in either academics or industry, that a second postdoc would be necessary if I wished to stay in research. There were also other reasons for my unhappiness, including pressure to publish, the difficulty in obtaining funding, long hours, and, of course, a salary that was less than ideal. I felt a second postdoc would do nothing to alleviate these hardships.

I became aware of the fact that friends and family were always asking me about news reports they had heard or read related to science or medicine—what did this mean or that mean. I realized that people outside laboratory research might also benefit from my knowledge of molecular biology. I became interested in increasing the public's awareness of biotechnology and began to collect biotech educational materials. I made a list of types of institutions that I thought might benefit from someone trained in molecular biology, which included, but was not limited to, school, publishing companies, law firms, venture capital firms, consulting firms, and public relations groups. I believed that all these institutions might need someone with my background to interpret or explain science.

Why would these companies or organization need a scientist? Law firms, for example, need scientists to interpret scientific data for forensic cases or patents. Public relations and venture capital groups need scientists to explain the significance of a laboratory breakthrough in order to interest the people they are trying to reach. Public relations firms must inform the public as to how a product may benefit them, and also answer questions and address concerns that the public may have about a particular type of technology or product. Venture capitalists will not invest in a company if they do not understand how the company will use a technology or a product to make money.

I spent several months developing a new networking base, as most of my contacts in science were at the lab bench. I made a list of names of people and companies from local biotechnology organizations, the World Wide Web, and newspaper articles that discussed a scientific breakthrough, a particular program, or relevant business news.

Making contact with these people was the hardest part and was an emotional roller coaster. The people I contacted fell into three categories. The first group consisted of people who wouldn't give me the opportunity to speak with them. Next, there were people who agreed to keep my CV on file in case they or others had a position that became available, but did not provide me with information. Finally, there were people who would spend a significant amount of time talking to me, providing me with information and names of colleagues who might have a need for someone with my background. Often these people were extremely impressed with my desire to create opportunities on my own. Almost immediately, I confirmed my suspicion that there was a need for scientists away from the lab bench. My network of contacts has continued to be of assistance to me even as I begin my new career.

Each informational meeting or interview was a learning experience. I always had to explain my reasons for leaving the bench, my ability to adapt to the new world I would be entering, and how I could contribute to the company or organization with which I was interviewing. Unlike an interview for a lab job, where it is possible to discuss science for the entire meeting, these interviews often covered many areas, and at times, because this was a career change, areas that I was not totally familiar with. Specifically, I was asked whether I could communicate my knowledge of science to people with little or no background in science and how I would accomplish this. After all, they would be hiring me to interpret scientific information, and if I couldn't communicate the information, I would be of little benefit to them.

Preparation for these interviews was key. I became familiar with trends or materials that were available about a particular interviewer, the company, and, equally important, the industry. Thus, when I was contemplating a career change to education, I became familiar with many educational resources that were available from biotech companies, the Web, and local education initiatives. If I interviewed in consulting, I became familiar with the stock market, the interests of local biotech companies, the business section of local newspapers, and business journals. You are not expected to be an expert in a field or area that you have not worked in, but becoming familiar with material will at the very least show interest, which in turn will send a positive message to the interviewer indicating that you will able to handle a career change. I would strongly recommend becoming familiar with areas that you believe may interest you before sending out letters seeking employment. First, this will help you determine if you are truly interested in a particular field. Second, it will allow you to become more knowledgeable about the field, without looking as if you memorized information before the "big exam" or interview.

I accepted a position as laboratory coordinator at Boston University School of Medicine's CityLab Program and as an instructor in the Biochemistry Department. CityLab is a biotechnology education program designed to give middle and high school students and teachers hands-on learning experience in biotechnology. My responsibilities at CityLab include managing the lab, troubleshooting scientific problems, designing additional experiments for students to do in the lab, teaching (at the high school, undergraduate, and medical school levels), and providing information on current techniques and overviews on subjects that teachers or students may have heard of through media reports. Although I didn't have experience in education, I was familiar with biotech educational materials and had a strong desire to communicate my enthusiasm for science to others.

The period before finding this position was a difficult one. Once I made the decision to explore alternatives, I still had to wait for the right opportunity, while continuing to carry out my research project. I found looking for a job a job in itself and spent several hours a night preparing. Upon making the decision, I had several thoughts. First, I came to the realization that my years of doing research would be coming to an end. I was not upset about this, as my reasons for leaving day-to-day research were very strong. However, I did reflect on the fact that I had spent most of my professional life training to be a researcher. Also, when starting any new job, you wonder if you made the right choice.

To date, my experience at CityLab has been very positive. I am in the lab with students and teachers sharing my enthusiasm for science. A lab background is necessary for this position, and my input is encouraged and respected. No regrets.[7]

Randy's colleagues were surprised but enthusiastic about his career transition. Surprised, because they had not considered or explored opportunities away from bench science. Enthusiastic, because they felt his new position was a good fit. More importantly, they were able for the first time to consider new opportunities for themselves. They discovered, by Randy's example, that they did not have to be strapped to the lab bench forever.

2.04 EVEN IN THE BEST OF TIMES

In the post-World War II era, after the Manhattan Project, rapid growth in research and development was fueled by the cold war; this was what colleagues have called the "golden age of science," when the United States experienced a very strong employment market for science and engineering professionals.

It was the best of times for many well-qualified professionals. Nevertheless, even then, many had to struggle with career transitions. A glimpse of their struggles can give us an idea of how hard it can be to change careers, even during an expanding job market.

A group selected by their professors as "outstanding" were awarded graduate fellowships at Columbia University in 1944–1945 and 1950–1951. They were followed up fourteen years later, when they were found to be on the highest rungs of their profession, technical specialty, or management. Their careers and career changes were monitored and analyzed.

Here are salient results of the study by Ginzberg and Herma.[8]

- The subjects included equal populations of physical scientists, social scientists, and those in humanities and the professions (law, medicine, engineering, architecture).
- Most attained a Ph.D. or advanced professional degree.
- They placed a high value upon career satisfaction, the nature of their work, and the opportunity for self-expression that work presented.
- About 58 percent followed a straight career path (entered and remained in one field and function, like chemistry research).
- About 29 percent followed a broad career pattern (shifted fields or moved into administration).
- About 13 percent followed a variant pattern (changed directions completely).
- Two-thirds met or exceeded their expectations for career fulfillment (independent of their value orientations or social type).
- Those considered by their professors to have "outstanding personalities" were likely to be at the top achievement level.

- Those considered by their teachers to have "colorless" personalities were much more likely to be at the lower achievement levels than those whose personalities had been assessed as "unattractive."
- Career self-realization was not a fully conscious process, but had to be learned from the alternatives encountered.

What does this say about pre- and postdocs, high-level professionals, and their job environments in the 1990s and beyond?

If two-thirds met or exceeded their career fulfillment expectations, then one-third didn't. This is consistent with what we see in the late 1990s—unemployment, disaffection, and dissatisfaction rates among scientists and engineers. So the more things change, the more they remain the same.

Personality plus ability equals achievement. This is also consistent with contemporary career success stories and career satisfaction trends. Anecdotally, we have noticed that candidates with equal abilities were able to tip the hiring decisions in their favor consistently, over many career changes, because of their pleasing, easy-to-work-with personalities, as you will also see from the career-change narratives below and in later sections.

In a recent biography, Franklin Delano Roosevelt was called a second-rate intellect, but a "first-rate temperament." Most corporate employers would rather work with a colleague who has both good ability and good temperament.

Each of the following career-transition narratives echoes many of Ginzberg's findings. Some of our career-change narrators are contemporaries, and some are intellectual descendants from the period he studied.

Vern Ehlers is a U.S. Congressman who evolved (or morphed) from a low-energy experimental nuclear physicist (Berkeley, 1960). His agreeable temperament emerges from a long conversation with him. A few excerpts reveal his interest in politics, public service, religion, and good fellowship.

VERN EHLERS
....
Transition from Physics to Politics

I became a candidate for the local County Commission, and I won by 113 votes out of about 6,000 on the Republican ticket. I went door to door handing out spruce seedlings that had a note on them saying, "Keep Camp County Green—Vote for Vern." It was part-time politics, and I could still teach and do research. But what happened is, once you get into politics full time, people really propel you into it further. One month later I ran for the state legislature, and one year later I ran for Congress. I really did not want to leave academia, and I never intended to get into politics, but as a Calvinist, I believe that "the Lord just put me where he wanted me to be." I could go back to academia in a minute, but I have no regrets.

The first pattern that pervades my turning points is religion; it has been a constant in my life, and it has assumed greater importance since I got into politics. My wife has chosen not to live in Washington, D.C., so I fly back home every weekend, and we go to church every weekend, which brings me back to reality, away from the hubbub of Congress, and puts my life back into focus. We Calvinists have been given a rough deal, but we have a very strong tradition of service to others. I still work on the church synod's world hunger project.

My advice is shaped by sixteen years of teaching at Calvin College and being educated as a liberal person, pursuing knowledge for its own sake. I've watched people who came here very focused on getting their engineering degree and going out to solve engineering problems. They were required to take liberal arts and humanities. Over time, I've watched as a disproportionate number of former students went on to become managers—their superiors said that they had a broad view and intrinsically valued the betterment of people, and it was good training for adaptability and versatility.

Physics is as much a liberal art as English literature is. We pursue knowledge for the sake of knowledge. People say, don't go into physics—the job market for physicists is bad. I say, get your doctorate in physics if you like it, and don't assume that you have to do physics, or only physics-related work. Physicists can be stockbrokers or politicians, and your training prepares you for much more. If you enjoy science, continue in it and go out and face the world. See what you can do to help.

I also encourage scientists to get involved in government or politics.

I must say that I am blessed by my abilities to enjoy my work, whether it's physics research, teaching, or politics. It's a privilege to do the kind of work I do and have done. I know that work is the glory of God. There are people who say, Why go to church? It's filled with hypocrites! Can you imagine a better place for them to be? And good fellowship is an important aspect of life.

Nathan Myrhvold, cosmologist and collaborator with Stephen Hawking (and now right-hand man to Bill Gates), is an example of Ginzberg's finding that career self-realization is not a fully conscious process, but has to be learned from the alternatives that present themselves, often serendipitously.

NATHAN MYRHVOLD
••••••••••••••••••••••

Transition from Quantum Gravity and
Cosmology to Microsoft Senior Vice
President

T he turning points in my life are apparent only retrospectively. Only afterwards did they prove to be turning points.

Literally by accident, I worked on a computer software program; it was a summer project. The goal was to develop mathematics software that would deal with mathematical functions and equations as easily as Word-Perfect deals with words. It was really intended to be a short-term diversion, not a career. But somehow venture capitalists became involved, and the next thing I knew we were a company. It just grew and grew, and finally we sold it to Microsoft, where I was supposed to continue on it. But I ended up developing Windows instead.

I was interested in mathematics, geophysics, and cosmology, and I got degrees from UCLA and Princeton, where I worked with Ed Witten and others in the field of quantum gravity and cosmology. I then went to work with Stephen Hawking for a year. There was really no rational economic basis to work in cosmology—there were maybe three jobs worldwide for cosmologists. I got one of them. I loved it. Hawking and I were trying to create a Schroedinger wave function for the entire universe. Very fundamental, almost philosophy. I never decided to move on. I wanted to be a physics professor. Cosmology was fascinating to me, and I still communicate with Hawking.

But this small software project, which doesn't exist now that it's merged into Microsoft, was never intended to be a career, and yet that's what happened.

I don't know if my knowledge of the conceptual language of physics has helped me to understand software or not. I tend to think in physics concepts, but others who know no physics do very well in software development. It's not clear to me whether concepts of physics are deeply meaningful or a convention. I don't think that learning physics was a drawback to working at a software company like Microsoft.

I suspect that after eleven years here at Microsoft, I'll continue to be here for a while. On the other hand, I am very interested in biology, paleontology, and all kinds of other things. I could imagine all sorts of interesting things to do, not competitive with what I do now.

I'm embarrassed about giving advice to others about their careers. Many scientists seem to get worked up about their own career situation. If you told me I would be working in "industry" when I was working on cosmology, I would have imagined that that meant I had to shovel coal or work in a salt mine. I just wanted to be a physicist.

When I look back, it seems that serendipitous events made a fool of my career plans. I'm not saying you shouldn't make career plans. I was uncertain about my own plans, but I was open to new possibilities. Even the best-laid plans go awry. The world is not simple or straight as we first imagine. So people should adjust their plans accordingly.

Role models did play a role in my career, but it would be hard to say what role they played. I remember that when I went to Microsoft, many of my physics friends thought I was betraying the religion, leaving the fold. Success in graduate school was determined more by what role model you selected for thesis advisor.

I do know people who are rainmakers, who say they are mystified about how success seems to have chosen them. Sure, they are "people magnets," but it's disingenuous of them to say that they don't know why or how they succeeded. They didn't do it by keeping their nose in a book.

We have noticed "rainmakers" (for example, in law firms) who claim that "business just comes to me and I don't know why." The implication is that they are very good at what they do and thus are magnets for new revenue. But a more prosaic answer is that when they are asked (as Celia Paul did for an article on rainmakers) how they spend their time each day, they answer, "On the telephone, talking to prospects." Yes, it is disingenuous of them to say they don't know, and, yes, they don't make rain by keeping their nose in a book—they go out looking for it.

Here's a career transition from theoretical physics to Wall Street that appears to be a "variant pattern," in Ginzberg's terms (a complete directional change). But that's not what this transition shows at all. Rather, the person found deep structural similarities between options pricing and quantum gravity or fluids. Perhaps you too can imagine deep structural similarities between what you do now and what you want to do next. Such a discovery integrates and synthesizes your many aspects, your transition, and you as a fully realized, fully functional individual.

Transition from Field Theory to Wall Street

I 've heard it said that academics never succeed in their first job outside academia because they first have to learn the lessons of an opposite social environment. I know quite a few very successful people who changed careers. I want to stress that this is not unique to scientists, because anyone may want to change career directions. The problems that arise, the impetus, the obstacles, are not special and not glorified.

The basic things that motivate people are obvious—a combination of uncontrollable forces in the job market and more qualitative effects, events, impressions, frustrations, and desires to move on. It seems strangely ordinary to have patterns that many go through. For example, I know a lot of people who left physics but were dedicated, loved it, made lots of sacrifices; some are embittered, some look back at that phase as a big mistake.

I have lost none of my fascination with physics. I still have close contact with physics people. I give seminars in my old field, in techniques and physics methods that can be used in the financial world. So it doesn't seem that remarkable that I decided to move on. I'm doing something that is equally as engaging as physics, if not more so. The work I do now, like the work I did in physics, uses equations, and the people are really smart.

I am motivated by fundamental problems of markets. Like science, markets are natural phenomena and randomness. What drives a market is a lot of different behavior: a lot is explainable after it occurs, some is predictable. The tools we use are tools for dealing with a lack of information—probability and risk. Risk is a measure of expectations about the future—transactional problem solving. It's similar to galaxy formation. Financial risk is expectations under certain contingencies and conditions, just like much of the structure of quantum field theory and statistical mechanics. Among the crowning achievements of our civilization are our profoundly incomplete understanding of quantum field theory and statistical mechanics.

We take expectations that are conditional on some event, such as valuing a complex set of marketplace options, and try to assess my company's exposure to the risk posed by exogenous events, mass market downturns. Even at the level of mathematical equations I use, there's also a need for assessing technology data, since I'm on the trading floor using three computers and scanning several other screens filled with changing information. I am also running models and their applications, developing pricing, doing risk management, designing algorithms, and supervising their implementation and coding.

The backgrounds of the physicists I worked with were homogeneous—they were all physicists. For the past three years at Lehman Brothers, the people I've worked with have been more heterogeneous, a wide range of different backgrounds—Ph.D. dropouts, Ph.D.s, economists, computer experts, academics of various stripes, teachers, mathematicians. In academia I did not have to contend with a corporate bureaucracy, but we have to get along, work cooperatively in a loose team culture, and although it's different from before, it's not such a great stretch.

I trade bond indices—an abstraction, a number that fluctuates—determined by the prices of every bond. Maybe 6,000 bonds. I trade that entire basket of bonds, and estimate its value. I trade with customers, other traders, investors, institutions. I will sell, determining what the correct value is of this security, offering it at a fair price. I'm actually selling my ability to determine a fair market value. I use measurements of a lot of things, fairly complicated, that determine the fair value of an index. I make many observations and decisions and synthesize them. Credit derivatives is a new area where we are becoming able to quantify and thus control or manage risk. We have invested heavily in this, based partly on models I've designed. Although it's hard to describe, we are basically offering this to a new financial market. It should not be surprising that information flow is at the heart of it. In theoretical physics, a diffusion equation is really developed to quantify our understanding and interpretations of data. Well, markets are data! In some way, a diffusion equation can describe heat moving—not the actual microscopic events taking place, but the average or macroscopic phenomena. In investments and in markets, the diffusion equation can value options, which are the values you put on contingent events or some outcome. It's one big fabric, and I don't see the problem-solving aspects as very different. What sets physics apart from meteorology or other complex phenomena is that physicists really had the hubris to go after what they deemed were the fundamental drivers in nature.

Physics gave me something that other applied areas of science did not—a potential to change my view of the world—and allowed me to wrestle with notions that affect my outlook in deep philosophic ways.

Why did I leave physics? When I first left physics in 1993, after working since 1987, I was seen as symbolic. I was the subject of several interviews in the papers, in magazines, and on television (NBC nightly news). The press was very interested in why a young physicist, who had, I guess, some sort of fairly high standing in the physics community would leave. I was a bit of a "poster boy" for this issue. For instance, in a *Scientific American* interview, I was quoted as saying, "I left academia for Wall Street in order to lose my cynicism."

This was partly true. I really had been cynical, but I don't want to give the impression that I'm bitter or angry at physics or physicists. I can be objective. The field has rotted from the inside out—now natural, human and social forces take precedence over physics. Physics was driven by experiment, science, and curiosity in Newton's and Einstein's time. Now you find that it's driven by getting approval by powerful figures in your field. It's become much more dependent on credentials, supply and demand for labor and teachers, a limited number of people who decide who gets money—it's incestuous. Imperfections will pervade any field. But physics had been spared much of that because every challenging new exciting result was testable, and not due to a person's popularity. Now physics is observational and theory tends to be unmoored, although theorists can still make a brilliant career. Academic fashion dominates physics now. The friends I talk to who are still in the field say that there is no sense of anything really being accomplished, or about the quality of physics being done. Someone commented, "Never has there been an age when so many smart people were doing so much useless science."

Physics is being outstripped by genetic science and computer science. Back in the days when physics captured people's imagination and excitement, Einstein was a celebrity, on a par with movie stars of today. Physics is, inexorably, becoming irrelevant. String theory is symptomatic: interesting mathematics, very esoteric, bold claims made, but no one has any illusions that it will be profound and exciting.

I don't think I would have been a physicist if I had not been inspired by its content. I never ceased to be inspired by what physics was. I lost my conviction about what physics could become. I was satisfied. I met all my personal goals. I did not climb up the career security ladder—that would have come—it was not my main interest. I had gotten my fill of it. My transition to Wall Street was due to a long-standing interest in economics. I had friends in New York who got me information, contacts, and eventually job interviews. I got the first job I interviewed for. I dislike networking strategically and developing contacts whose sole purpose is to advance my career. You should see the parade of interview subjects who come through here, who have perfected their handshake, staring into your eyes, giving you their business card, who have learned the "right" way to network. It's all very tiresome, based on form and not on content. Yet you have to compromise. It's necessary but not pleasant; since we live in a social society, you always have to monitor the norms of society. In coming to Wall Street, you have to put the uniform on; you won't get a job here if you appear in jeans and a T-shirt. The eccentric type of physicist who will not change outward appearances, forms, or manners just will not have a chance here.

How well do you get along with others? How well do you get things done? How well do you concentrate on substance rather than form? Do you adapt? When I see people who worry about their career paths, their rank, their compensation, who the boss is—these people are not using their best energies on content.

You have to work well with people in teams. You have to be effective in deploying other people. I can't write my own C code—others have to do that. I'm satisfied in both of my careers. I experience great exhilaration and great frustration. I am still inspired by the accomplishments of physics. Our picture of the universe—string theory, black holes, the large-scale structures—is very beautiful and profound.

Perhaps you have guessed that this individual is a highly productive, exceptionally gifted scientist-turned-options trader. Some people are in awe of his credentials (Ph.D. Stanford, Harvard, Institute for Advanced Study, 45 papers published in five years). His career resilience places him at the upper tail of a normal distribution of scientists. His cynical views of contact making and the current science scene are independent of his own accomplishments, versatility, and career well-being. Although he scoffs at networking, perfect handshakes, and good eye contact, his "people skills" are clearly intact, his social intelligences are the equivalent of his scientific/mathematical intelligences: considerable. Our next morpher actually morphed herself and her career several times, and qualifies for the title "polymorph" as well as persistent.

Transition from Biology to Editor
to Publishing to Grant Administration
to Writing

About halfway through graduate school, you kind of get into this tunnel—you know, there's no light at either end, and you start to wonder, is this really how I want to spend my life? I kind of flip-flopped on it a few times. In the end I basically decided, probably about a year before I was ready to finish, that I didn't want to do a postdoc. I was tired of working at the bench, kind of burned out, kind of thinking that I wanted to do something more general. When you're doing research, your focus is so narrow, and I really liked to be more of a generalist to know less about more things rather than everything about this one thing. And I decided that to me, to work sixty or seventy hours a week was a bit much. To me the payoff just wasn't big enough to justify working that hard.

But I really didn't know what else I was going to do. I'd always had strong language skills. I was never that narrow in my focus like many scientists are.

The way I found out about this job was a fluke. I started brainstorming, and I said, OK, if I could do anything in the world, a fantasy job, what would I do? And I thought, well, gee, I'd really like to work at the zoo. Zookeeping. That would really be a lot of fun. Then I backed off and said, OK, in serious terms, what kinds of things could I do for the zoo that would make sense?

Grant administration came to mind because I'd been doing some of that for the genome project, talking to the people in Washington and making sure we were doing everything correctly and had approval. That was one thing—they must have some type of research grants.

The other thing that came to mind was fund raising. I started to think, well, when I was an acquisitions editor, part of that job involved not just knowing science but going out and wining and dining people, talking them into things. A lot of it was building a rapport, nurturing people. That's kind of applicable for fund raising.

I called up someone who was a higher-up in the Institute and I said, here's what I'm thinking, what do you think? She said, that sounds like a really good idea, and the people who do that here are—and she gave me the names, and I called the person who is now my boss, and she agreed to meet with me. As soon as I told her I had worked in publishing, she said "Can you write?" and I said, "Well, I can fudge it." She said, "We need a science writer—we lost our science writer and we've been freelancing a lot of stuff, and there are some people who can kind of fake it, but they're not scientists, so let's talk about this more."

I left my last job on a Friday, and I came in Monday and started this job, and that was about two years ago. It's worked out well—I've been really fortunate.

Not only did she exceed her expectations in an activity she hadn't planned to enter, but she displayed conspicuous absence of shyness in pursuit of her contacts. We will discuss exponential interviews in Section 3.11.

The following narrator had multiple career transitions, from academia (Harvard) to industry (Bell Labs), and eventually back again, to Columbia University. The Harvard faculty advised him against his first move, but he decided that the "best reason not to teach was that I couldn't imagine teaching without real-world experience. It seemed obvious."

But organizational life taught him some lessons about personality and people dynamics.

Transition from Biophysics to Industrial Research to Geology

After about six years I was asked to be department head. Most places offer you this kind of job without transmitting any wisdom—you have to relearn what everyone else knew.

Major learning and creating impact clearly demands skills other than lab skills. To be a manager somehow without any instruction was difficult. I had a responsibility to make things work with my boss. I had assumed that power came from the bottom, and friction from the institution. Now I was the agent of the institution. I had to listen to institutional concerns, program the issues. I would work from the top down, rather than from the bottom up. An example would be my attitude when someone was underperforming, I would not be sympathetic. Bell Labs had a management model adopted from the university culture.

Exxon had set up a new lab, trying to position itself as an energy company, not an oil company. In 1981 I joined Exxon as director of the physical sciences lab. This was a level above where I had been, and I was exposed to the business side of a large corporation. Major learning was necessary to realize that the top of the company was in control, and that being right—the disease of physicists—does not work with people, emotions, feelings, and the corporate culture. You have to feel comfortable about knowing when to shut up, and feel a need to do what the company thinks is important. I felt I had to balance being smart when I expressed my disagreement.

After a while, I began understanding the Exxon corporate culture. It was an extremely well-managed company, and it made a big effort to teach me and help me adapt. Management was very professional. In 1986, the company downsized, there was a change in leadership, and they cut the lab back. The energy leaders lost power to the oil men in the company. In fact, the headquarters was downsized by a factor of four, and the corporate lab by a factor of two. I came to respect these arguments, since the leaders understood that these upheavals were not just another economic cycle—it was really a new era, a new transition, a global economy. Every boss above me either was terminated or left. I was made senior director, with a budget of $100 million. It was a fundamental transition.

I negotiated for the lab and stabilized it by strategic planning. I had moved high up, but I felt too far up to remain content without the technical work. I started to think about change. It was all meetings.

It's very hard for people brought up in one era with one set of principles to come into a new era where the old principles don't work. Science had been an enormously successful enterprise. To give that up for a new customer-oriented activity was not in the cards for most people who had spent their whole life in the golden age of science. It would be naive to think that universities would benefit from the experience and could change.

Physics is really a great discipline for the mind, for problem solving, abstraction is a useful talent, and breadth of exposure makes it easier to build diverse careers.

Here are his conclusions, based upon his several satisfying transitions: (1) You have to learn new things on your own for each new job or career. (2) For most career paths, attributes beside scholarship are very important. You need to communicate to the nonexpert (the public or management) what you're doing and why, and communication is really undeveloped in the science community.[9] (3) Once you're out of the lab, you need to work in groups, to forgo individual contributions in favor of the group's. Disrespect for other disciplines is rife; in the hierarchy of the sciences, it seems that many practice "disdain downward." (4) It's very hard to predict what will happen to you in your career, but learning to make transitions will be more important for all of us.

So we are beginning to hear recurring themes of career-transition attitudes, behaviors, and strategies that pay off. We will find more threads in the fabric of career well-being in the following sections. This will lead us to an inventory of career well-being attributes, against which you can measure yourself.

2.05 BEYOND CREDENTIALISM

A Harsh and Narrow View of Credentialism

The "Law of the Instrument" is an aphorism about the expertise we develop as credentialed professionals: "Give a small boy a hammer, and you will notice that everything he encounters needs pounding."

A harsh and narrow view of expertise is that it is, or can be, a form of addiction. Experts can represent any viewpoint, no matter how absurd. This law is sometimes stated in the form, to every Ph.D. there is an equal and opposite Ph.D.

To extend our career health metaphor, not only do addicts have trouble without their "hit," which provides a "high," but also they exhibit an "addictive personality." Worse still, we see young scientists "anaesthetized" by their mentors. ("They lied to us.") A visit to a meeting of Alcoholics Anonymous or another "twelve-step" programs reveals that many of those who are recovering alcoholics become incessant users of tobacco and coffee. They have exchanged one habit for another. In health terms, they are still hooked. In career terms, this shows how hard it can be to give up a career or specialization that satisfies many needs, and gives us pleasure. But our Ph.D.s can be a burden, as the following limerick teases:

> *Graduate school was no breeze*
> *Weighed down by our Ph.D.s*
> *We collapsed from the strain*
> *Alas, it is plain*
> *We are killing ourselves by degrees.*

In a broadside against credentialism, James Fallows[10] remarked, "Professions now represent America's surest thing . . . an entrepreneurial society is like a game of draw poker: you take a lot of chances, because you're rarely dealt a pat hand and you never know what you have to beat. A professionalized society is more like blackjack, and getting a degree is like being dealt nineteen. You could try for more, but why?" An answer is that our professions and credentials are no guarantee of desirable employment. Because increasing fractions of the labor force are provisionally employed "contingency workers," it's draw poker for more and more of us.

Riverboat Pilots' Association

Among the career change champions—those who have changed careers one or more times, enjoying satisfaction and success— some have not obtained a doctorate. Yet they thrived, prospered, and fulfilled themselves. Therefore, in your transition to a new career, you can also flourish without a doctorate in your new career choice.

In his book *Life on the Mississippi*, Mark Twain described how the riverboat pilots attempted to make themselves into a monopoly. The expansion of the West created a boom in the steamboat business. Any farmhand could sign on as an apprentice pilot and depress the labor market for pilots. So the pilots formed a guild or association, recruited members, and exchanged information on the river's changing sandbars and currents.

"Now came the perfectly logical result. . . . The outsiders began to ground steamboats, sink them and get into all sorts of trouble, whereas the accidents seemed to keep entirely away from the association men," according to Mark Twain.

The insurance companies insisted upon association men as pilots. Steamboat owners agreed to successively higher wages, passing the cast along to the passengers and freight handlers. The pilots prospered until the steamboat industry overpriced itself and was destroyed by the railroads. Fallows[11] adds, "the association and the noble science of piloting [riverboats] were things of the dead and pathetic past!"

Doctorates as Union Cards

Doctorates have been called "union cards," reflecting a view that their possession was a permit, a license, or (at a time in the dead past) a guarantee for work in one's specialty. Attainment of a doctorate was a demonstration of a certain level of competence, knowledge, discipline, and research ability. It was also entry into an association of like-minded individuals, like the riverboat pilots. If the steamboats lost out to the railroads, the railroads subsequently lost out to the airlines, and the airlines may be losing out to the Internet and developments like videoconferencing.

Another view of the doctorate is that it bestows a certain professional status (but not necessarily stature). Professional status was once a form of insurance, "a familiar and cherished part of the American achievement ideal . . . the professional now represents America's surest thing."[12] But if everyone has a sure thing, who is going to take the risks?

The doctorate is not the only way to succeed in science and technology. A number of the career changers we spoke to have no doctorates. Yet they were satisfied and successful career changers; some were career-change champions. As you see from the following career-transition narratives, they thrived, prospered, and fulfilled themselves. They demonstrate career resilience and career well-being.

One political scientist explains: "When I was working on the Hill, and considering alternatives, I looked for jobs on committees, as congressional administrative assistants, and I remember being told by one potential political employer: 'Look at that stack of papers on my desk; those are people willing to work for free.' I realized I had 'credentialed' my way out of the job market."

Our next narrator prospered precisely because he had no credentials. He went to MIT in physics as an undergraduate, and after seven years at Stanford in physics, he was getting to the point where he had to decide whether he wanted to stay in academia. He decided that merely looking at postdoc appointments was not enough. "I had to look a few jobs moves ahead, so I decided to apply for jobs. I don't like wasting my time."

Transition from Relativistic Scattering Theory to Options Models

In 1987, I realized that the key issue for me was that academia was not a viable career. Since the Ph.D. was relevant mainly for an academic job, I realized I did not need to finish the Ph.D. Although my thesis on relativistic scattering theory was hard conceptually, I did not feel comfortable in presenting work that was not correct or the best I could do.

A small boutique options firm in Chicago, O'Connor and Associates, had placed an ad that said "graduate science students welcome." I went to their presentation. I had no background in finance, but I was intensely excited. The head of research was a physics Ph.D. The firm had a lot of cool problems. I flew out to Chicago and the guys there wore jeans, they had refrigerators full of free beer to help yourself. They said I could spend half my time doing what they wanted, and the other half doing whatever research in trading I wanted to do.

The center of the finance business is in New York or London, where the "A" teams are. So I came to New York.

I started modeling options. Think of it as a set of solutions to partial differential equations with boundary conditions set by the market. This was all applications from physics.

The people with decent skill sets in any quantitative discipline, especially physics and engineering, will always find a place to apply those skills in a business, especially a money business. But in business, you have to figure out why you are in a room with a group of other traders. You have to be able to switch back and forth from technical to financial to strategic matters very quickly, without getting disoriented. We have lots of programmers who are good producers of computer programs, but they stick to the details only. I work as the risk manager for the equities division, as a senior vice president to our managers worldwide.

I have to have the right level of focus and change quickly when I don't. A lot of scientists struggle with this, with interpreting what is needed when, what's the relevant level of focus, and how to communicate this. You can really leverage your problem-solving skills the more you can do this. Some of us are fast runners, some are fast talkers. But the greatest problem solvers can be useless unless they have these kinds of communication skills.

Here's another satisfied changer, minus a doctorate.

Transition from No Ph.D. in Animal Behavior to Comedy Writer of Science-Based Programs for Museums and TV

I wanted to get a Ph.D. in animal behavior, specifically elephants; because summers I worked at Zoo Atlanta. But while I was a student, I also wrote comedy sketches and did improvisation with a college theater troupe.

I found this was great fun, a blast. I did it as a hobby. I researched the field of comedy writing, and discovered that it was very difficult to find work. So I started giving free shows, writing and performing my own material for children at schools. I really enjoyed it very much. If I was bad or made mistakes, I figured that they were getting entertainment from me for free. I was learning. A friend filmed me, and I watched the films to see how I could make the performances better. I developed a style.

I was able to do a lot of this humor and writing because my parents were very funny. My father is a physician, and he used to tell great stories in any accent. My mother was a Ph.D., my sister's a Ph.D., my brother's an MBA. Being funny was always rewarded by laughter.

But he never abandoned science. He says he's glad he didn't go into a scientific career as a researcher or get a Ph.D. "I love any chance to write whatever I want to for kids, in any venue. People see my shows and I hear them say, 'I don't know if my kids liked it, but I liked it.'"

Here's a woman who went to Smith College, majored in math, and did that only because she loved it. "I'd say if there's any kind of theme in my career, it's been that I've gravitated toward things that I enjoy, and I'm lucky enough that that's worked for me. I'm not sure that everyone is that fortunate. I have the bachelor's degree only. I did go through an honors program, so I graduated with high honors in math, but I didn't go on to graduate school."

Transition from Mathematics to McDonnell-Douglas to NIST

I did some informational interviewing, and that turned up an offer of a job doing computer programming and computer-related activities at McDonnell-Douglas.

I was lucky enough to have a job that sent me to standards meetings, where I had a lot of interactions with other companies and government, and was able to co-chair different committees that I was involved in. I always felt that if you are going to participate, it's better to have a leadership role where you're more visible. I think that really did help.

There was a representative from NIST who participated in some of those meetings, and he knew of a job opening in NIST and suggested that I apply for it. It was just funny to find this group at NIST who cared vehemently about that standard process, the coordination process. From that lab, I ended up getting involved with Sematech, which has a framework for integrating manufacturing applications. I ended up working out a collaboration between Sematech and NIST, and at the heart of that collaboration was the framework technology.

One of the pieces of advice someone at McDonnell-Douglas gave me was to change jobs every three years and change careers every nine or every eleven. I don't think I've actually changed careers, but I have changed positions about that often, and things have worked. Moving around is actually a good idea. I feel that way even though I'm not sure if this last move I'm making is the right move or not, because I'm giving up a position where I at least had a lot of prestige and monitored a lot of funds. There's been a lot of excitement in being here.

One thing that's helped me a lot is networking—just being involved in organizations that span different companies or government agencies so that I have broader visibility outside of NIST. It's certainly been a plus to have those kinds of connections. They say you never know who your next boss is going to be. Someone that you hire could turn out to be your boss. That actually happened in my case.

She found that by doing what she enjoyed doing and what she excelled at, she was able to gain visibility. This led her to make good public presentations that strengthened her communications skills and her career-transition abilities.

Here's a naval architect and marine engineer who was so attached to English literature that he left his specialty for a year to satisfy his intellectual curiosity, and then returned to pursue a Ph.D. he never got.

He studied and designed propellers for the U.S. Navy's David Taylor Model Basin, while studying hydrodynamics at Johns Hopkins at full pay.

Transition from Naval Architecture and
Marine Engineering to English Literature
and Back

I spent a great deal of time on my dissertation topic, "Mechanics of Cosseret Surfaces" (about substances like liquid crystals with local directionality) on weekends, evenings. One day, I just decided to give it up. To quit. And I did. Both Columbia and Johns Hopkins were intellectual paradises, and excited the parts of me that love learning. I had no regrets about quitting; maybe it would be nice for my children to be able to say that I got a doctorate, but for me its only use would have been if I had ever wanted an academic position. I didn't. It had no effect on my career. I moved freely with professionals and professors in the field the rest of my life.

When I returned to David Taylor, I was head of the Hydrodynamics Branch, about twenty professionals reported to me. I had more scope in numerical fluid mechanics, physics of viscous fluids and cavitation, and analysis. From 1970 to 1980 was the happiest time of my career.

Eventually he was made editor of the *Journal of Ship Research*, which combined his love of mathematics and the written word. He followed his instincts.

Now that we have visited some flexible career transitioners, we have found common ground. We will look at *your* ability to segue from one career to another in the section of the book on renewal.

Our Web site[13] can direct you to complete details of the above career-transition narratives, plus a transitioner from political science to social science to a professional society director, plus other case histories.

2.06 GREENER PASTURES?

Scientists and engineers, especially younger postdocs, say that physicians and attorneys, no smarter than they, are sitting on top of the world. After all, the average compensation of doctors and lawyers is several multiples of the average salary of science and technology professionals.

We counsel high-level professionals, including attorneys and physicians, whose incomes can be an order of magnitude greater than scientists' incomes . . . and whose career dissatisfaction is as great, or even greater.

As many as two-thirds would not recommend their own profession to their children. Almost half would not, given the choice, enter the same profession again. (By the way, the United States has 5 percent of the world's population but about 70 percent of the world's attorneys, and about half of the world's scientists.)

One of our career-change champions says that the attitude of academics toward their corporate counterparts is, "If you're so smart, why aren't you poor?"

And Ginsberg and Herma,[14] in their study of accomplished professionals, remark, "Since accomplishment based upon endowment seems to be effortless . . . it is sometimes felt that it does not deserve special awards."

However, as the following case studies of an attorney and a physician show, their grass is no greener than ours.

CASE STUDY
•••••••••••••••••••••••••
The Dark Side of Surgery

Dr. Oberon (not his real name) is a thoracic surgeon in his mid-forties. He has held a number of academic appointments connected with hospitals and has published several dozen clinical/research journal articles.

However, he has held five jobs in nine years, which appears excessive even to him (the average is about two). He is highly conflicted about walking away from a career that he says he is very good at, and that is a source of self-esteem and immediate gratification.

His family was filled with physicians who believed medicine was "a calling," "the holy grail." His younger brother, whom he envies, is "a major investment banker."

He says he "loves his patients, but loathes administrators and cardiologists, has trouble with the system and getting along with others because of the politics and the moral stance of hospitals and managed-care contracts." He complains, "Heart surgeons are not well-adjusted people." He seems to have lost his altruistic ideals and feels "devalued." He says his physician father was "the last angry man," an idealist. He refers to himself as a "hot reactor."

He has considered alternative careers in creative writing, medical broadcasting or communications (as a radio/TV medical expert), and management consulting in the burgeoning health-care cost-containment field. He says he wants to be his own boss.

He has written a screenplay (as yet unsold) to demonstrate his belief that hospital administrators are basically corrupt.

His strongest values are "earnings," "independence," "status/prestige," "moral fulfillment," and "satisfying his calling."

Assessments show him to have a very high academic focus and high extroversion. His orientation scales suggest that he pursue leadership, law/politics, financial services, writing, or culinary arts. His occupational scales suggest that he pursue a career as an attorney, financial planner, manufacturer's representative, CEO/president, advertising account executive, writer/editor, or emergency medical technician. Other assessments suggest that he puts his best efforts into his work, that he is forceful, original, and conscientious; and that he perseveres in holding clear convictions about how to serve the common good.

He asserts that he is "a consummate doctor," and the work itself has "high melodrama," especially when the patient goes home "resurrected" through a transplant. Nevertheless, he feels that he has "virtually no control," since he can't operate outside the confines of a hospital. He says, "It's easier to be God than to have a God over me."

"I am at the bottom of a food chain that begins with the primary care physician who refers to the internist, next to the cardiologist, and then finally to the surgeon." He finds the surgeon's "life-style is lousy," with very long hours and very high stress.

· ·

CASE STUDY
· ·
High Income as an Insufficient Reward

Mr. David (not his real name) is a partner in an old-line law firm, specializing in highly structured project-finance transactions for large electric power and petrochemical plants.

He is in his early forties, earning $350,000, and although he is happily married, he finds that "something is missing" from his work life. He says he "lives inside my head" and leads an intensively introverted and introspective life, has ulcers, and has personal relationships that are "strangely impersonal, somewhat like Bill Clinton's."

His highest values are "creativity," "independence," and "intellectual challenge." He also values "time freedom" and "uniqueness of a new assignment."

He has very superior abilities: mental, linguistic, English usage, spatial visualization, and mechanical comprehension. He was magna cum laude at Harvard and at Princeton. But he has an unusual ability to lull himself and mesmerize others into considering all possible options in any given decision, which in career terms tends to paralyze him, foreclosing action.

His strongest and most enjoyable skills are "research," "data handling," "management", and "analysis." Others are entrepreneurial, persuasion, and follow-through.

Assessment instruments show very high interest in creating and design, in analyzing, and in producing, especially activities like "farming/forestry" and "plants/gardens." His academic focus is very high, and his extroversion (interest) is very low. On the occupational scales, he shows high interest and skills as an architect, landscape architect, fashion designer, chef, liberal arts professor, or some other "creating/producing" occupation.

Other assessments suggest that he has a highly original mind and a great drive to organize a job and carry it through, and is skeptical, critical, independent, determined, and sometimes stubborn.

His wife earns substantially more income than he, and encourages him to pursue his interests, but his ability to see so many sides of every issue he faces seems to immobilize him right now. Nevertheless, he needs to generate enough income from his new career direction to feel independent—"at least $150,000."

He has thought about being a landscape architect, a garden designer, the attorney-founder of a small law firm, or a management consultant, and about doing something to benefit the world, doing something socially useful, or building something. He has read many books on career change, but has been unable to "break out."

....

What career advice would help each of these ?

THE STRUGGLE: CAREER SATISFACTION BY TRIAL AND ERROR

Finding career satisfaction is rarely a fully conscious process, according to Ginzberg and Herma on their study *Talent and Performance*. They observe that much of the journey toward career self-realization "is not known to the individual either at the time it is happening or even in retrospect."

So it is important to decode or deconstruct the parts of the process that are unknown to us.

Time is likely to unveil some elements of this career-transition process, Ginzberg suggests, that "were shrouded because the individual was too involved to perceive connections or too inexperienced to be able to assess them correctly."

The purpose of presenting case histories and career-change narratives is to make this process explicit under as many different conditions as possible. Our exercises on renewal are designed to provide a system, a logical sequence of steps that help you fast-forward through the nuances of the transition process.

Without decoding, the process proceeds as it does in most careers: by trying actual career paths, by testing actual career alternatives we encounter during the job search or the career transition—essentially a Darwinian struggle to learn by trial and error how we fit into suitable career niches.

The struggle can be guided or self-directed, solemn or joyous, and can take months or years. We suspect that most of us cope with our own career problems as well as we cope with our health problems. We may muddle through, if we do it alone, as the following case study shows; or we may move through smoothly and with alacrity, like many of the champion career changers.

CASE STUDY
······················
A Scientist as Self-Healing Career Changer

Mr. Russ Salamani failed at his first effort to obtain a physics Ph.D., and received a master's degree in nuclear physics instrumentation.

His first job as a physicist was at IBM, working on the effects of nuclear radiation on electronic components and the propagation of gamma rays and neutrons through the atmosphere. After two years, the large organization he initially enjoyed felt impersonal.

He applied for an opening as assistant professor of physics at a small college, and began teaching undergraduate physics and mathematics. He enjoyed this for six years, and students found him to be "tough but fair" and a stimulating, often inspiring lecturer. He began graduate studies at a third-tier university part-time, and after two years completed a theoretical dissertation on high-energy nuclear pair production. His work was published in archival and international journals.

He sought a position in industry, since he was denied academic tenure and wished to increase his income to support a growing family. He began at a large research facility specializing in applied research on communications and power systems. After two years, he was let go because of his low productivity. He searched for other jobs in allied industries, but to no avail.

Remembering a social acquaintance who worked at a small research center, he called and was invited to join after an interview. The work was highly unstructured, a departure from his previous employment. He was able to write several papers that were eventually published, but he was again let go after two years during a downsizing.

On his own, with few job prospects at hand, he continued to write articles, which brought him consulting assignments with high-technology companies that needed his emerging skills in writing and marketing. He began to understand that teaching was a form of selling ideas, and he knew he had been a good teacher. He became keenly interested in how to sell high-technology products and services. He persuaded a book publisher that his ideas about technology and science were publishable in book form for a mass audience, and he thrived on the opportunity to speak publicly and to publicize the books he wrote.

Concurrently, he was securing consulting assignments with a variety of firms. These included management consulting projects for a large computer company, an assignment for a large foundation, and other assignments for financial organizations. He learned to make contacts on the telephone and face to face, and to use one set of contacts to find other contacts, by tapping his outgoing personality. He found and obeyed his demon.

A book publisher hired him to help market its books. An investment banking firm hired him to learn merchant banking—mergers and acquisitions.

But by his mid-forties he was adrift, his career was going nowhere, he was the victim of a midlife crisis and depression, and he had no clear career direction. He sought professional help, but this appeared to make matters worse by undercutting his self-confidence. He turned to religion, which gave him some small comfort after his parents died.

He began to do volunteer work, initially helping others who found his background compatible with their own.

His salvation and redemption ultimately emerged from "the healing power of helping others," as he regained his confidence slowly, harnessed his abilities—inspired by protégés—and he eventually became extremely active, productive, and satisfied in a teaching career.

·······················

2.07 ON BEHALF OF INTEGRITY, AMBITION, AND SELF-MARKETING

Joseph Epstein has observed[15] that to educated people, ambition is pointless at best, and vicious at worst. It is a "perverse quality to possess in an unjust society," arising from a lack of ability. The more educated one is, Epstein says, the more hopeless and unjust the ambitious self-promotional life seems. These attitudes and feelings are also shared by those people who are depressed (clinically or situationally) and echoed by others whose education and training bring them little satisfaction, or who are educated beyond their abilities to be satisfied.

However, among our career-change narratives, wholesome ambition appears to be ingredient of behavioral, cognitive, moral, and career health.

Indeed, Norman Podhoretz, in his autobiography *Making It*, referred to ambition and the craving for material success among academics and intellectuals as a "dirty little secret" that was regarded much the way sex was in the Victorian era. He asserted that he was an openly ambitious intellectual at a time (the 1960s) when ambition was considered provocative to academics and intellectuals; this was quite a bold confession then. He brought the dirty laundry out in the open for our scrutiny, and helped make ambition a subject fit for discussion, much as sex is now. (Sociologists say that in the 1990s, people speak more openly about matters sexual than about matters financial. On the other hand, we have noticed that some people will talk more readily about their *sex* problems than about their *career* problems.) A residue of negative associations still clings to ambition and self-promotion, especially among young academics, intellectuals, and some attorneys and physicians. Their career expectations and the need to *appear* satisfied with their career often make open career-problem discussions off limits, even taboo. To these populations, "careerism" and "opportunism" are the enemy of achievement and ascendence based on merit.

Academics and other credentialed professionals who care about appearances and political correctness will maintain privately that if one experiences stirrings or pangs of ambition, it is best to keep these (taboo) yearnings well hidden. Although it is not widely appreciated or believed, even budding Nobel laureates have been known to lobby for the prize or to urge friends to lobby for it on their behalf.

"Perhaps the one novel that no serious writer in America would care to write today is one about a man who sets out to succeed in life and does so through work, decisive action, and discretion, without stepping on anyone's neck, without causing his family suffering, without himself becoming stupid

or inhumane. . . . [This is] no basis for a novel because there is no conflict. But anyone who knows the world at all knows that to set out with legitimate ambition and to achieve what no one has set out to achieve without diminishing oneself is to have led a life filled with conflict."[16]

Benjamin Franklin was such a man.

A Genius for Life

He was also a man of many achievements, "accompanied by constant good fortune," possessed by a genius for life, for living, and for excelling at many careers—as a shopkeeper, printer, scientist, inventor, statesman, revolutionary, and "part-time philosopher." He experimented with lightning. He invented the Franklin stove. He initiated the first public library in the United States. He had abundant gifts—of energy, industry, patience, practicality, opportunism, ambition, and a "knack for turning everything to personal advantage."[17]

He was an earlier, amplified version of the career-change champions whose narratives appear throughout this book.

Benjamin Franklin teaches us that "human felicity is not so much produced by great pieces of good fortune that seldom happen[,] as [it is] by little advantages that occur every day." He also teaches us that life itself resembles a kind of plastic, a "substance within the power of each of us to mold." Several of our career-change narrators present modern variations on this theme.

Uriah Heep, Jay Gatsby, and Sammy Glick are literary stereotypes of ambition and cunning, or despicable deviousness and vulgarity, or single-mindedness and animal energy, or hot-blooded desire and attention to appearances—all traits and characteristics that many of us, and many other credentialed and educated people as well, tend to scorn. They personify William Hazlett's remark: "Fortune does not always smile on merit." In the public eye, selling ranks low and science ranks high. Rarely do they coexist well in the same person.

Ambition is an "ardent desire for rank, fame, or power" or "the fuel of achievement."[18]

Alfred Adler insisted that ambition is intrinsically healthy, "innate, a necessary and general foundation of the development of every person." "In the end, forming our own destiny is what ambition is all about."[19]

Fuel and Oxygen of Achievement

Ambition is a positive, productive driver of career progress and your career transitions.

Despite the low opinion that many credentialed professionals have of salespeople and selling, it is possible to market oneself with dignity and integrity—and it is necessary (but not sufficient).

Each of us is unique (just like everyone else). Thus, each of us has to find his or her own style and comfort zone of selling our skills and ourselves, self-promotion, and marketing—just as scientists have had to find their own style of doing science, research, and discovering (see "Strategies for Discovering" in Section 3.12).

Make a list of your objections to (1) being ambitious and (2) selling yourself. By making your objections explicit and comparing them to the narratives of our career-change champions (see especially the ones below), you may find that you can overcome your inhibitions or those objections by hitchhiking their realistic optimism, career satisfaction, and success. It's another form of gaining strength from their strength. It's a form of modeling behavior, acting "as if" you are someone else until it feels natural. On the other hand, if your style or your true self is not compatible with ambition and self-promotion, you may simply have to push yourself, tunnel through, or behave counter to your normal impulses and compensate.

Integrity Marketing and Selling

If ambition is the fuel of achievement, then marketing is its oxygen.

Buyers demand honesty and trust; but the used car salesman stereotype and Willy Loman in Arthur Miller's tragedy *Death of a Salesman* have done a disservice to the practice of selling with integrity and dignity.

If the seller and the buyer are considered adversaries—one wins and the other loses—it's no wonder that selling has a bad name. Selling is far too important to be left to the salespeople.

A major component of selling is gathering information: to identify potential buyers (*not* to push unwanted merchandise upon an unwitting sucker), and to understand what are the latent and overt needs of a potential buyer. Persuasion is virtually unnecessary when the buyer needs the product or service. And modern marketing emphasizes skill at *searching* (see "Strategies for Discovering" in Section 3.12) and *finding* the right client. In career terms, this is finding the right job or career.

The table below compares traditional and nontraditional (ethical) selling.[20]

Function	Traditional Selling	Non-manipulative Selling
Information gathering	Prospecting, small talk, fact finding—little time spent	Planning, meeting, studying—much time spent
Presentation	Pitching—more time spent	Proposing—little time spent
Commitment	Closing, overcoming objections—much time spent	Confirming—little time spent
Follow through	Reselling—little time spent	Assuring—much time spent

For-profit corporations, nonprofits, and academic institutions all invest substantial resources in selling. Airplane manufacturers invest some 5 or 6 percent of their revenues in selling their products to the airlines. As a percentage of revenues, the cost of sales varies: For the coal and steel industries it may amount to 3 to 5 percent; for the computer hardware and software industries, it may range from 20 to 40 percent; for perfume and jewelry, it may perhaps be as much as 50 percent. Academic institutions also invest heavily in recruitment of students. And academic researchers write grant proposals, a significant investment.

Why not invest a similar percentage of your income-producing time in marketing yourself and your skills, talents, and interests? That such an investment of time and activity protects your career investment may not be obvious, but it is reasonable, and you can make the investment without diminishing your substantive knowledge or sacrificing your honor, integrity, and dignity.

Ethics of Selling

Here are the values and ethics that are compatible with ethical marketing or selling, whether you are selling a product, marketing a service—or purveying yourself.[21]

1. Selling is an *exchange* of value.

2. Selling is something you do *for* and *with* someone (not *to* someone).

3. Understanding people's *needs* and *wants* must always precede any attempt to sell.

4. Develop *trust* and *rapport* before any selling activity begins.

5. Selling techniques give way to selling *principles*.

6. *Integrity* and *high ethics* are the basis for long-term selling success.

7. A salesperson's *ethics* and *values* contribute more to sales success than do techniques or strategies.

8. Selling pressure is never exerted by the salesperson. It's *exerted only by prospects* when they perceive that they want or need the item or service being sold.

9. Negotiation is never manipulation. It's always a strategy to work out problems . . . when prospects *want* to work out problems.

10. Closing isn't just a victory for the salesperson. It's a victory for both the salesperson and the customer.

A friend, a pharmaceutical lawyer, maintains that marketing and selling are among the highest creative endeavors and "art forms" evolved by humankind, a wholesome and integral part of being alive. But that's him. What about you? If you resist integrity selling, dignified self-promotion, for any reason, read on.

Entrepreneurial Talent

Entrepreneurial talent develops not only physical capital, but also "metaphysical capital." This may be in the form of a mental image of what you and your career should look like when you make it through the Darwinian job market (or "the valley of death," as Andrew Grove, head of Intel, puts it) to the other side.

Entrepreneurial talent is an ability to shift resources "from areas of low productivity and yield to areas of high productivity and yield," according to the nineteenth-century economist J. B. Say.[22] The following career narrators demonstrate this by their *behavior*, that is, to serve a market you have to understand what the market wants, and give it to them. The purpose of a business is to serve its customers, and if it's also well managed, it will incidentally run at a profit.

Marketing scientific instruments to an often antibusiness academic culture presents special challenges. "They were always putting 'truth and excellence' ahead of 'listening to the customer,'" as one career changer says. "This attitude comes back to bite people," he explains, and it propelled his own career make-over into software development. But marketing to satisfy customers[23] can make entrepreneurs prosperous, as the following vignette demonstrates.

HARDING WILLINGER
....

Transition from Dental School to Tropical
Fish Tank Supplier

I was a predental student at NYU for two and a half years. I never finished my bachelor's degree because I was drafted into the Army during World War II. When I came out of the service, I went to work with my brother Alan.

Alan was a hobbyist working in a pet shop. Somehow he met a man who was making electrical immersion heaters for tropical fish tanks that hobbyists kept their fish in. This was right after the war, when parts, supplies, and many consumer products were unavailable. Nevertheless, this man was able to scrounge enough materials and parts to make and sell a few hundred heaters a week.

Alan brought me in to help them make and package the heaters and deliver them to pet stores and jobbers. I knew all of his customers. I knew exactly where to buy the parts. I knew how to make and sell these fish-tank heaters. Because of who he was, I had no pangs of conscience about doing exactly what he did and supplying his customers.

My uncle was a very successful dentist (which is why I started on a predental college major). He had an extra room in his Bronx dental office. He loaned us the space, and we were in business! We started making and selling these heaters. We knew there was a market, and we sold a dozen here, a gross there, and began to improve and differentiate the product.

I am good at marketing, sales, strategy, and pragmatic solutions. I understand what motivates people. Our objective was to try to get the pet store wholesaler or distributor to purchase as large an order as possible from us so that their warehouses would be full—and they'd be motivated to sell as hard as possible. All my marketing was directed at motivating them to buy huge quantities. I did it by extended dating and steep volume discounts for quantity.

If I were to offer advice, I think that most start-up businesses like ours are undercapitalized. In starting out with a new business, you should look very, very hard for the greatest leverage, using what you know of the marketplace.

My son-in-law was a Wall Street trader who, when asked, says, "I'm not making much money, but I don't like the work." I say, "Who says you have to like work?" The important thing for me was to make enough money so I could do what I liked. I had to be *good* at what I was doing so I could be *successful*. Then I could do what I liked. But you can get trapped in what you don't like if you live beyond your means and then have to keep doing it. You don't have to like your work to save enough money to quit and start your own business. This is a capitalist world we're living in, and we can make what we want of it. By 1994 we were doing $44 million in sales and sold out to Warner Lambert.

The view that we must "love what we do and the money will follow" is a recent one. Generations of our predecessors succeeded at work they didn't like, so that they could do what they wanted. Here's a young man who started his company in order to take a break from his academic career at M.I.T.

Transition from Computer Science to Entrepreneur

I'm not really atypical of someone in my field. I had an early and natural affinity for computers and computing. I got my first computer when I was thirteen or fourteen, and before that, calculators or whatever I could get my hands on. My father, actually most of my family, are physicians, so I did have a certain amount of push to go into medicine, but by the time I was halfway through high school, I realized that I was going to go into the sciences—almost certainly into computing.

I said I wanted to do computers, so Dad said "You have to go to MIT, then." I showed up at MIT and was scared to death. Suddenly you're no longer by default in the upper half of the intelligence curve.

I started off in the normal computer science program, but they have an accelerated master's program where what you do is a co op with a company, you work with a company for three summers and a semester, do your research work there, write a thesis, and get out. That's the program I was in. I should have gotten a master's and gotten out in five years, but the thing that happened in that experience was that I realized that going along that path, and just getting a job as a computer programmer was just absolutely not what I wanted to do. I horrified . . . commuting out to the suburbs, an hour out. It was really . . . *deadly* as a job and as a career path. So when I came back to MIT, I checked all the rules and found there was nothing that said I had to write my thesis and leave. I was accepted as a computer science master's student, and that was that. They couldn't really throw me out. So I refused to finish the thesis. That was the first thing I'd ever done that was steadfastly "against the rules." I kind of surprised myself.

I ended up starting to hang out at the Media Lab. I finished up my master's work there and started in the Ph.D. program. I had really diverged from any kind of scientific work in the research I was doing. By then I was studying computer music with a composer. My two advisors in the media lab are in artificial intelligence and a composer. Music has been a strong interest my whole life; my mother, in fact, was an opera singer, so I've been classically trained. I ended up spending about five years in the Media Lab, two of them finishing up my master's and three in the doctoral program, and I ended up leaving through a combination of things. By then, I'd really immersed myself in media technology, media arts and sciences, really applications- and design-oriented, which I enjoy tremendously. I think all of us knew that there was something big on the horizon, but none of us knew it was the Internet. Then there were a lot of things happening. It was a great time to get out and stake a territory in it. I had spent ten consecutive years at MIT, and that's a little too much for your mental and physical health. I needed a break. I guess to a certain extent, I started the company to be a potentially temporary break from my academic career. At this point, it's pretty unlikely that I'd ever go back. That was in 1992.

The company itself is doing tremendously well, especially this year; we have about eighty employees now. My partner and I still own most of it. It's been quite a ride. There's a real generational thing going on. I spend a lot of time hiring and recruiting now. The age range in engineering goes from 17, literally (there's an amazing student we've hired, finishing his senior year in high school, who's on par with any engineer in the company), to 47 or so. There's a real break at around 27. I'm in my thirties, but maybe I fall somewhere near that line. A lot of younger people coming in are a lot more comfortable socially, with themselves, with what they're doing. The stereotype of people in computers as having turned away from other human beings is going away to some extent.

At MIT, the healthy respect for starting companies was a nice thing. If you looked at most of the computer entrepreneurs my age who came out of MIT, mine's not that unusual a story. A lot of them stayed on and got degrees. Entrepreneurship is around—it's part of the culture. So many of the large companies were started by MIT graduates, Digital and Hewlett Packard.

One thing I try to get across to people is that, looking back, what made me reticent to do this was really fear of the unknown. There really wasn't anything...there was no great magical business sense or power or knowledge that I was lacking that, if I had had, I would have felt comfortable. For example, a scientist might be inclined to think, "Gee, I spent fifteen years, easily, learning what I know now. I didn't spend those fifteen years learning about business, or about entrepreneurship, so I can't do this." But it's just not true. Nobody starts companies having the background in it. It's very true. All of business school is about running a large established corporation. There's nothing about starting one. There is no formula for it. I know so much more now than I did five years ago. But looking back five years ago, I thought "Oh, geez, there must be something I don't know." It's not true. I think that the barriers are really mental, confidence. You have to suspend judgment internally and just do the thing, go for it. The downside if you fail is really pretty small. You usually don't have much to lose, especially if you're just coming out of graduate school or something like that: Chances are you've trained yourself to live on nothing.

The motivation for starting his company, what we can call "academic fatigue," had very little to do with his company's success. Learning how to take chances and risks, what outsiders see as imprudent or even dangerous, is not perceived as risky by the risk takers themselves.

SUMMARY OF CHAPTER 2

In this section, you met some of our career-transition stars, superstars, and just plain folks. You learned that they struggled with internal and external hindrances to their career transitions. You learned that credentials (or lack of them) are not a factor in making a transition. You saw that by teasing out many case histories' common themes—career attitudes, behaviors, and practices—you can objectify your own level of career well-being and benchmark it against others' levels and your own level at a later time. You now know how to select those elementary components of career well-being that you think need work and find out how to improve those aspects of your career wellness, resilience, versatility, and potential for career renewal.

In Chapter 3, we will decode the meanings of each aspect of career well-being. You will perform career exercises or "calisthenics" that will strengthen your career muscles. You will use new muscles in new ways. You will, in effect, learn how to write your signature or throw a ball with the hand you do not normally use.

NOTES

1. Bernice T. Eiduson, and Linda Beckman, editors, *Science as a Career Choice* (New York: Russell Sage Foundation, 1973).
2. Ibid. p. 3.
3. Ibid. p. 11. Emphasis added.
4. Ibid. p. 13.
5. Ibid. p. 187.
6. Glaser, B.G. ibid., pp. 619, 656.
7. Randy Krauss, "Leaving the Lab Bench, *The Physiologist* Vol. 39, No. 5, 1996.
8. E. Ginzberg and John Herma, *Talent and Performance* (New York: Columbia University Press, 1964).
9. Aside from C.P. Snow's two cultures of science versus arts and humanities, there is a third culture—scientists who are excellent communicators, writers of highly commercial books.
10. James Fallows, *Atlantic Monthly,* December 1985, p. 49.
11. See *Huckleberry Finn.*
12. Fallows, 1985.
13. www.harbornet.com/biz/office/sct001.html, or www.toa-services.net/sct001.html
14. Ginzberg and Herma, ibid.
15. Joseph Epstein, *Ambition* (New York: Dutton, 1980).
16. Ibid.
17. Ibid.
18. Ibid.
19. Ibid.
20. T. Alessandra et al, *Non-Manipulative Selling* (Englewood Cliffs, N.J.: Prentice-Hall, 1987).
21. Ron Willingham, *Integrity Selling* (New York: Doubleday, 1987).
22. As quoted by Peter Drucker in his book *Innovation and Entrepreneurship.* HarperBusiness, NY, 1993.
23. Mark Twain explains how he became a millionaire. He bought an apple for a penny, squeezed it to make apple juice, sold the juice for two pennies, bought two applies . . . and then received a telegram saying that his wealthy uncle had died, leaving him a million dollars.

C h a p t e r

3

·············

RENEWAL

·························

3.01 WHAT TO ASK YOURSELF WHEN DEVELOPING A CAREER PLAN

A mentor told us that teaching was, "Show them what you're going to do; do it; show them what you did."

You are now ready to enter the domain of self-assessment, question-naires, inventories, and exercises. You will take your own pulse, check your own blood pressure, test your reflexes, and measure your own muscle strength, weight, and height. You will determine who you are, in career-transition terms, so that you can generate and select a range of career options that are compatible with who you are. Your previous career decision-making patterns, your values, your skills, your interests, your favorite skills, and how to evaluate them, sift them, and sort them out—all will come under our intense scrutiny.

When you have uncovered a range of options compatible with your pref-erences, we will show you how to develop and pursue career-transition strategies to get where you'd like to be.

Along the way, as in Chapter 2, we will visit a number of scientists, en-gineers, physicians, and others who will tell you how they did what you are going to do.

When you are finished, you will understand career health. We have looked at its components, especially what you can change and what you

can't change. Now we will do some warm-up exercises to help you flex your career-transition muscles.

You must ask yourself some very personal and probing questions, and reflect upon your answers. This process will help you begin to develop a new career plan. Answer those questions that you can answer, in a narrative form, and circle the numbers of those questions that you need help in answering. *The questions you have difficulty in answering reveal the areas that you need to focus upon in order to develop your career plan.* We recommend that you start and maintain a confidential "career-transition diary" or "journal," intended to capture your detailed jottings, musings, information, ruminations, data, contacts, reflections, wisdom, and angst about your forthcoming change. Use a nonlooseleaf notebook similar to the notebooks you would use in a laboratory for collecting and interpreting technical or experimental data. This journal will record data concerning your experimental journey to a new career or job. (The following responses to the questions were given by Donna Ferrandino, who completed the SCT program.)

1. What gives me real satisfaction in my life and work?

    In work, I like to feel that whatever I am doing, it somehow has a positive impact, no matter how minor, and serves some useful purpose. For example, I would not want to develop or sell cigarettes or bombs. I feel satisfied when I am recognized for a job well done and am appreciated by my boss or organization. I feel satisfied when I am able to interact successfully and on a pleasant basis with others—bosses, coworkers, clients, etc. I feel satisfied when I am adequately compensated for the work I am doing.

In life, I again feel satisfied if I am doing something worthwhile, and not negative. I like to have a positive impact on my own life, and to positively affect or help others when possible. I like to interact closely with family members and friends, and I feel satisfied when others are happy with me and what I am doing. I do not like to cause conflict, but I will not be pushed around. I am satisfied when I can reach a balance between work, relationships, learning, hobbies, and relaxation, and have variation in my existence.

2. How do I want to live my life?

I used to be a workaholic, but I no longer wish to live that way. I have come to value having free time to visit and go out with family members and friends, and to paint, read, and relax. I want to live a life that is balanced in all aspects: physical, emotional, mental, spiritual. I want to be healthy in every way. I want to spend time with my parents, sisters, nieces and nephews, friends, significant other, dogs. I want to live with a positive attitude, and look forward to each new day. I want variety and not to be bored. I want to work, but not to be a slave to the job, and not to live paycheck to paycheck or on the edge, as I have been doing for too many years.

3. What is success to me?

Success is having balance in life: enough worthwhile work, enough play, enough physical activity, enough time devoted to personal relationships, enough money to not have to fret over every bill and emergency, enough time to do the things I want to do. Success is doing my job well, while also doing the other things in life well. Success is being happy with my situation and satisfying my own standards, which are usually high.

4. What do I enjoy about my job? What do I dislike?

I don't have a job now, but I have had many different ones in the past, so I will speak from these past experiences.

I enjoyed working with pleasant people I got along with; being appreciated and compensated for doing an excellent job; having variety in my job; not being tied down to one office, one room, one location; knowing that I could advance and learn more and better things as time went on; being challenged and not being in a rut; not doing drudgery work (bookkeeping, making arrangements for things, running errands, etc.). I enjoyed doing work when I felt I was making a positive contribution of some kind to someone, and that I was not just being asked to spin my wheels for no reason.

I disliked boring work, unless I was in the mood to relax my mind; I disliked attending meetings, which are usually a complete waste of time; I disliked being on the telephone a lot; I disliked working with people who were mean or lazy, or back-stabbers; I disliked working in the same place with the same people for too long; I disliked being taken for granted, or being discriminated against for being a woman doing a "man's job." I disliked knowing that I would be doing the same tasks indefinitely unless I pushed or stood up for myself; I disliked having to "prove" myself in several jobs, and being condescended to. I disliked being underpaid and overworked.

5. Do I want to remain in science, engineering, medicine, or technology?

I once felt that science was a noble profession, and that scientists served a good and a higher purpose. I found out that this is not always so. I also found out that certain branches of science are looked down upon and underpaid, and that science, in general, is not nice to women. I would like to remain in science if I can do worthwhile work, not lab work with a bunch of rats; if I can be adequately compensated for my knowledge, expertise, experience, and talents, which are considerable; if I am not tied down to a desk, lab, office, or room.

6. What skills have I developed?

Scientific skills I have developed are the ability to find a balance between logical and intuitive thinking to solve problems; the ability to approach problems and tasks in a stepwise way, breaking them down into smaller problems and tasks, while not losing site of the overall picture; the ability to organize my tasks, my work space, my projects; the ability to express myself, summarize problems, report results, etc., in a concise, clear, understandable manner, with economy of words. I have learned math, abstract thinking, dealing with abstract and concrete projects; learned to separate the theoretical from the practical, and to know what will work in a situation. I have learned how to be mechanical when necessary; how to be detail-oriented when necessary; how to apply solutions to solve problems.

Nonscientific skills I have developed are being creative in solving problems; doing a thorough job, and following through on a project until the end; overcoming obstacles, such as nasty supervisors, jealous coworkers, and prejudice; excellent writing skills; good people skills; the ability to work with, collaborate with, and get along with all kinds of people from all walks of life, and all kinds of backgrounds. I can work

with minimal supervision; can concentrate deeply when necessary; can be efficient and organized; can apply common sense to solve problems; can anticipate problems before they arise; can see the "big picture," but keep track of details along the way.

7. Which skills are transferable to nontechnical fields? Which fields are most appropriate to my skills?

   I think that all of my skills are transferable to nonscientific fields.

   I am not sure which fields are most appropriate. Perhaps writing or editing for a scientific journal or magazine for scientists or the public; working in public relations for some group that promotes health in some way; developing ideas and ways to produce healthy products; research in health or medicine. I need more help in defining possible fields.

8. Which options match my interests, personality, and values? (What is a "good job" for me?)

   What would not be a good job is one in which I am tied to a desk, lab, or room; any kind of lab work that I have to do myself (I could oversee lab projects); one where I would not be able to interact with people; one where I was working for a company/project/employer that does not promote health (cigarettes, liquor, meat, etc.) or positive values (destroys the environment, exploits people, produces useless products, etc.). Being a college professor would not be good; I don't fit well into that environment.

Options that might be good are writing consumer information for a company or writing for a magazine or journal that promotes healthy living and good values; doing health-related research with people, designing, carrying out, and reporting results, i.e., doing the whole project, alone or with others; being an administrator for a health agency, an academic institution in science or health, or a company that produces appropriate products.

I need more help with this question.

9. How can I develop a realistic plan to change my career?

I do not have a career right now. But I did have one as an industrial hygienist, and I now want one more related to nutrition and foods or to medicine. I got an advanced degree. I am participating in the SCT program. I have applied for jobs that I think I would like. I have time to spend on developing and carrying out a plan to get a new career going.

I need more help in answering this question.

10. What risks will I have to take (or what will I have to sacrifice, what do I have to invest) to make my career change?

I am sure I will have to relocate, which involves the aggravation and expense of moving. I am already without money, so I will go deeper in debt. I will have to risk failing at something entirely new in middle age. (I have not failed at any job in the past, but it is always a possibility.) I will have to become part of a very fragile and changeable job market, and I will have little or no security. I will probably have to sacrifice the freedom I have had as a business owner and then a graduate student: to set my own hours, order my own priorities, work in the middle of the night if I want to and run errands during the day, etc.

These are merely examples of warm-up questions to prepare you for a detailed and microscopic examination of your skills, interests, and values, and obstacles to your next move. If you were talking to a career professional (or a physician), these questions would represent your first "intake" session (your medical history). In career health terms, your answers to these questions may reveal some career problems, issues, and ailments that you will address step by step.

The following career-transition narrative is an example of the types of questions individuals ask themselves while contemplating their career transitions—in this case, from physics to neuroscience. How did he answer the above questions?

Examine and reflect upon the kinds of questions the career changer below asked himself in his own voice as a narrative case history. You will be able to write such a narrative when you have completed your own career change. His narrative is intended to stimulate you to write your own career-transition or job-search narrative once you have successfully completed your own transition. It's intended as career calisthenics to "prime your pump" and start your juices flowing. As you read, consider (1) the career changer's answers to the above questions, (2) other questions he raises, and (3) your answers and any new questions his narrative suggests.

JOSEPH ATICK
....

Transition From High-Energy Physics To Computational Neuroscience

I would say that going to the Institute for Advanced Study was one of the key factors that convinced me to leave physics. When I was at Stanford as a graduate student, I still entertained some doubts about my judgment of the field and my reading of the signs of decline. I thought, perhaps I am not seeing what is going on in Princeton, where the gods of this field are. I went to Princeton looking for that vision, and what I found there reinforced my doubts and my resolve to leave physics. The second key factor was *opportunity*. I needed a stable place where I could make the transition. I was offered assistant professor jobs at several places, and at that time I turned them down because I knew that at most universities, academic freedom is a myth. You are not hired to work on anything you want. Typically you are hired because some senior person sees you as an heir to his or her little domain. This person wants you to work on what he or she hired you for. This is, of course, all subtle but very effective. So I knew very well that if I left IAS and got a job as assistant professor, any change in career would have to wait until after tenure. The idea of working on problems that I saw as irrelevant to reality was so horrible that I could not accept any of the offers. Instead, I accepted an offer to stay at the institute, not as a postdoc, but in one of those five-year long-term positions. Since this was not a tenure track, no one at IAS could pressure me in a substantive way—all they could do was complain about my switch, and I got used to that.

Knowing that in principle I had five years of guaranteed employment gave me the opportunity that I needed to make the switch. I took advantage of it immediately, and made my move as abrupt as it could ever be. I knew that hesitation could push me back to a compromise that I would have regretted later.

Looking back, I believe my move out of physics is among the best things I have done in my life. I was alive again and active and excited about what I was doing. Do I recommend that people do this? No, unless you do it with your eyes wide open. The move has not been easy. In my new field, I worked two to three times harder than I worked in physics. In physics I was known—out of twenty-five papers I wrote in physics, only one came back with a referee report asking for revision. In computational neuroscience I could not publish a single paper for two years. I had to fight every step of the way to explain myself. It took enormous effort to achieve some level of acceptance within which I could function. (Out of a total of thirty papers in computational neuroscience, I would say twenty had to be revised at least once before being accepted.)

So if you measure the success or failure of a move in terms of comfort and security, then I failed. On the other hand, if you measure success in terms of personal satisfaction and contributions to real science, then I think I have succeeded. One thing that is very clear to me is that my work in the new field has a much bigger impact than my work in physics. I know because I am the editor-in-chief of the journal *Network: Computation in Neural Systems*, and so I keep up with the directions of the field.

Thus anyone contemplating a move should assess his or her personality before making the move. *Do you function well under pressure, and can you survive a struggle?* If yes, then abrupt career moves between different scientific disciplines are the roller coaster for you. If not, you should do a more traditional move.

We have selected a stellar career-transition narrator to stimulate and inspire you and to help you discern clues to the process. (Later on you will visit other narrators who fall closer to the middle of a normal distribution of career transitioners, like most of us; this would represent scores on our "Career Well-Being Inventory" of about 50 to 70 percent.)

It's clear that this person's transition is as difficult for him to navigate as yours is for you. The style and content of your transition will be uniquely your own. What can you learn from him and his transition about you and your transition?[1]

Just like life, career transitions are not a few preliminary conclusions. (We never promised you a rose garden.) Career transitions are navigable and doable to the extent that you are motivated (read between the lines of the narrative). Career transitions are personal and professional discontinuities, inescapable like old age. A career transition is not for wimps.

We have archived additional career-transition narratives relevant to this topic on our Web site (www.harbornet.com/biz/office/SCT001.html), including career transitions (1) from liquid crystal researcher to marketing to fiber optics financial analyst to teacher, and (2) from pediatrics to corporate development in a managed-care operation.

3.02 CAREER DECISION-MAKING PATTERNS

....

*F*ocus Exercise

Use this focus exercise to look at how you make career decisions. You will uncover patterns that may have led to problems in your present job, career, or work environment. It is very likely that you will alter some of these patterns as you utilize the methods in this book, and as you develop systematic and effective methods of career planning.

1. When did you first think about becoming a professional in your specialty, and why?

   _____

   _____

   _____

   _____

2. From childhood to the present, what else have you thought about or imagined doing?

   _____

   _____

   _____

   _____

   Why haven't you pursued these alternatives?

   _____

   _____

   _____

   _____

   _____

LIFE CHOICES

3. For each of the following "life choices," fill in the blanks with the choice you made (first column), the alternatives available to you at that time (second column), the rationale you used for your actual choice (third column), and in retrospect, how you feel about your choice now (fourth column).

Choice	Alternatives	Rationale	In Retrospect

College:

_____ _____ _____ _____
_____ _____ _____ _____
_____ _____ _____ _____
           _____ _____ _____
           _____ _____ _____
           _____   _____
                                 _____

Choice	Alternatives	Rationale	In Retrospect

Major:

_____ _____ _____ _____
_____ _____ _____ _____
_____ _____ _____ _____
           _____ _____ _____
           _____   _____
                                 _____

Choice **Alternatives** **Rationale** **In Retrospect**

Graduate or Professional School:

Choice **Alternatives** **Rationale** **In Retrospect**

Professional or Technical Specialty:

Choice **Alternatives** **Rationale** **In Retrospect**

First Position after Graduate School:

Choice	*Alternatives*	*Rationale*	*In Retrospect*

Second Position:

Choice	*Alternatives*	*Rationale*	*In Retrospect*

Third position:

The following is a sample Career Decision-Making Pattern completed by Walter Niles.

	Choice	Alternatives	Rationale	In Retrospect
1. College	Caltech	MIT, RPI, Stanford	Best program	Glad I went; excellent preparation
2. Major	Biology	Physics, EE, Math	Interesting problems, more opportunities	Perhaps a double major, with EE
3. Grad School	Wisconsin	Berkeley	Able to pursue problem I was interested in	I enjoyed Madison, and learned much
4. Scientific Specialty	Neurophysiology membrane biophysics	Molecular biology	Able to continue pursuit of problem of overriding interest	Glad I chose these options
5. First Position	Albert Einstein College of Medicine postdoc	Harvard postdoc	Opportunity to work with world-renowned membrane biophysicist	Perhaps a little too single-minded, began to limit options
6. Second Position	Rush Medical College instructor in physiology	None	Wasn't paying attention	Should have made this one short
7. Third Position	Rush Med. Coll. assistant professor in physiology & biophysics	None	(Mis)perceived opportunities for advancement	This was a big mistake; soft-money, no support from dept. chair, snake pit

81

4. Looking at your answers to item 3 above, what factors most influenced your decision making?

_____

_____

_____

_____

_____

_____

5. Did you ever consider leaving graduate school, or your specialty, and why?

_____

_____

_____

_____

_____

_____

6. What influenced your decision not to leave?

_____

_____

_____

_____

_____

_____

7. Up until now, what obstacles have prevented you from leaving your present position?

_____

_____

_____

_____

_____

8. Have you noticed pervasive feelings of optimism or pessimism about your career?

_____

_____

_____

_____

_____

_____

9. What can you conclude about your career decision-making patterns that will help you to make this transition effectively?

_____

_____

_____

_____

_____

• •

Something that is not always visible to us is the optimism or pessimism that lies just beneath the surface of our career decision making patterns.

Many of us go through periods of high and low energy during our quest. Sometimes these fluctuations are situational, sometimes they are systemic. Sometimes they resemble a bad cold, sometimes a burst of enthusiasm similar to what you feel after a good workout. The bad cold may not be under our control, but the workout is.

To an extent, one can alter these feelings by facing them openly. The following chart reveals some research findings on what's good about pessimism and what's bad about optimism. Now, reflect upon whether optimism or pessimism informed, or drove, your career decision-making patterns.

What's Bad About Optimism? What's Good About Pessimism?[2]

OPTIMISM	PESSIMISM
Good	*Good*
Optimists have fewer infectious diseases than pessimist.	Pessimism heightens our sense of reality.
Optimists have better health habits than pessimists.	Pessimism endows us with accuracy.
Our immune systems may work better when we are optimistic.	
Optimists live longer than pessimists.	
Optimists believe that good events have permanent causes, and bad events have specific causes.	

OPTIMISM	PESSIMISM
Bad	*Bad*
Optimists tend to "blame" themselves for good things, and to blame the outside world for bad things. They internalize the good and externalize the bad.	Pessimism promotes depression and inertia (rather than activity) in the face of setbacks.
	Pessimism feels bad (blue, down, anxious).
	Pessimism is self-fulfilling (even when success is attainable, pessimists do not persist in the face of challenges, and therefore fail more frequently than optimists).
	Pessimism is associated with poor health.
	Even when pessimists are right and events turn out badly, they still feel worse (they convert predicted setbacks into disasters, and disasters into catastrophes).

A few words about clinical depression. Some individuals discover that they cannot pull themselves out of a long-term episode of career distress, discouragement, or negativity. This is common, and so if you experience long-term career "blues," you are not alone. You may wish to examine this closely. Many job searchers are reluctant to discuss these matters, but they should not be considered unusual or taboo. Please see Section 3.17, "Good Career-Planning Habits and Hygiene."

This sparkling and vivacious young woman has made several transitions with versatility. See if you can tease out of her narrative her career decision-making patterns, in order to prepare yourself for uncovering your own.

Transition From Optical Engineering To Polaroid To Congressional Fellow To NIST To Trade.

The timing sort of worked out. Part of this was by design, not by accident. I was working with this guy that I thought might make a good Ph.D. advisor, and he was also my boss's boss. So, I started working at Polaroid in

January and I was enrolled in the program by September. I was at Polaroid for ten years, and of that ten years it took me seven to get my Ph.D. The good thing was that by the time I finished, when I applied for the AAAS Congressional Fellowship, I could say without lying that I had fourteen years' experience working as an engineer in the field, but at the same time, I was a recent Ph.D. graduate. That combination helped when I applied for the Congressional Science Fellowships, because for the one that I got, they wanted more recent Ph.D.s, and yet having a more industrial background helped me, because the committee that eventually hired me wanted people with backgrounds, not just people who had never worked at all.

All my time at Polaroid, I was relatively happy, but nothing is perfect. I enjoyed my job, I enjoyed what I was doing, but I wanted to do something where I could integrate the engineering and technical background with something larger, sort of societal. The Congressional Science Fellowship seemed like a fine combination, although to be honest, I didn't know what I was getting myself into. It was kind of a wild shot: I applied for all of these things, and I prayed and prayed and prayed and hoped for the best.

Landing one was really neat. It was as much of a surprise to me as to anyone else. Polaroid gave me a leave of absence to go away for a year. When I decided to even apply for it, I talked to my boss and said I wanted to take a break, wanted to do something like this, and I was afraid that he'd think I was unhappy. I wasn't unhappy, but I thought it would be neat to do something different. I was getting, in my heart, a little stale. We remained very good friends. In retrospect, he tells me now, "I should never have let you apply because I knew you wouldn't come back." I assured him at the time that I would come back, and I meant it. I did go back to Polaroid, but I only went back for a few months and then I left again.

I have to be very honest and admit that I miss certain aspects of optical engineering. I haven't totally let go yet. In the big picture, I feel that I've done the right thing, that I'm in the right position—all the good things. But on the other hand, I had worked really hard within my field to get to a stage where people were starting to respect me professionally.

So that's where I am. I don't know what I'm going to do for the future. Right now, I'm sort of too new, still. I don't have any big plans for my next career moves. Working in the private sector for many years and then ending up in the government as a federal employee is change enough, and working for a department that every year Congress wants to cut, make it disappear—it's kind of a different environment.

When you're an immigrant family, you've left a whole country and you adapt to a new environment and culture and language and so on. When I was thirteen, it was kind of a big shock to learn a new language and get used to a new country. So, in some fashion, it's a little like that. That sounds melodramatic, but I changed states, changed careers. I did feel very lost at first, for six months. What helped is that I've gone through that sort of trauma before.

I listened to the self-help tapes. I'm forever analyzing my strengths and weaknesses and writing goals. I've always done this. I have the one-year plan and the five-year plan. I make a lot of lists. All along I was always ticking in: What skills do I have? What skills am I lacking in? If you're at a stage where you're changing paths, it's really important to do a self-assessment. Do it honestly as to yourself, look at your skills, your assets, your liabilities. Can you take a risk? Can you afford it? Will you be starving? I super-analyze everything. By the time I jump, I've figured out plans A, B, and C, and just in case those don't work out, what would be plan D? I think that for the most part it works out better for me that way. If you're a recent graduate and you're thinking of changing, I think it's important to do that self-assessment. What do you want? What if you can't get there? How many years will it take? Then follow it through.

Did you see patterns in her transitions? Would you agree that they include ambition and integrity (see Section 2.07), optimism and energy, timing, a quest for synthesis of her many interests, public service, a talent for "judging right about imperfect materials" (see Chapter 1), good decision-making capacity, ability to sustain conflict or losses and rebound, honest self-appraisal, and a willingness to weigh alternatives planfully and in detail?

Now, what are yours?

At our Web site[3] you will find additional career-transition narratives: (1) from physicians to company start-ups, (2) from biology research to high school teaching and administrating, and (3) from oil and gas exploration to energy analysis.

3.03 VALUES: PERSONAL PRIORITIES

In the previous sections, you have asked yourself critical questions designed to help you understand your career decision-making patterns and how they determined your present career condition. Perhaps these patterns were not completely obvious to you at the time you made these decisions.

Our goal here is to continue the important task of bringing these often-latent drivers of your career aspirations up to the surface for your conscious scrutiny, and to focus your attention on what you want.

The purpose of this section is to help you identify, define, and rank-order or prioritize the most important aspects of your work, your lifestyle, and your career. Simply put, the exercise is asking, What do you want? What are the aspects of work that are intrinsically satisfying to you?

Some common issues to address when determining what you value most are: How much money do you really need to feel financially secure and to maintain your chosen lifestyle? What would your typical workday be like? What type of environment would you like to work in? What would your fellow employees and/or clients be like? And how would work fit in with your personal life? What does a balanced life mean to you?

....

Instructions: From the list below, choose the five items that are most important to you (i.e., what do you want from your work?).

A. High Earnings Potential
   (be able to purchase luxuries of life you want)   _____

B. Job Security
   (be assured of keeping your job and salary)   _____

C. Friendships
   (develop close personal relationships with people
   from work)   _____

D. Benefits Available
   (health, tuition, reimbursements, discount services)   _____

E. Rapid Advancement
   (opportunities for growth/promotions from work well
   done)   _____

F. Socially Useful Work
   (contribute to betterment of world)   _____

G. Creativity
   (artistic or intellectual expression)   _____

H. Making Decisions
   (use judgment, have power to decide courses of
   action, policies)   _____

I. Public Contact
   (day-to-day contact with clients or colleagues)   _____

J. Status and Prestige
   (derive status and prestige from work)   _____

K. Teamwork
   (collaborate with others)   _____

L. Self-Employment
   (own/run a business)   _____

M. Regular Work
    (establish a routine with structured assignments)   _____

N. Autonomy
    (work with little direction from others)   _____

O. Variety
    (change work responsibilities frequently)   _____

P. Regular And Predictable Hours
    (maintain same daily work schedule)   _____

Q. Travel
    (travel 20 percent or more each week or month)   _____

R. Congenial Atmosphere
    (have pleasant, relaxed environment with friendly
    colleagues)   _____

S. Intellectual Challenge
    (perform work that is intellectually stimulating)   _____

T. Fast Pace and Pressure
    (work in a busy atmosphere with frequent deadlines)   _____

U. Risk Taking
    (work in an environment of adventure, excitement, or
    high stakes)   _____

V. Independence
    (work without significant direction)   _____

W. Geographic Preference
    (be able to live in the city or region of your choice)   _____

X. Competition
    (engage in activities that test your abilities against
    others' abilities)   _____

Y. Power and Authority
    (exercise control and command respect)   _____

Z. Time Freedom
    (free time in your work or day)   _____

AA. Influence People
    (be in a position to change attitudes or opinions of
    others)   _____

BB. Job Tranquility
    (avoid pressures and "the rat race" in job role and
    setting)   _____

CC. Supervision
    (be directly responsible for work done by others)   _____

DD. Help Others
(be involved directly with helping individuals or small
groups) _____

EE. Affiliation
(be recognized as a member of a particular organization) _____

FF. Change And Variety
(have work responsibilities frequently changed in
content and setting) _____

GG. Exercise Competence
(demonstrate a high degree of proficiency in job skills
and knowledge) _____

HH. Aesthetics
(work in a visually pleasing environment) _____

II. Moral Fulfillment
(feel that your work is contributing to ideals you feel
are important) _____

JJ. Work on Frontiers of Knowledge
(work in research and development, generating
information and new ideas in the academic, scientific,
or business communities) _____

KK. Location
(work close to your home so you don't have to
commute long distances) _____

LL. Other Values
(add anything you wish) _____

Now list the five values that you ranked as *most important*. Call these your "top
five" values.

_____
_____
_____
_____

_____

Which of your top five values do you find in your current job?

_____

_____

Which of the top five are missing in your current job?

_____

_____

Is it possible to find all of your top five values in one job, or are they contradictory? If they are contradictory, how would you change them?

_____

_____

_____

_____

_____

_____

_____

_____

_____

_____

_____

_____

_____

_____

• •

What would you conclude are the values and personal priorities of the following engineer-turned-attorney? What might he now give as his top five values? Did he have them in his prior incarnation as an engineer? Does he reveal any incompatible or contradictory values? How did he deal with them?

Transition From Engineer To Engineering Malpractice Attorney And Productivity Lawyer

I have degrees in mechanical engineering and industrial engineering, and I'm a licensed professional engineer.

I never abandoned engineering, nor did I depart from practicing engineering. I am an engineering malpractice attorney. When you see a product failure, either the engineer who designed it was at fault or whoever built it made a mistake, a technical flaw. I really added a new career.

Most attorneys are not schooled in engineering and so will not be able to analyze the failures easily. But by combining both engineering and law, I am able to evaluate failures quickly and less expensively than others.

I speak "engineering." It was my mother tongue. I can read blueprints. I know technology. I can talk to any opponent's experts without needing an interpreter, because I didn't give up engineering—I expanded my background to embrace litigation that relies on engineering. There are many good product liability lawyers who are not engineers, but only a handful of lawyers (usually patent lawyers) are technical people. I have a clear advantage, since I really understand the technical components and issues.

I was not disgruntled at being an engineer, although I think engineering had an impersonal aspect and was rather narrow—being at the drawing board. I see a larger diversity of human behavior and more variability of people in the law than I did in engineering.

It's such a personal thing—choosing and changing careers. I'd say it's a given that we find something that we enjoy, since that's a major motivation. Also, it's very important to be self-sufficient. There's no luck involved for me in finding that my talents and satisfactions always lived well together. Being around when circumstances and opportunities came up was less luck than being in tune already, and willing to take a chance. Self-employment works well for me because I found a market for something I liked that I'm good at.

Many highly theoretical scientific skills can also exist in a person who has lower-level practical skills, like wiring, plumbing, fixing things.

My brothers were both very helpful to me, since they are very knowledgeable about both business and me. When I made decisions, they were always available, and so were many others.

The biggest career obstacle is maintaining a balanced life. No matter how intense your career is, the key to having a good life is balance between your work and everything other than work. A lot of young people forget this. If you devote your time only to your career, even if you're successful you'll have a one-dimensional life—busy relationships, divorce, alienated kids. If you're focused only on your career and everything else takes a back seat, that to me is a career failure. If you have a full and balanced life—strong personal interests outside of work, hobbies, kids, making time for family—that to me is a career success.

I don't regret that my work interferes with the rest of my life and that the rest of my life interferes with my work. They don't because of balance. I resist greed. I make all my dealings honest. It's means more to me to know that I'm a winner at the balanced life. A case is important, but it's just a case. They say that the law is a jealous mistress, and that work is never finished.

But I make time. The only substitute for "quality time" is time. I call it controlling my calendar. I never let my calendar control me. Each year I

> take my kid's school calendar to my office and block out scheduled school events on my office calendar. I have only one calendar, and it's at the office. My secretary is trained to say, "He's not available." She's not to give any reasons: courtroom appearance, fishing, picnic, school visit.
>
> I had really good role models in both law and engineering. I probably have a stronger affinity for engineering than for law, but they're almost equal. My partner is stronger in law than in engineering, so we have a really good marriage. And we spell each other, so the other can vacation with family and balance work with all the rest of life.

It seems clear that he has as a very high priority "leading a balanced life." Although he says his engineering work was "impersonal," he expanded his engineering to "embrace litigation," a highly interpersonal activity. So he has morphed into a person who truly balanced his life in being able to call upon multiple preferences. Can you do this? How?

Our Web site[4] contains an additional career transition: from physician to venture capitalist.

3.04 SKILLS

Now that you have examined your values, you must inventory *all* of your skills. Career transitions call for unusual combinations.

As a scientist, engineer, or technical or medical professional, you possess a rich variety—a bushel basket—of skills (among which are the skills you most enjoy using) that are transferable to other careers. Analyzing what you do *best* and what you find most *satisfying* is an essential step in determining which job or career will be most *suitable* to you.

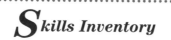

Skills Inventory

The central discovery every person must make, Max Weber said, is to "find and obey the demon that holds the fibers of one's very life." The goal of this skills exercise is to help you understand what you (1) know how to do, (2) like to do, and (3) want to learn how to do. The Skills Inventory is a complex, difficult, but critical tool in the career-planning process.

This exercise is divided into two parts. Please follow the instructions for each part carefully. Allow several hours to complete it. You may find it advantageous to complete the Skills Inventory in two sittings.

PART I

Step 1 Write down *twelve* life experiences under the heading "Life Experiences/Accomplishments Important to You." Consider life experiences or "accomplishments" of any size. The experience or accomplishment does not have to be important to other people, but *must be powerful to you*. List *specific* experiences/accomplishments that will easily divide into discrete actions for analysis. Good examples:

1. Wrote article for specialist journal on . . .
2. Designed research project, equipment; obtained grant . . .
3. Operated complex equipment, e.g., . . .
4. Developed specific software, e.g., . . .
5. Organized a book reading group, or volleyball league
6. Created computer model of . . .
7. Wrote popular article on . . .
8. Painted a picture of . . .; composed/arranged music . . .
9. Photographed a landscape, person, scene . . .
10. Created a successful marriage . . .
11. Managed a team to...supervised a group to . . .
12. Built a home . . .
13. Invested or managed funds . . .

To the extent possible, select experiences/accomplishments emphasizing the different dimensions of yourself: your work life, education, sports, hobbies, even a personal relationship or other aspects of a *balanced life*.

Step 2 From your list, choose the *six* experiences that you *most enjoyed*. On a separate sheet of paper, describe what you did to accomplish each of the six. *Be specific, listing each step in great detail*. For example, if your life experience/accomplishment was to design a research project that resulted in a grant and/or published article(s), then the detailed supporting steps might be:

1. Scrutinized and absorbed the relevant literature.
2. Contacted published experts in the field.
3. Developed relationships, collaborations.
4. Organized, staffed, and participated in resulting research project.
5. Established data collection procedures.

6. Contacted a company to establish a consulting relationship.

7. Drafted grant proposal, with budgets, collaborators, milestones, etc.

8. Organized a special conference.

Each of these detailed steps (in support of a larger accomplishment) can be further subdivided into its component elements. In this way, specific skills (itemized below) may be teased out of the background noise, brought to the surface, converted from subtext into text, and inventoried. This process will help to make the transferability or portability of those skills evident to you. Later, you will rename these and use them to present yourself in a new light in your own words.

PART II

Step 1   Examine the numbered columnar description-list of skills, the first group of which is headed "Follow-Through Skills," on the first page of the Skills Inventory (which follows "Your Life Experiences"). Create a grid or matrix as follows: Consider the full description-list of skills (173 items) to be column zero on the left side of each page, with columns one through six to its right. At the top of each of these six columns, write the name of one of your six most-enjoyed life experiences (Part 1). Read through the entire list of specific numbered skills, and place a check mark in column 1 next to any described skills that apply to experience 1. Now, repeat the check-off process for your second experience in the second column, your third experience in the third column, and so on, until you have completed all six experiences. You will thereby identify specific, potentially transferable skills associated with each of your most enjoyable and powerful life experiences. Complete this process for all of the 173 skills described in the Skills Inventory.

Step 2   After completing this process for *all six experiences*, please use the section (following Skills Inventory item 173) headed "Your Strongest and Most Enjoyable Skills" to review the inventory and to summarize the general and specific skills that you have checked most often for *all six experiences*. On some pages you will have checked all the boxes. On other pages the checks will appear to be randomly distributed. Analyze the patterns. Seek out those skills that show up regularly along rows. *These are skills that are common to all of your most-enjoyed life experiences or accomplishments.* Clusters of columnar checks may indicate that you have skills that are describable by the group heading. (You may wish to go back and replace the check marks with a numerical rating on a scale of one to ten to reveal the "global ability" or "intensity" of your strongest and most-enjoyed skills. In this case you will sum the rows and columns to find your patterns.)

You are going to translate *our words* for these skills into *your own words*. This will help you bring them to the surface of your consciousness and readily draw upon this self-knowledge with ease and fluency during (job and informational) interviews—in your own words, using your own normal, comfortable, conversational vocabulary.

Write the skills you have used most consistently in the section entitled, "Your Strongest and Most Enjoyable Skills." For the 173 specific skills, simply write the verb associated with each of your most consistently used skills in the space provided. Then, *describe that skill in your own words,* so that you will be able to talk about the skill fluently (as appropriate to the setting and context) when presenting yourself. Ask yourself if this list reflects your abilities and the skills you like to use. If it does not, add those that are not included, so that you have a complete inventory. You will later use all the skills inventoried in presenting or marketing yourself in a new career direction.

Step 3 Write a list (at the bottom of the same last page) of the specific skills you wish to develop further in your next job or career.

Step 4 Finally, you may wish to share these completed pages with a close colleague or, if you are stuck, with a career management professional.

LIFE EXPERIENCES/ACCOMPLISHMENTS IMPORTANT TO YOU (Please see instructions)

1. _____

_____

2. _____

_____

3. _____

_____

4. _____

_____

5. _____

_____

6. _____

_____

7. _____

_____

8. _____

_____

9. _____

_____

10. _____

_____

11. _____

   _____

12. _____

   _____

FOLLOW-THROUGH SKILLS

1. I **follow** instructions and use previously established plans or procedures.
2. I **complete** projects within time and budget constraints.
3. I **identify and cultivate** contacts who help me achieve my goals.
4. I **find ways to execute** a task more efficiently.
5. I **go around** the established procedures and practices to get the job done. I improvise.
6. I **finish** an unpleasant or difficult project.

MANUAL DEXTERITY SKILLS

7. I **am able to use** tactile sensitivity.
8. I **am able to do** manual work precisely.
9. I **am able to do** physically demanding work.
10. I **can use** my hands to create a product.
11. I **can build, assemble, set up or install,** something.
12. I **can fix, repair, or modify** something.

SKILLS IN MANAGEMENT

13. I **delegate tasks and schedule** work for others.
14. I **set** performance standards.
15. I **select** the right talent for a particular job.
16. I **coordinate** multiple tasks and projects.
17. I **act** as a buffer, protecting people from organizational politics.
18. I **gain** the participation of people from different departments and organizations.
19. I **build** effective teams to get a job done.

SKILLS IN WORKING WITHIN OTHER CULTURES

20. I **interact** successfully with people of different cultures and with different customs.
21. I **adapt** my behavior to suit those of another culture.
22. I **am resourceful** in learning and using new customs to **help bridge** national, religious, or regional differences.
23. I **am flexible and do not force** others to adhere to my values and way of operating.

24. I **speak** foreign languages.
25. I **write** foreign languages.

PHYSICAL AND/OR COMPETITIVE SKILLS

26. I **assess** my opponents' strengths and weaknesses, and my own.
27. I **employ** my physical coordination and ability.
28. I **can compete** with others and/or myself.
29. I **develop** ways to improve my competitive performance.
30. I **extend** my physical limits and test my strength, courage, and endurance.
31. I **recognize and take advantage of** situations where I can win.

DATA-HANDLING SKILLS

32. I **process** information accurately.
33. I **organize** information **and create** systems for its storage and retrieval.
34. I **remember** detail.
35. I **manipulate** data as needed.
36. I **deal with** many details successfully.
37. I **can survey** large amounts of data **and locate** errors or inconsistencies.

ENTREPRENEURIAL SKILLS

38. I **seize** opportunities to apply new ideas.
39. I **direct** new organizational start-ups.
40. I **recognize** the practical use for concepts, theories, research, or ideas.
41. I **turn** an idea into something tangible.
42. I **design** projects **and/or develop** programs.
43. I **implement** new programs.

SKILLS IN WORKING INDEPENDENTLY

44. I **work** effectively without direction or supervision from others.
45. I **set and meet** my own deadlines, budget constraints, and quality standards.
46. I **move** into totally new situations on my own, **and** I **initiate** successful actions and relationships.
47. I **seek** further responsibilities **and create** new opportunities for responsibilities.

SKILLS IN INNOVATION

48. I **can invent or develop** new strategies **and improve** on earlier strategies.
49. I **can modify or apply** new approaches to old problems.

50. Based on available information, I **can form** a diagnosis.

51. I **can conceive and develop** imaginative ideas or approaches.

52. I **can intuitively perceive** something that is not apparent to most people.

ANALYTICAL SKILLS

53. I **can identify** the parts that compose the whole, e.g., the steps that go into the process, the various factors contributing to the problem.

54. I **can create and test** a hypothesis and strategies.

55. I **can compare, analyze, review, evaluate, and screen** new solutions or services.

56. I **can develop** ways to evaluate the success or effectiveness of strategies, designs, meetings, procedures, services, etc.

57. I **can dissect** ideas and services.

58. I **can separate** the relevant from the irrelevant, the important from the unimportant.

RESEARCH SKILLS

59. I **can obtain** information from published sources.

60. I **can interview** people to obtain necessary information.

61. I **can determine and locate** the best sources for specific types of information.

62. I **can design** a process for collecting information.

63. I **can plan, organize, and categorize** a lot of different information into a useful pattern.

64. I **can discover** patterns by scrutinizing data.

65. I **can use** several different methods and checkpoints to track progress and confirm results.

SKILLS IN NEGOTIATION

66. I **can differentiate** the important from the less important needs of others.

67. I **can recognize** opportunities and structure compromises.

68. I **can develop** strategies for obtaining a favorable negotiated outcome.

69. I **can convince** diverse groups of people to work together and compromise in a way that satisfies each person's critical needs.

70. I **can negotiate** between contending groups or conflicting individuals.

71. I **can clearly identify** my needs, feelings, boundaries, and areas open for negotiation.

PROBLEM-SOLVING SKILLS

72. I **can remain** calm when faced with unexpected or difficult situations.

73. I **can maintain** a sense of objectivity when problems arise.

74. I **can improvise** under stress and act as a troubleshooter.

75. Before proposing solutions, I **collect** all relevant information **and define** the problem.

76. I usually **choose** a solution that is accepted by others.

77. I **can explore and assess** the viability of a wide range of potential solutions.

NUMERICAL/FINANCIAL SKILLS

78. I **can plan, prepare, and administer** budgets.

79. I **manage** my money or others' money.

80. I **use** numbers or symbols as a tool for solving statistical and other problems.

81. I **have prepared** financial reports.

82. I **can use** numbers and statistics to develop a concept or show a trend.

83. I **can recognize** discrepancies among numbers and investigate the causes of these discrepancies.

ENCOURAGEMENT/INSPIRATIONAL SKILLS

84. I **encourage** people to seek further knowledge or experience.

85. I **facilitate** people's process of self-assessment, goal setting, and action planning for personal/professional development.

86. I **encourage** others to take risks and to learn from successes and/or failures.

87. I **evaluate** people's performance or effectiveness and give useful feedback on their strengths and weaknesses.

89. I **help** people develop their own ideas and insights.

90. I **help** people overcome problems that prevent them from doing good work.

HUMAN RELATIONS SKILLS

91. I **work** well as a team member, motivating fellow team members and workers, sharing credit, and expressing appreciation.

92. I **can see** situations through others' eyes, deal effectively with many different people, and appreciate others' ways of doing things.

93. I **handle** difficult people well and work well in hostile situations.

94. I **care** for others, aiding them in their life situations or raising their self-esteem.

95. I **provide** good, timely, courteous service to a client, customer, or patient.

96. I **earn** the trust of another, enabling her or him to speak openly and honestly.

97. I **create** climates conducive to social interaction.

TRAINING/EDUCATING SKILLS

98. I **can design** a strategy or program to help someone learn something new.

99. I **can motivate** others to learn.

100. I **can organize and administer** training/educational events and materials.

101. I **can explain, demonstrate, instruct, model, or inform.**

102. I **can facilitate** group discussions.

103. I **can assess** others' learning styles and tailor the training approach.

BUSINESS/RESEARCH WRITING SKILLS

104. I **can draft** a clear, concise memorandum or brief.

105. I **can write** clear, concise letters or reports. I can accurately document steps, procedures, decisions, etc.

106. I **can write** directions that readers can easily follow.

107. I **can proofread and edit** effectively.

108. I **can write** articles that report events.

109. I **can write** a textbook, scientific article, news report, documentary, etc.

SKILLS IN PERSUASION

110. I **can influence** others' ideas, attitudes, and needs.

111. I **can sell** ideas, theories, and strategies to others.

112. I **can promote or sell** products or services, **and** I **help** others see how the service or product will meet their need.

113. I **can influence** others to alter their behavior or opinions.

ARTISTIC AND DESIGN SKILLS

114. I **can develop** visually pleasing items, e.g., photos, sculpture, paintings, graphic arts, architecture, etc.

115. I **can apply** my sense of color, shape, and design.

116. I **can design** comfortable and functional work/living space (interior and exterior).

117. I **can conceive, develop, or select** audiovisual presentations, e.g. film,, slide-tape, transparencies.

118. I **can conceive** visual representations of ideas or concepts.

119. I **can apply** musical knowledge to produce, compose, or select music.

CREATIVE WRITING SKILLS

120. I **can write** promotional materials by using words creatively.

121. I **can describe** people, scenes, and events vividly and originally. I **can tell** a story in writing.

122. I **can write** poetry **and/or develop** poetic images or themes.

123. I **have written** novels, plays, poems, screenplays, short stories, etc.

124. I **have moved** people through written words to feel emotions.

125. I **can express** my feelings in writing.

PRESENTATION SKILLS

126. I **have made** presentations to groups, delivering information or speeches.

127. I **have emceed** public meetings or ceremonies.

128. I **have demonstrated** the use of items, products, or services.

129. I **have led** workshops, eliciting discussion from participants.

130. I **am poised** in public appearances, able to deal with a difficult situation, representing the organization/group to the public.

131. I **have built** upon audience responses, moods, or ideas.

132. I **can use** humor to warm up an audience.

LISTENING SKILLS

133. I **can hear and** effectively **utilize** information or opinions that differ from mine.

134. I **can ask** questions in a probing but nonoffensive manner.

135. I **can paraphrase and summarize** what someone else has said.

136. I **can hear or utilize** unspoken nuances, **respond** to unasked questions, **and address** another's unexpressed feelings.

137. I **can let** others direct material to be discussed without forcing them to talk about my area of interest.

138. I **can demonstrate** attention through appropriate nonverbal communication (e.g., maintaining eye contact, nodding in agreement).

GENERAL COMMUNICATION SKILLS

139. I **can use** easily understood language and words appropriate to the listener.

140. I **can present** my ideas in a logical, orderly, coherent, and integrated way.

141. I **can provide** clear explanations of difficult or complex concepts, ideas, or problems.

142. I **can represent** another's point of view effectively.

143. I **can use** good timing to gain maximum impact for my ideas.

144. I **use** facial expressions and body movement to express ideas and feelings.

INTERPERSONAL COMMUNICATION SKILLS

145. I **deal** effectively with conflict, confronting others effectively on difficult matters.

146. I **counsel** others in decision making or problem-solving.

147. I **can communicate** my feelings to others.

148. I **can respond** to others' needs, feelings, boundaries, and areas open to negotiation.

149. I **can clarify** misunderstandings and give clear directions.

150. I **can adjust** my communication according to the individual with whom I am speaking.

COMPUTER SKILLS

151. I **am fluent** in the most simple computer languages.

152. I **am comfortable** with a PC.

153. I **am comfortable** with e-mail.

154. I **can use** advanced computer software and languages.

155. I **work** well with sophisticated computer hardware.

156. I **can program** in BASIC, C+, C++, or other languages.

157. I **can figure** out how to install and troubleshoot any computer hardware and software.

158. I **am on-line** several hours a day; I **access** information on the World Wide Web; I **surf** the Net.

159. I **use** many sophisticated Internet capabilities.

160. I **access** on-line chat groups, MOOs, news groups, and on-line search engines regularly and enjoy this very much.

161. I **am fluent** in a variety of standard computer software programs (e.g., WordPerfect, Lotus, Excel, Quicken).

162. I **effectively complete** a task and learn new software and hardware easily.

163. I **modify** standard programs.

164. I **create** computer programs.

165. I **follow** developments in the computer field.

166. I **know** new and useful software and hardware.

167. I **appreciate** salient new software and hardware.

168. I **train and teach** others how to use a computer.

169. I **introduce** computerized systems into workplaces.

170. I **debug** software.

171. I **troubleshoot** hardware.

172. I **diagnose** computer malfunctions.

173. I **solve** technical glitches.

YOUR STRONGEST AND MOST ENJOYABLE SKILLS

General Skill Category	Specific Skills (verbs)	Other Words That Describe This Skill
1. _____	_____	_____
2. _____	_____	_____
3. _____	_____	_____
4. _____	_____	_____

SKILLS YOU WANT TO DEVELOP FURTHER

1. _____ _____ _____
2. _____ _____ _____
3. _____ _____ _____
4. _____ _____ _____
5. _____ _____ _____

You will be referring back to this summary in later exercises.

Here are some examples of individuals who understood how to use their skills to change their careers.

Can you determine what this extraordinary narrator, a mathematician-turned-computer entrepreneur, would rank as his strongest and most enjoyable skills? How was he able to deploy his mathematics and computer skills in the service of two challenging (and extremely successful and satisfying) careers?

DAVID FOX

Transition From Applied Mathematician To Neural Networks

I was always doing applied mathematics, taking courses solving real problems. No one else would take these problems, so I just did them for the fun and challenge of it. Who knew these were "career preferences"? It just came naturally.

While studying for my orals, I was a computer operator, a job I worked at on the night shift. NYU had a policy at this time that you couldn't be a full-time student and have a job at the same time. But I had this job and I had to study for my orals—and there was no way to study while running the computer because I had to keep getting up and changing the tapes. We had Fortran and punched cards in those days. It just bugged me that I had to change these tapes and dump every few minutes, and so could not study for my orals. I looked at the octal codes, and I rewrote the Fortran and assembler to remove the rewind instructions—so now I could run five or ten jobs at once. I remember I used to sit cross-legged on the consoles studying. A math professor came by and asked how I did it. He invited me to go with him to General Motors and do the same bragging. GM offered me $5,000 to do the same thing for them, and it was the first batching of jobs anyone had apparently ever done. No one would ever think of changing IBM codes or machines, but I did it for the pure joy of solving a problem.

I was always nuts about mathematics problems. I could not believe anyone would actually pay me to do this—it was recreation.

If I were to look back, I would say that the pattern of my behavior and career changes shows that I was always an outsider, always disagreeing with the majority views, and always arrogant and charismatic enough to think I was right. I have inherent curiosity about everything associated with computers. I even have elegant new ideas for key-word searching on the Internet.

I have learned how to manage our company's managers. I tell them to take good care of the people who work for them, and complain to the people they work for. It's the opposite of what most managers do. I call this "smile down and bitch up." It works.

If you guessed the following skill clusters, you begin to understand his value system: follow-through, management, entrepreneurial, working independently, innovation, research, negotiation, problem-solving, numerical, human relations, persuasion, general communication, and computer skills. Not only is he wealthy in skills, but he has also converted those into financial wealth.

Now, how about your skills? Are they convertible into "currency"? How well you do this will depend upon how well you are able to understand, consolidate, and incorporate our career well-being calisthenics.

Our Web site[5] contains the following career transition narratives: (1) from stellar atmospheres to commercial software, and (2) from physics to science policy administration.

3.05 TAKING STOCK: A PRELIMINARY CAREER EVALUATION

In previous sections of this book, you have explicitly determined your career decision-making patterns, your personal priorities or values, and your strongest and most enjoyable skills. You can use this information to evaluate your career and to decide whether or not to change directions. You may be asking, "But what else can I do, other than what I am doing now?"

After completing the patterns, values, and skills exercises, approximately half of those considering a new career decide to stay in a field that draws upon their scientific, engineering, and technical skills. This is a successful outcome because these exercises were valuable in focusing their next career move—a step that usually involves changing their work environment. This exercise, "Evaluating Your Career," will help you to pinpoint where your job dissatisfaction lies, to clarify what directions are most appropriate for you, and to decide whether you should make a career change or change your work environment.

· ·

*E*valuating Your Career

1. Look at your values exercise. Is your current career or job satisfying your most important values? (If you are not now working, go to item 2.) Check one answer.

   YES: _____ All *or* _____ Most

   NO: _____ None *or* _____ Few

   If you answered "None" or "Few," could you change anything in your present job so that it would satisfy your top five values?

   _____ Yes _____ No _____ Not Sure

2. List all the elements that you like and dislike about your (current or) most recent job environment. Refer to your answers to the values exercise (Section 3.03).

Likes	*Dislikes*
_____	_____
_____	_____
_____	_____
_____	_____
_____	_____
_____	_____
_____	_____
_____	_____

   Could you change positions within your field, or even outside of science and technology, and thereby satisfy your top five values?

   _____ Yes _____ No _____ Not Sure

   If yes, what changes would you make?

   _____

   _____

3. Check those environments that would most closely fit your values.

   • Corporate _____

   • Government _____

- Nonprofit   ____
- Foundation   ____
- Consulting   ____
- University   ____
- Industrial   ____
- Entrepreneur   ____
- Other   ____
- Combination   ____

If you are or were in an environment that you did not check, how would the new one have to differ to meet your values?

_____

_____

Name and describe other potential environments.

_____

_____

Are there any alternative careers that might meet your top five values?

_____ Yes   _____ No   _____ Not Sure

4. List all the day-to-day activities that you like and dislike in your current or most recent job. Think in terms of the skills exercise you did earlier (Section 3.04).

Likes	*Dislikes*
_____	_____
_____	_____
_____	_____
_____	_____
_____	_____
_____	_____
_____	_____
_____	_____

Now look at your skills exercise results. Does your current or most recent job utilize most, if not all, of your most enjoyable skills? Check one answer.

YES: _____ All   *or*   _____ Most

NO: _____ None   *or*   _____ Few

If you answered "None" or "Few":

A. Could you change anything in your present job (or have changed anything in your most recent job) that would allow you to use more of your most enjoyable skills?

_____ Yes   _____ No   _____ Not Sure

If yes, what changes would you make?

_____

_____

B. Could you change positions within science, technology, engineering, or medicine in order to use more of your most enjoyable skills?

_____ Yes _____ No _____ Not Sure

If yes, what changes would you make?

_____

_____

What different areas of specialization are you interested in?

_____

_____

C. Are there any alternative careers outside of what you are doing now that might utilize more of your most enjoyable skills?

_____ Yes _____ No _____ Not Sure

If yes, describe them.

_____

_____

_____

_____

_____

_____

_____

OPTIONAL EXERCISE: METAPHOR

Write a metaphor that describes your feelings about your scientific career. (Example: Being a scientist, engineer, or medical professional or running a lab is like being captain of a ship; sometimes it's smooth sailing and everything is going just right, and other times it's very rough and you hit the rocks.)

OPTIONAL EXERCISE: BULLETIN BOARD EXPERIMENT

Imagine that you are looking at the bulletin board in your current job or position. What items are posted on this bulletin board? Now imagine you are viewing the bulletin board of your "ideal" or "dream" job or career. What items are posted?

_____

_____

_____

_____

_____

OPTIONAL EXERCISE: YOUR "DECLARATION OF INDEPENDENCE"

Look at the exercise creating your specific career plan, your "theory of victory," and how to allocate your resources according to your values and interests. (See Section 3.17 for details.)

• •

Business as a Calling

Vocation derives from the Latin "to call," and "callings" to an occupation (clergy, science, medicine) may come from above or below the deeper layers of oneself.

Can business be a calling?[6] The characteristics of a true calling are the following:

1. Each calling is unique to each individual.
2. A calling requires more than desire; it may require talent.
3. A true calling reveals its presence by the sense of renewed energies that we feel.
4. Callings are not easy to discover.

Since many businesses, especially small ones, grow jobs faster than universities and the academy, perhaps you can find niches that match your latent or "deep structure interests" and the "core functions" of business work.[7]

One way to determine your suitability to a business career is to examine your latent or deep structure interests, values, priorities, and skills using an assessment instrument specifically designed to examine this: the Business Career Interest Inventory (BCII), developed by Butler and Waldroop. The business "core functions" you may measure, your own deep structure interests, are application of technology, quantitative analysis, conceptual thinking, creative production, counseling and mentoring, managing people, enterprise control, and influence. The BCII is neither a clinical nor a complete diagnostic tool, but it may help you evaluate your interests vis-à-vis the fundamental activities that support a business career. It is no substitute for your imagination or your own judgment.

The following individual, who morphed himself and his career several times, is unusual in that he had to do introspection into his own needs and drives. Can you imagine how he would respond to this exercise? Is business a calling for him?

Transition From Clinical Psychologist to Comptroller Of Psychiatric Clinic to Head of a Managed-Care Company

As a child of the Depression, I chose a profession that was close to money: I became an accountant. I worked for a small firm and developed a private practice evenings and weekends. An early client was an outpatient psychiatric clinic. As the clinic grew, I became more interested in it as a client, and the clinic offered me the job of comptroller.

The Long Island Consultation Center, as it was called in the mid-1950s, was delivering psychiatric services. Because I was helping to administer and direct the clinic, I began to see that superficial administrative decisions had a big effect on clinical decisions, and vice versa. I felt guilty about my lack of clinical knowledge, so I went to graduate school (Long Island University) at night, and got an MA in clinical psychology and an internship.

Now I had two degrees, accounting and clinical psychology, and I began to see that mental health clinics needed help with their intersections, between accounting and clinical practices. So I began consulting for many of them, working seventy-five hours a week.

I realized I needed to know more about organizational behavior. I thought a Ph.D. would open doors and establish my credibility. So I went to NYU and obtained a doctorate in public administration of health care. In fact, I developed an entire curriculum for NYU in this area. I found administrative, executive, and organizational work very exciting, and it had the potential for large impact, more so than clinical work.

I always had energy and an eagerness to try new directions. I next moved into federal government. NIMH had a special teaching fellowship for one year in public administration. I ended up staying there for fourteen years (1967 to 1981), until the Reagan years. John Kennedy had established the National Committee on Mental Health Care, with centers around the country; I was active on this legislation. I got to be highly visible and controversial, responsible for some $200 million per year in spending. It was a very heady experience to have an effect on NIMH with my writing and speaking—extraordinary! It was an experiment in intergovernmental relations that I spent seven or eight years doing. (Previously it had been the responsibility of the states.)

I again got eager to move on. We had neglected training clinicians. We had assumed that clinicians were going to acquire the expertise to run community mental health clinics. They couldn't. We set up a staff college at NIMH to teach people how to handle administration, finance, and personnel for these clinics.

The staff college of NIMH developed courses for our own staffs and wide programs for others. But Reagan had no interest in these programs, so in 1981 I came to California to be the president of an HMO. This came to me through a personal contact, a friend who was a medical director. He asked, and even though I had no ideas about HMOs, I said, "What the hell," and I stayed with that HMO for another six or seven years. (That seems to be my threshold of boredom.)

I became the president of a high-technology firm named General Parametric. The company had a creative computer genius who developed presentation graphics and video displays to use with a PC and its software. You could make up graphs and charts, slides, hard copy. I was asked by the guy who made these happen if I would be on the board of directors. In two years the company grew very quickly, and it went public in the late 1980s. I was, as they say, "present at the creation."

My current company is US Behavioral Health, which works on contract with large employers (like Levi Strauss and others) to provide special counseling help for those employees who are addicted to drugs or alcohol. We have 1600 employees, many of whom have clinical degrees. They are on the phone twenty-four hours a day, seven days a week. They have computer access to all the clinical records while on the phone; they listen to the nature of the case, often an emergency, and then refer the patient to one of 35,000 clinicians on call. We manage these benefits for some seven million people nationwide. We have a very sophisticated system, and I've written a book on the subject, *Managed Mental Health Services*.

I think it's important to have a sense of oneself, to do some introspection. A major factor in making my positive transitions was my personal needs and drives. I think it had little to do with my ability. At each juncture, I felt, "I *need* to do that." I had very personal imperatives that gave me the initial impetus to change.

There are a lot skills that scientists have that can be adapted and transferred to other responsibilities, such as administration. The book by Pelz and Andres, *Scientists in Organizations*, addresses these issues, which intrigued me. Superficially, a transition from science to administration would seem to be quite difficult because of the substantial differences in the behavior of successful administrators. Scientists usually need to have control; the same is true for clinicians. But administrators and executives depend on cooperative behavior if they are to be leaders. Your success depends entirely on other people—and introversion and control don't work. For example, it's clear that if people are not interested in pleasing me, they can defeat me.

I was not relatively happy at all times, in all careers, but my transitions were motivated by personal concerns. My need to change careers was connected to my infatuation with the process of discovery and learning. It was a process of going into a new environment, asking questions, and getting answers. I had to expose myself to new people, new techniques. I usually move on every six or seven years, and it's often out of boredom. I can tell when I'm ready to move on because I usually write a book that caps that phase, then leave the field.

Obviously, business was a "calling" to this transitioner. His answers would be different depending on which career he was answering for. His versatile energy, optimism, and willingness to try new career directions are praiseworthy, but clearly "serendipity" can be a code word for "highly talented, and therefore a magnet for good career opportunities." His upscale career well-being radiates brilliantly from his narrative, as does his impatience to move on to new levels of self-discovery and engagement with real-world problem solving. His deep structure interests on the BCII are notably high.

3.06 NONTRADITIONAL CAREERS USING SCIENCE/TECHNOLOGY SKILLS

Choose Your Strongest Skills

Now that you have identified skills that *may* fit into the career(s) that interest you, choose up to five of your strongest skills. These should be consistent with those from your list in step 3 of the skills exercise in Section 3.04. Use the space under I below to list these skills. In II, describe each skill and show how you use it. You may select examples from both work and leisure-time projects and activities.

For example: "The Black-Scholes equation is a financial options model that resembles a diffusion equation like the Schroedinger or thermal diffusion equations. . . . I started modeling options. . . . Think of it as a set of solutions to partial differential equations with boundary conditions set by the market. This was all applications from physics. . . . Risk control is more like a collection of transactions, more like statistical mechanics. . . . Mathematics is an extremely useful tool and discipline. All I did was to find an environment where I could do this as a career. . . . I work as the risk manager for the equities division, as a high level consultant."

A second example: "While I was a student, I wrote comedy sketches with a college theater troupe. I found this was great fun, a blast. I did it as a hobby. I researched the field of comedy writing and discovered it was very difficult to find work. So I started giving free shows, writing and performing my own material."

Another example: "In addition, I volunteer several hours of my time a week to a local crisis hotline. I counsel crime victims over the phone. I calm them when they are very upset and comfort them during a crisis situation. Furthermore, I advise them to get additional help if needed."

As you can see, more than one skill area can be found in each paragraph. In the first example, "mathematical skills" is one main skill chosen, yet others ("consulting" and "analyzing") are in the descriptions. Skills in the second example include both "writing" and "comedy," and in the third, "counseling," "comforting," and "staying calm to help others in a crisis".

In addition, a skill such as "advising" can be used in different venues, such as on Wall Street doing options and risk analysis, in hospital administration, or providing human resource services in a corporation, depending on your values and interests.

I. My Five Strongest and Most Enjoyable Skills

    1. _____
    2. _____
    3. _____
    4. _____
    5. _____

II. Write a paragraph for each skill listed (in I above) that illustrates how you have used that skill (see example above). Use a separate page for each skill.

A *lternative Careers*

Instructions: Go through the "starter" list of alternative careers (below), and check the box next to any area that interests you. Do not think about whether or not you would be good at it, or if you have the correct education, etc. Just think about what interests you. All skills listed below can be found on the skills list in Section 3.04 (both broad skill areas and the specific skills listed are used). A more detailed list of nontraditional careers, and their requisite skills and characteristics, can be found in "Careers for Chemists: A World Outside the Lab:[8]

This is simply a "pump-priming" exercise. Freely select other options that feel logical and comfortable. The appendix contains a much more extensive list of industry groups, locations, and other career search selection criteria that you can scrutinize after you have finished this "starter" list.

- ☐ **ADVERTISING:**
  - ☐ *Account executive*: negotiating, influencing/persuading others, advocating, budgeting.
  - ☐ *Copywriter*: written communication skills, creative expression.
- ☐ **ADMINISTRATOR:** data-handling skills, organizational skills, managerial skills.
- ☐ **AGENTING:** influencing/persuading others, negotiating, observing people.
- ☐ **ART DEALERSHIP:** negotiating, influencing/persuading others.
- ☐ **BUSINESS MANAGEMENT:** managerial skills, organizational skills, data-handling skills, human relations skills.
- ☐ **COLLEGE ADMINISTRATOR:** managerial skills, organizational skills, data-handling skills, human relations skills.
- ☐ **CONSULTING:** oral communication skills, analytical skills, human relations skills.
- ☐ **CORPORATE TRAINER:** oral communication skills, writing clearly and concisely.
- ☐ **COUNSELING:** human relations skills, problem-solving skills.
- ☐ **EDITOR:** organizational skills, written communication/conceptualization skills.
- ☐ **ENTREPRENEUR/BUSINESS OWNER:** managerial skills, organizational skills, oral communication skills.
- ☐ **EXECUTIVE RECRUITER:** influencing/persuading others, human relations skills.
- ☐ **FINANCIAL ANALYST:** data-handling skills, analytical skills, communication skills.
- ☐ **FREELANCE WRITER:** written communication skills, working autonomously, discipline.
- ☐ **FUND RAISING (DEVELOPMENT):** influencing/persuading others, organizational skills.
- ☐ **HOSPITAL ADMINISTRATOR:** managerial skills, organizational skills, data-handling skills, human relations skills.

☐ **HUMAN RESOURCES (PERSONNEL):**

☐ *Recruiting*: oral communication skills, human relations skills.

☐ *Benefits*: data-handling skills, advising.

☐ *Compensation*: data-handling skills, analytical skills.

☐ *Labor relations*: oral communication skills, written communication skills, human relations skills.

☐ **INSURANCE BROKER:** oral communication skills, data-handling skills.

☐ **INVESTMENT BANKER:** negotiating, influencing/persuading others, data-handling skills.

☐ **JOURNALISM:** written communication skills, data-handling skills.

☐ **LOBBYING:** oral communication skills, human relations skills.

☐ **MARKETING:** oral communication skills, analytical skills.

☐ **MARKETING RESEARCH:** analytical skills, written communication skills, data-handling skills.

☐ **MEDIATOR/ARBITRATOR:** oral communication skills, human relations skills.

☐ **NONPROFIT/FOUNDATION EXECUTIVE:** managerial skills, organizational skills, oral communication skills.

☐ **PATENT ATTORNEY:** analytical skills, communication skills, problem-solving skills, computer skills.

☐ **PUBLIC RELATIONS** (*corporate communications, government relations, public affairs, consumer affairs*): oral communication skills, written communication skills, research.

☐ **PUBLISHER:** managerial skills, organizational skills, data-handling skills.

☐ **PROFESSIONAL SOCIETY EXECUTIVE/ADMINISTRATOR:** human relations skills, presentation skills, management skills.

☐ **REAL ESTATE BROKER:** persuading others, negotiating, data-handling skills.

☐ **SALES:** influencing/persuading others, data-handling skills.

☐ **SCIENCE POLICY ANALYST/RESEARCHER/ADMINISTRATOR:** research skills, analytical skills, working independently, presentation skills.

☐ **STOCKBROKER:** influencing/persuading others, data-handling skills.

☐ **TEACHING:** making presentations, advising.

☐ **TECHNOLOGY FIRM ADMINISTRATOR:** data-handling skills, organizational skills, managerial skills.

☐ **THEATER PRODUCTION:** negotiating, influencing/persuading others, organizational skills, managerial skills.

☐ **VENTURE CAPITAL:** analytical skills, research skills, presentation skills, communication skills.

Your training, background, and experience have grounded you with broad scope and various skills. As a result, numerous careers are available to you. Think about which careers would dovetail with your values and your skills.

Below, write the names of the careers you checked off that interest you. Add the names of additional industry groups from the Appendix. Next to each named career, describe those skills you have that would be useful in that career. You will find a list of selected books that will help you explore your career options in the appendix.

1. _____

   _____

   _____

2. _____

   _____

   _____

3. _____

   _____

   _____

4. _____

   _____

   _____

5. _____

   _____

   _____

• •

You will compare these options with your interests in Section 3.07. In Section 3.08, you will conduct a systematic scan of all likely career options and rank-order them.

Now that you have a clearer sense of your own skills, we will look at how others have adapted their skills and transferred them to nontraditional careers. By "nontraditional" we refer to those careers for which scientific or technical training and skills are useful, but not required.

Many scientists, engineers, and technical and medical professionals do nontraditional work. The career transitions narrated below provide a sample of nontraditional areas, along with descriptions of the major skills required. Most careers require more than one skill; some require very many skills.

The next transition is one of the more extreme cases in that the narrator went into physics for purely arbitrary reasons (a romantic interest at the time was a mathematician who suggested it). But more importantly, because he is a committed Marxist, he wanted a specialty as far away as possible from politics, and therefore "safer" to do. (He actually ran for vice president of the United States on the Communist ticket with Eldridge Cleaver.)

Transition From Physics
To Public Interest Law

I tried to get college teaching positions in the 1970s, but there were no jobs available. This was very different from the mid-sixties, when I got three excellent college teaching offers.

So I drove an airport limousine for a while, and then was invited to a summer institute at the University of Wyoming, designed to retrain college teachers to be high school teachers. I was offered a teaching job, but it was withdrawn when the school discovered that I ran with Eldridge Cleaver. The American Federation of Teachers helped me to institute a lawsuit against the school for breach of contract. I won mitigated damages in the lawsuit but did not accept the position.

Instead, I was hired on a civil rights matter through friends at the ACLU and UAW to work full-time in the human resources department of the local county government. Getting a full-time job with a liberal salary and full benefits made all the difference in the world to me, since I had been depressed and lonely during this difficult, turbulent period of insta-bility. I worked on employment discrimination cases during the day and studied law four evenings a week for four years. I continued after law school to work on civil rights cases, disability, negligence, and prisoners' rights. The judges, other attorneys, and even the clients I represented left much to be desired intellectually, however.

I loved arguing and debating cases, and I still do. Both physics and law gave me the chance to express my natural tendencies to be adversarial and intellectually stimulated.

For the narrator, the common ground between physics and law was sim-ply that both gave him the chance to express his natural tendencies to be ad-versarial, intellectually stimulated, and combative. He says, however, that judges, other attorneys, and even clients he represented "left much to be de-sired intellectually."

The next nontraditional career transition (or "variant" pattern, in Ginzberg's typology; see Section 2.04) is a man whose consistent life theme was to define his own destiny. (When George Gershwin asked Maurice Ravel to teach him composition, Ravel said: "Why be a second-rate Ravel when you can be a first-rate Gershwin?")

KEN RIND
••••••••••••••••••••••

Transition From Nuclear Chemistry To Biotech Venture Capital

I produced fission of silver with high-energy (300 mev) proton bombardment at the Nevis Cyclotron of Columbia University for my Ph.D. in nuclear chemistry.

I was offered a job at the City University of New York. City College was expanding its physics programs, and I was supposed to be given a laboratory and lots of equipment to do nuclear research. When I arrived, I asked, "Where's my lab?" The department chairman showed me a big hole in the ground. I said, "What's that?" He said, "We ran out of money." I left after two or three years. There was nothing I wanted to do without a lab there, but I realized all that equipment I had used earlier was unique and expensive.

I started to look around for what I could do without a lab. Others ahead of me at Columbia in physics had gone to work at Quantum Science and its Samson Fund, a high-technology stock market operation run by Mirek Stevenson, who had worked with Charles Townes on lasers. Mirek went to IBM to try to build a working laser there. His lab assistant dropped the crystal and broke it, so he ended up working on the world's second working laser. He left.

His wife was an MBA and securities analyst, and she encouraged him to use his technology training on the stock market. Her firm helped investors to select and analyze technology stocks. I was there during the mid 1960s. One of the firm's clients was the Rockefeller family. Laurence Rockefeller hired me to work with the family's investment people on the stock market. I was advising people about semiconductor companies. At that time, there were only about six or seven firms in the United States doing high-technology venture capital. I helped form the National Venture Capital Association in 1973. (Now we have about 200 member firms and about 600 venture capital people.)

In 1970, I was recruited by Oppenheimer and Company, a Wall Street stock brokerage firm. Originally, Oppenheimer wanted me to be a "research department" to cover technology stocks. I turned this down because I was really interested in venture capital. I had served my apprenticeship at Rockefeller, and had already switched over to venture capital. Eventually Oppenheimer offered me a partnership. There were not a lot of science and technology types like me working in the financial community in those days. From 1970 to 1976, I worked there about half of the time on venture capital and half time on corporate finance.

By 1974–1975, Wall Street had gone more or less bankrupt. There were no venture capital funds available. The pension funds could not invest in venture capital until 1978, when the law was changed to permit it, and then the venture capital business exploded.

In 1976, I started Oxford Ventures with a colleague, Cornelius Ryan, who had an MBA from Wharton, knew computers, and had worked at Travelers, RCA, and Burroughs. A second partner was originally a civil engineer who got an MBA at Harvard Business School. We searched for several years for biotech partners, and eventually, in 1987, we found Alan Walton, who had been a professor of biochemistry at Case and Harvard.

Today, about two-thirds of our deals are in biotech, and about one-third in services and instruments. We've invested in some seventy-three companies; about twenty-six went public and thirty got acquired. Industrywide among venture capital funds, about 10 to 15 percent of the companies venture capital firms invest in go bankrupt, about half lose money, and only a small percentage make money.

I think that all of my career transitions were made to control my own destiny, to attain more freedom. Maybe this originated with my father, who was an independent businessman, a customer's peddler, who sold dry goods door to door. He represented himself, selling goods that others had manufactured.

I would say that people should not be afraid to learn a new subject. If you have a Ph.D., business is trivial. But you need to have or develop a personality that is outgoing. I had to learn how to speak publicly, to meet people, to make contacts. Of course, if you're not like this and cannot become like this and you want to change careers, and work, say, on Wall Street, you can do it. Just sit in a room, learn about stock options and warrants, and write computer code until you understand it well.

I have a temperamental disposition to work hard. I'm not afraid of learning new things. I worked hard to learn about fission and spallation reactions. I worked hard to change, and I was not afraid to change.

He fulfilled himself so successfully that he is unable to retire. He says he cannot decline the new opportunities that continue to present themselves. He's now helping Israel develop new software and biotech companies in conjunction with some twenty-eight technology "incubators" using 1200 Russian refugee scientists.

Now consider Dr. Sheldon Silverstein, who has two satisfying careers. By day he's a pediatrician, and by night a stand-up comic.

SHELDON SILVERSTEIN
••••••••••••••••••••••••
Transition From Pediatrics To Stand-Up Comedy

I got my medical degree in 1985 at Downstate Medical Center in Brooklyn and did my internship and residency in pediatrics at Kaiser Foundation Hospital and California Pacific Medical Center.

I was working twelve hours a day at clinics, but four or five nights a week I was doing stand-up comedy turns on "open-mike" nights at Catch a Rising Star and Holy City Zoo (where Robin Williams got his start).

I took a four-year leave of absence from my residency to start my career as a full-time humorist. I studied with a professional comedy coach. During my leave of absence, I also wrote a book about an autistic sibling.

I found that medicine and humor work well together. Humor can provide perspective to alleviate the stress, alienation, and panic most patients experience in the medical office or hospital. Humor helps ease pain by relaxing and distracting the sufferer and elevating his or her mood, which influences pain perception. Putting laughter into a diagnosis, or bedside manner, has measurable value. I joke that I keep my patients in *stitches*, or I *inject* them with humor.

I returned to my pediatrics residency in 1990 and launched Stand-Up Medicine Seminars, which is a lecture bureau for my medical talks and speeches. I present a talk called "The Healing Power of Humor in the Medicine Practice" at medical staff meetings and educational conferences, and as an after-dinner keynote speaker at special events.

I left stand-up comedy night-clubs because the level of humor was sinking. I didn't want to do sex and drug humor.

But I now have two satisfying careers; I'm fortunate. One foot is in comedy, and another is in pediatric medicine. I can tickle the children's and their parents' funny bones. I also set broken bones. Laughter and humor are important: A hearty laugh is an aerobic workout—without the sweat suit.

I'm writing a book filled with serious medical information in a lighter *vein* called *Medical Handbook for Dummies*.

Many physicians are writers, such as Michael Crichton, author of *Jurassic Park*; William Carlos Williams, the poet; Richard Seltzer, a surgeon turned writing teacher and author of essays, and Oliver Sachs, author of *The Man Who Mistook His Wife for a Hat*.

My father, who was a dry cleaner in Brooklyn, felt that getting an education was a buffer against "taking crap" from people. But I discovered that a higher level of education, like I got in medical school, entitles a degree holder to a higher level of crap. I should have realized this earlier when I bumped into my own childhood pediatrician. I told him I was studying to be a pediatrician, and he advised me, "Don't be a schmuck." *Of course, if you make a mistake in medicine, it's serious. In comedy, it's funny.*

The Humor Project (110 Spring Street, Saratoga Springs, NY 12866, Telephone: (800) 600-4242, WWW: http://www.wizvax.net/humor/) has a catalog of over 200 humor books, videos, audiotapes, software, and props to amuse, amaze, delight, inform, and help individuals and organizations to incorporate humor into their work. All of us need humor in our lives. Indeed, a sense of humor and equanimity is a recurring theme among fulfilled career transitions, and restores balance to our lives. If intellectual activity is our strength, it can also be our weakness.[9]

3.07 YOUR INTERESTS: FUTURE SKILLS DEVELOPMENT

If you have clearly defined your values and skills, yet cannot choose alternative fields to explore as possible job or career choices, use the following exercises and career narratives to generate ideas. The exercises are designed to stimulate you to bring to the surface and record your interests, latent and obvious. *Interests* differ from *skills* in that skills exercise familiar, favorite, and strong "muscles," such as those muscles you employ in hobbies, avocations, and leisure pursuits. (You will have identified your skills in Section 3.04.)

Your *interests* are future skills that you wish to develop further. The question each of the two narrators below faces is, "How do I develop my interests into future skills?" or "How will I pursue my interests?" Your interests can lead you to consider a general career area that will give you satisfaction. However, your interests change and evolve as you do, like a moving target. You can enjoy and flourish at several different careers, as some of our narrators explain.

Several of our career-change narrators describe how their values and skills pointed to careers that diverged from their initial science specialty: analyzing technical stock portfolios for a large insurance firm, marketing engineering or technical products, starting and running a biotech venture capital firm; becoming a humorist, newspaper reporter,. or songwriter. With so many changing environments to choose from, you may be confused. If a major hobby outside of scientific work was following the stock market and investing, the choice of a financial environment is appealing. If a major non-scientific or outside interest was making people laugh, the choice of comedy writer is natural. Note the twists and turns that the following career-change narratives reveal, and as you read them, think how you would write your own career-change saga. The exercises follow the narratives.

The young woman below, who eventually morphed from biology to science journalism, took a circuitous route of development. Notice how much she struggles to make her transition.

Transition from Biology to Science Publishing, Administration, and Science Writing

I went to Wisconsin as an undergrad and majored in biology. I knew then that I was interested in genetics, I'd been interested in genetics since I was a sophomore in high school. I was very certain that I'd be on a research path for my entire career. I graduated and went on to Stanford for a doctorate in genetics. I guess I knew all along that I wanted to go to the bay area for graduate school.

About halfway through graduate school . . . you kind of get into this tunnel—you know, there's no light at either end and you start to wonder is this really how I want to spend my life? I kind of flip-flopped on it a few times. In the end I decided, about a year before I was ready to finish, that I didn't want to do a postdoc. I was tired of working at the bench, kind of burned out, and thinking that I wanted to do something more general. When you're doing research, your focus is very narrow, and I enjoyed being more of a generalist; know less about more things rather than everything about this one thing. And I decided that to me, to work 60 or 70 hours a week was a bit much.

But I really didn't know what else I was going to do. I'd always had strong language skills. I had seen ads for *Nature* and *Science* editors, so that was the first thing that occurred to me.

I mentioned it to my advisor and he said, yeah, that sounds like something to look into. Right about that time I was starting to talk to people, about "I'm not sure I want to continue in research and I don't know what I want to do." It just so happened a friend of a friend worked for a textbook publisher, and she said "*My boss has a Ph.D. in zoology and he's working in publishing. Maybe you should talk to him.*"

I went and talked to him, and he was very encouraging, and told me about what he did, which was developmental editing. Textbooks have a lot more to them than just a scholarly book, where people just write it and go. He loved what he was doing and told me scholarly publishers also hire Ph.D.'s to work as editors, so that's another place to look.

I went to the library, and identified all of the publishing companies in the United States specializing in science. I got 101 names and addresses and sent off resumes and cover letters and I got a call from Academic Press.

It turned out they were just about to place an ad in *Science.* I went down there for an interview. We hit it off, and they decided to hire me as an *associate acquisitions editor. I spent two years there. After the first year I was promoted up to acquisitions editor.*

That job entailed thinking of new projects, keeping an eye on science, what I thought people in the field would purchase.

There was a lot of travel in the job, going to meetings, which was great, after being cooped up in graduate school for six years with little money to go anywhere. I was on the road, staying in nice hotels, wearing nice clothes, it was all very refreshing. It was really nice. I was making a lot more money than my friends who had gone on to postdocs.

I enjoyed it for a couple of years. I got the feeling that the corporate way of life was not for me, so at that point I did something rash. I just decided to go back into the lab. I needed the change. I went out and found a job very easily, given my background. I found a job and worked with a young PI there. That was going fine, but he had not planned that well and he had agreed to take on a postdoc before he had hired me, and counted on her getting a fellowship, which she didn't get. So he was running out of money, so I began to look for something else.

I was going to continue in labwork in that way, off the tenure track. *I sent out resumes, and I just happened to send a resume to George White at the Genome Institute,* because of the genome money. He called me up and he said "I really want to talk to you because I'm interested in your background—you have a *science background and an administrative* one as well. I've got this huge genome project and I don't have time to attend to all of the management details, and I wonder if you'd be interested in stepping back outside the lab again and helping me manage this, manage the people, the budget, and all that."

Well, that sounded great—I could still be in the lab, but not working at the bench. So I said, yes, I'm very interested. That's what brought me to the Salk in La Jolla. I loved the Institute and the surroundings—it's beautiful, all these cliffs, over the ocean, and the people were friendly . . . it has a special kind of character to it, a family kind of character, due to it being founded by a Nobel laureate. People here feel really proud to be part of the Institute—

it's very good, being around here, and I was attracted to that. It just kind of clicked, I was really happy.

That position lasted for almost three years and then the PI got an offer to go elsewhere. He decided to leave and at that point I started thinking, well, gosh, I had this great job and now what's going to happen.

Landing this position was a fluke. I never set out to be a writer and I had no formal experience in writing, although the publishing job entailed some writing: whenever I decided to pursue a project that required approval by the management. They were marketing folks and book production people—they didn't know science. At that point I'd have to translate and explain the need for the project and why it was significant to scientists, and that all had to be in lay terms. But that was good practice, and when I came to this job, I said, yah, I do have science writing experience. But the way I found out about this job was totally a fluke.

I started brainstorming, and I said, ok, if I could do anything in the world, a fantasy job, what would I do? And I thought, well, gee, I'd really like to work at the zoo. Zookeepers. That would really be a lot of fun. Then I backed off and said, ok, what kinds of things in serious terms could I do for the zoo that would make sense?

Grant administration came to mind because I'd been doing some of that for a genome project, talking to the people in Washington and making sure we were doing everything correctly and had approval. That was one thing—they must have some type of research grants.

The other thing that came to mind was fundraising. I started to think well, when I was an acquisitions editor, part of that job involved not just knowing science but going out and wining and dining scientists. A lot of that was building a rapport, nurturing people. That's also applicable to fund raising.

When I was working for George he had agreed to host a large meeting, which was about one hundred people coming to San Diego and basically he threw it all in my lap and said "I don't want to know anything, do this for me." So I had expertise in dealing with catering people, hotel people, managing an events. So I felt that was all applicable to fundraising too. Plus I knew science, and practically any organization in science has to raise money. Having a scientific background certainly can't hurt.

I called a higher up in *the Institute and I said, here's what I'm thinking, what do you think? She said that sounds like a really good idea, and the people who do that here are—and she gave me the names, and I called the person who is now my boss. As soon as I told her I had worked in publishing,* she said "Can you write?" and I said, "Well, I can fudge it." She said "We need a science writer—we lost our science writer and we've been freelancing a lot of stuff, and there are some people who can fake it, but they're not scientists, so let's talk about this more."

So it just worked out. It was really fortuitous—I never knew that there was a position here that would suit me. So I stepped right into it. I left my last job on a Friday, and I came in Monday and started this job, and that was about two years ago. It's worked out well—I've been really fortunate.

Notice too that she is not yet set in a lifelong career. She is still growing and evolving.

The next narrative reveals a very talented man who was doubly burdened: (1) He had too many interests, and (2) he had the brains to develop those interests in many different directions. His career problems were intensified by winning a MacArthur Prize Fellowship.

ROBERT SCOTT ROOT-BERNSTEIN
....

Transition From Biochemistry To History and Philosophy Of Science, To Physiology

I'm probably the most bizarre person you ever met. I was probably born an artist, but I knew I could never make a living at it. I do have visual ways of thinking and organizing ideas.

As an undergraduate at Princeton, I wanted to do and learn everything. The way I could do that was to major in biochemistry, so I majored in that. But the chairman of the department yelled at me, "There's only one reason to be a biochemist, and that's to be a biochemist."

I had an unorthodox view of biochemistry, at variance with the way they taught it. I knew biochemistry was not for me. Maybe more likely was mathematics or theoretical biology, or history and philosophy of science from the point of view of a scientist—those were the choices I considered. I decided to get a Ph.D. in history (also at Princeton), and I wrote a dissertation on the history of physical chemistry. I also wrote some theoretical biology papers; I was a teaching assistant in biology to keep the doors open. I knew that I'd have problems getting a job, since there were none in the history or philosophy of science. The view then was; if you're a science practitioner, history and philosophy of science is a no-no. So I simply went to the top. I contacted CEOs of major corporations and foundations. I found Jonas Salk, and the Salk Institute offered me a job. Jonas liked odd-ball backgrounds like mine, and he let me do bench work *and* history/philosophy of science because he was also looking at human evolution of culture. He let me play in both fields.

Then I got a MacArthur Prize Fellowship (1981–1986), which only exacerbated my career problems.

I wrote my book *Discovering*, and I was looking for connections between science and art. I was able because of this (as I'll explain) to develop a theory of immunity, and to discover a patentable drug for arthritis that others hadn't noticed.

For the last fifteen years, I had no credentials in whatever work I was doing. I was always "learning on the fly," learning how to learn, using new ways of looking at things.

At Salk I was working on interactions between proteins that no one was addressing. Crick and Pauling said you can't have them, and you can't figure them out. But once you understand it, it's really easy. Since they said no, others avoided the topic. I was looking at autoimmune diseases like MS. I had isolated a segment of protein that was the cause of the disease, but no dose of this protein fragment by itself could cause the disease. Yet with an adjuvant acting as a sort of catalyst, it could. The adjuvant in combination with the protein fragment would work, and the adjuvant or the fragment without the other would not. They were like mutual causes of the disease in complex or cocktail form.

Then I had an unexpected observation. I took a bunch of vaccines and mixed them up with a bunch of tuberculosis and others in vivo. The entire experiment was a total waste—nothing happened. Except, as Sherlock Holmes said, the most interesting part of all was that the dog didn't bark. I was giving rats arthritis. One rat did not get arthritis. What was different was a specific viral vaccine (now being patented) against arthritis in animals and humans. It turns out people had seen and ignored this in humans for fifty years. There is related material that has the same effect, and I saw that the dog was not barking. I wouldn't have seen this if I hadn't done this unusual experiment, and thought of the taxonomy of scientific theories (like "turn it on its head" or Langmuir's principle). I also advise companies on how to solve problems using strategies for research.

I always asked myself, where do you want to be? In a lot of my discussions I had to think of where I wanted to be to get to the end point I wanted. My dad told me, "Always keep your options open," and it was a lot of work to keep my options open, but I did it.

At Salk, because of the MacArthur Fellowship, they cut me out of their budget, and then they closed down in 1983 in the third year of my fellowship. So I needed a home. I had a number of choices. I tried to find a real job at a university. The MacArthurs were pretty new then, and no one knew what they were for. People wanted me to start out as an assistant professor like anyone else, and work my way up in a traditional discipline. I had no papers published in biology. I had to ask myself, Do I do what I don't want? Or do I live off the MacArthur and do biology?

I moved to LA, where an old mentor who worked at the VA hospital gave me lab and office space. I had contacts at UCLA, and I made new contacts—I met maybe 100 new contacts (most people did not turn out to be helpful, although the MacArthur did help open doors). I had written an article on science and art, and it was the dean of fine arts at UCLA who called *me*, saying that he had a big plan for me—to revitalize the UCLA fine arts program by taking in people like me and others with fine arts backgrounds, and some with demonstrated creativity in both science and art. He took somebody from Disney, an animator, a techie metallurgy person to think of new ways to do sculpture—all odd things. I didn't know any of the others he contacted, but he wanted a new honors program, "Creative Processes in Science and Art." I must have had breakfast, lunch, and dinner with over fifty people at UCLA. It was amazing! All of them wanted to get their two cents in, to see if I knew what I was talking about.

About six weeks into my course, that dean left, and the chancellor axed the whole program. The course got high reviews on melding science and art. But I was on my sixth year of the MacArthur. I had spent all my savings. I literally had to have a real job.

I got three offers. One was an endowed chair, a full professor at the newly formed George Mason University (formerly a junior college)—with no equipment, but it was a biologist position.

Another was Michigan State University, where I am now a full professor (at age 43), but I started as an assistant professor with equipment, and began to work from the bottom up. I have no regrets now, but there were problems then. I had a joint appointment in the natural sciences and history/philosophy of science. The university cut this department a year and a half after I got here, which is why I'm a professor of physiology. I must say I entered the physiology department with a chip on my shoulder, but it all worked out.

Probably flexibility, keeping my options open, was very important. I had a goal of where I wanted to be, and I was willing to take steps toward my goal, or sidesteps toward my goal. The next career is not one's last career. None of the jobs was a fundamental answer for me or my career problem. I never found or will find that answer.

It's interesting. At Harvard or Princeton they have people like Stephen Jay Gould who can work in almost any discipline he wants. Here, we have intense territoriality: If you haven't demonstrated your competence by getting a Ph.D. or postdoc, you can't even use our equipment! At Harvard or Princeton they assume an undergraduate is capable of using their equipment—it's OK. Here, they ask—even if you're 50 years old—are you qualified? Are you sure you know how to use it? Why ask me? I guess that's another example of parochialism in the academy.

I guess learning how to learn was very important to me. If you can do this, you can operate in any field. Also, you have to know how to deal with people, what tools you will need to master a field. This gives you the ability to bridge fields. I'm trying to put together my thoughts on this into a "tools for thinking" approach. It's hard the first field you enter, but it gets easier with each new field.

Here's a person interested in bench science, history and philosophy of science, connections between science and art, immunity, arthritis, physiology, and theories of discovery. What is special about this man is that he was able to indulge virtually all his interests sequentially, and many simultaneously. What questions did he ask himself that you can ask yourself about your potential future skills development, your interests?

● ●

NOW IT'S YOUR TURN

1. What do you do in your free time, or what would you like to do if you had more free time?

_____

_____

_____

2. What topics, subjects, or issues do you enjoy talking about, reading about, studying, etc.?

_____

_____

_____

3. From childhood through college, what did you want to be "when you grew up"?

_____

_____

_____

4. If you did not have to work for a living (if you won the lottery or a MacArthur), what would you do with your time?

_____

_____

_____

5. List five of your strongest interests that you were able to identify. If necessary, reread the narratives and reflect upon your interests for several days.

_____

_____

_____

6. What types of jobs or careers might utilize these interests? Brainstorm. If the well has run dry for the moment, review other career-change narratives in the book; let your mind freely associate with the narrators' circuitous career paths for inspiration.

_____

_____

_____

· ·

In the section that follows we will introduce you to a systematic way of examining job or career options.

3.08 CAREER OPTIONS EXPLORATION, RESEARCH, AND TREND TRACKING

Overlaps

You are going to search for, and to find, the overlap(s) between your internal *preferences* (your top five skills, interests, values, and favorite skill cluster) and the *external marketplace niche realities*.

Your Preferences

Top five values (Section 3.03)

Top five skills (Section 3.04)

Top five interests (Section 3.07)

Actual activities you most enjoy doing; clusters of your favorite skills (Section 3.04) [You will create Research Grid 1.]

Marketplace Niche Realities

Industries or economic sectors [You will create Research Grid 2.]

Work environments [You will create Research Grid 3.]

Job requirements [You will create Research Grid 4.]

Additional specifications [You will create Research Grid 5.]

From the overlap (or discovered coincidences) of these two groups will emerge your most likely career options. But first, you must go through several rounds of guessing career options, comparing them with marketplace niches, second-guessing and comparing, third-guessing and comparing, and so on, until you zero in on your most likely career options. Since this can bewilder anyone, we have broken the process down into small steps.

Career Options Exploration (and Research)

From the previous topics, you should have developed some ideas about career options that interest you. Your next step is to further examine and refine these options, using methods we call career options exploration or career options research.

Before you begin to explore your career options, however, your values, skills, and interests should be clear to you. Often they are not, and it is at this point that many people consult a career counselor to help clarify and objectify these complex and difficult issues. (Career testing administered and interpreted by a professional may also be very useful to you.) You may need to review or redo the earlier exercises on values, skills, and interests (Sections 3.03, 3.04, and 3.07). Career options exploration, coupled with informational interviewing, will help you explore many jobs—*before* you make a decision to leave your present job or career. The information you collect serves three purposes:

1. You will see what types of jobs or careers exist that are compatible with your values, skills, personality, and interests. This expands your options so that you can make an informed decision about your next move. Since you may feel that you made a mistake choosing your present career path, expanding your options also gives you a sense of optimism, energy, and forward movement. (If the job or career resembles a lock, and your résumé resembles a key, you are studying the lock in a way locksmith does—to design a key that will fit the lock and open the door for you.)

2. You will come to understand the potential new career or job on a day-to-day basis. What is it *really* like to be what you *think* you want to be?

This will dispel myths and assumptions about other people's careers and jobs that may have misled you in the past.

3. You will use the information you collected to prepare you for your informational interviews (Section 3.09). *Later*, you will start your job search, design and write your résumé; and obtain—and prepare for—job interviews.

There are many approaches to see how well a job or career fits or harmonizes with your values, skills, personality, and interests. They may include intuition, informational interviewing, reading career books, brainstorming sessions, and browsing on-line or in a career library or bookstore. Some are simple and obvious; others are complex.

If you simply jump in to the options generation process, you can get bogged down. Here are a sequence of steps to help you organize this process.

· ·

OPTIONS ALGORITHM

1. Make a "first guess" at several career options.

2. If you have too many options (say, more than five), you will need to narrow your number of options.

3. If you have too few options (say, only one or two), you will need to expand your number of options.

4. Read case vignettes and narratives from this book (or others) of people like you who have changed careers, and compare your own options with theirs.

5. From the five previous sections (your values, your skills, taking stock, nontraditional careers, and your interests) make a list of the *actual activities* you most enjoy doing, the clusters of skills you most enjoy using, or your favorite skills—for example: (1) writing, (2) managing, (3) selling, (4) corporate research development, (5) teaching, and so on. We will call these preliminary preferences (Pref. 1, Pref. 2, and so on).

6. Similarly, select *work environments* or *economic sectors* that appeal to you (see what you wrote in the three previous sections: evaluating your career, nontraditional careers, and your interests)—for example; (1) advertising, (2) investment banking, (3) industry-specific research and development, (4) the nonprofit sector, (5) the academic world, (6) small company start-ups, (7) large corporate environments, (8) foundations, (9) government.

7. You may already have "second-guess" specific career options that you want to explore. These options may arise from your instincts, from previous experiences or exercises, or from a combination of your choice *preferences plus niches* list. List these.

8. The previous seven steps should be done **before** you begin to scrutinize sources of career information, so that you do not confuse information gathering with option se-

lection. It is common to be overwhelmed or distracted from your quest when you examine source materials. (It may be that you are trying to do too much at once.)

9. The following specific "framing" questions will clarify your choices of marketplace niche realities.

Items 10 through 15 continue later.

FRAMING QUESTIONS

I. Work Environment.

A. **People.** What type of people are involved in this type of work/industry (management, support staff, colleagues, clients, competitors, customers, etc.)?

_____

_____

_____

_____

_____

B. **Workplace.** What are the circumstances (hours, typical pressures/stresses, overtime, travel, geographic location, attractiveness of workplace, typical size of the organization)?

_____

_____

_____

_____

_____

C. **Career path.** What levels can you attain in this type of work/industry (typical hierarchy, advancement, average salary ranges)? How marketable is this experience?

_____

_____

_____

_____

_____

D. **Outlook.** What are the current trends in and future outlook for this type of work/industry?

_____

_____

_____

_____

_____

_____

_____

II. Job Requirements

  A. What credentials are needed (education, training)?

_____

_____

_____

_____

_____

_____

  B. What skills and characteristics are required?

_____

_____

_____

_____

_____

_____

  C. What are some of the different job titles and/or specialty areas?

_____

_____

_____

_____

_____

III. Additional Specifications

  A. What is the product or service provided by this type of work or industry?

_____

_____

_____

_____

_____

_____

_____

B. What type of ongoing training is necessary (reading professional journals, taking classes, licensing, etc.)?

_____

_____

_____

_____

_____

OPTIONS ALGORITHM (CONTINUED FROM 1 THROUGH 9)

10. Now go back to your list of (1) preferences and (2) niches, and attempt to revise, alter, shorten, or lengthen the third-guess options based upon your responses to the framing questions.

11. You are now ready to compare your third round of options with external information sources—without the distraction of "toggling" or "dithering" between states of confusion (similar to "hunting" in feedback loop systems).

12. Relatively simple sources to begin with are the U.S. Department of Labor's *Occupational Outlook Handbook*, and the *Dictionary of Occupational Titles (I & II)*,[10] which give you (a) short descriptions of many, but not all, occupations and (b) references to additional sources. These sources *are one example only* of how to proceed to begin to answer the framing questions. The methods and principles apply to other sources you will need to scrutinize. For example, another is *Jobs '97: The Essential Job Hunting Guide*,[11] which gives the career outlook for occupations, industry forecasts, and a regional roundup.

13. Answer the framing questions using the first informational source (in this case, say, the *Occupational Outlook Handbook* or *Jobs '97*). Answer them as completely as possible. Note any gaps in work environment, job requirements, or additional specifications.

14. Use additional sources to fill in these gaps. These sources may be found in the appendix, under "Selected Books to Help You Explore Your Career Options," and (a) in Sections 3.09 and 3.12; (b) in a well-stocked career library; (c) in a well-stocked bookstore; (d) through informational interviewing and contact research; (e) and online (see "Use and Misuse of the Internet" in the appendix).

15. The following sequence in the algorithm is optional, but it may clarify your choices.

Research Grids

This will help you to *weigh* the importance of your top five values, top five skills, top five interests, and your favorite skills and activities against marketplace niche realities. Here's how.

> *Example: Let's say that you are interested in preliminary explorations of advertising, writing, management, investment banking, sales, and consulting. You can sort these preliminary preferences as follows:*
>
> *Exploration List 1. Actual activities (or what you want to do)*
>
> **Pref. 1:**   *Writing*
> **Pref. 2:**   *Management (or managing)*
> **Pref. 3:**   *Sales (or selling)*
> **Pref. 4:**   *Corporate R&D*
>
> *Exploration List 2. Industries (or where you want to do it)*
>
> **Pref. 1:**   *Advertising*
> **Pref. 2:**   *Investment banking*
> **Pref. 3:**   *Industry-specific R&D*

You will enter your own actual activities on a photocopy of the blank Research Grid on page 137, and the preferred industries on another photocopy of the Research Grid. On page 136 you will see *for illustrative purposes* how the items on exploration list 1, actual activities (above) *are entered as an example* of what you are to do on page 137.

Please notice that the boldfaced numbers **Pref. 1, Pref. 2, Pref. 3,** etc., which represent your preliminary preferences, are keyed to two grids, which also have boldfaced numbers **(Pref. 1, Pref. 2, Pref. 3,** etc.) under the columns headed "**THEIRS.**"

Using this example as a guide, generate two lists below: (1) actual specific activities that you enjoy, and (2) the industries you would feel comfortable in. Be inclusive and instinctive.

Preliminary Interest Exploration List 1: Actual Activities

(For transfer to a copy of the Research Grid on page 137, under column headed "THEIRS")

Pref. 1 ——————————————————————————————

Pref. 2 ——————————————————————————————

Pref. 3 ——————————————————————————————

Pref. 4 ——————————————————————————————

Preliminary Interest Exploration List2: Industies

(For transfer to a copy of the Research Grid on page 137, under column headed "THEIRS")

Pref. 1 ——————————————————————————————

Pref. 2 ——————————————————————————————

Pref. 3 ——————————————————————————————

Pref. 4 ——————————————————————————————

Scrutinize **Sample Research Grid**: Actual Activities (page 136) to see how the example arrives at *highest* compatibility (TOTAL = ı15) to **Pref. 4**, Corp. R & D, and the *lowest* overlap (TOTAL = +7) to **Pref. 1**, writing.

Now, begin to fill in the column headed "**YOURS**" following this example, inserting your top 5 values, your top 5 skills, and your interests from 3.03, 3.04, and 3.07 into photocopies of page 137. You will quantify and compare the compatibility of your *internal* preferences (values, skills, interests, and favorite skills) with the *external* marketplace niche reality (industries, work environments, job requirements, and additional specifications) on these and successive grids.

For Illustrative Purposes

Sample Research Grid: Actual Activities

	YOURS (fill in before you begin research)	THEIRS ACTUAL ACTIVITIES (fill in during research)			
		Pref. 1	Pref. 2	Pref. 3	Pref. 4
Top 5 Values		Writing*	Management*	Sales*	Corp. R&D*
1.	Independence	+3	+1	+2	−1
2.	Status and prestige	+2	+3	+1	+1
3.	Regular hours	−3	+2	−3	−1
4.	Intellectual challenge	+2	−2	+1	+1
5.	Creativity	+3	−3	+2	+1
Top 5 Skills					
1.	Communications/ written	+3	+2	+3	+3
2.	Organization	0	+3	+1	+2
3.	Problem solving	+2	+2	+2	+3
4.	Investigating	+2	−2	+2	+3
5.	Delegating	−3	+3	+2	+1
Your Interests					
1.	Sports management (Little League)	−1	+1	0	0
2.	Tennis	−1	+1	0	+1
3.	Skiing	−2	0	0	+1
4.	Piano/jazz	−1	0	0	0
5.	Reading about Civil War	+1	0	0	−2
TOTALS:		+7	+10	+13	+15

*These items are here as samples, for illustrative purposes only, transferred from the example on page 134. Your *actual* entries will be transferred from your own exploration lists 1 and 2 (page 135), to the blank version of this grid on page 137.

Legend: Degree of overlap, harmony, or compatibility between you and your choices

Scale: +3 = Highly compatible, harmonious overlap
        +2 = Somewhat compatible, harmonious overlap
        +1 = Barely compatible, harmonious overlap
         0 = Neither compatible nor incompatible, neutral
        −1 = Barely incompatible, inharmonious overlap
        −2 = Somewhat incompatible, inharmonious overlap
        −3 = Highly incompatible, inharmonious overlap

Please Make Photocopies For Personal Use

Research Grid: _____

	YOURS (fill in before you begin research)	THEIRS ACTUAL ACTIVITIES (fill in during research)			
		Pref. 1	Pref. 2	Pref. 3	Pref. 4
Top 5 Values 1. 2. 3. 4. 5.					
Top 5 Skills 1. 2. 3. 4. 5.					
Your Interests 1. 2. 3. 4. 5. TOTALS:					

Legend: Degree of overlap, harmony, or compatibility between you and your choices

Scale:
+3 = Highly compatible, harmonious overlap
+2 = Somewhat compatible, harmonious overlap
+1 = Barely compatible, harmonious overlap
 0 = Neither compatible nor incompatible, neutral
−1 = Barely incompatible, inharmonious overlap
−2 = Somewhat incompatible, inharmonious overlap
−3 = Highly incompatible, inharmonious overlap

Please make five photocopies of page 137, and give them the following titles: Research Grid 1: Actual Activities; Research Grid 2: Industries or Economic Sectors; Research Grid 3: Work Environments; Research Grid 4: Job Requirements; Research Grid 5: Additional Specifications. Follow the sample research grid procedure. If you find that your answers are incomplete, seek additional resource material about your targeted jobs from the list of selected books, bibliography, library, bookstore, or information interviews, and make note of these gaps below. "I need additional information about . . ."

_____

_____

_____

_____

_____

_____

Some of these gaps may be filled in during your informational interviews, described in Section 3.09.

Examine the list of "Selected Books to Help You Explore Your Career Options," located in the appendix. Place a check mark next to those books on the list that appear to cover the actual activities and industries that are of greatest interest to you. To locate these books, find the career library closest to you. Such libraries are sometimes affiliated with career counseling programs at universities or colleges. Local career libraries can be very helpful. Make sure to avail yourself of the services of the career librarians, who are very knowledgeable about these resources. Make note of any jobs or industries that are not included in this list and ask your librarian for assistance. Also, large chain bookstores will carry most of the career hardcovers and paperbacks. See Section 3.12, "Job Search Research," and the appendix.

Trend-Tracking

In the coming years, there will be two types of workers: (1) the "front-line information user" and (2) the "back-line information provider."[12]

The first are focused on meeting customer needs and problems; they are team-based, and their skills and specializations are secondary to customers' solutions and specializations. Career paths for this kind of work are customer-focused, decision- and action-oriented, with a tendency to long-term employment, continuity and security, multifunctional roles, new skills acquisition in the service of clients or customers, direct value-added work (doing, not how-to-do), ability to read customer needs readily, and leadership flexibility (ability to change roles as needed by client), with an emphasis on experience over education and credentials.

The second are focused on their expertise or profession, are true "knowledge workers," are temporary or project-oriented, tend to be highly specialized, do indirect non-value-added work (somewhat behind the scenes), and are systematic, educated, and credentialed.

You can set up your own system for tracking[13] perishable trends using your research skills. One method, advocated by Gerald Celente, is to gather information from reliable news sources in the context of what is happening around you and creating your own "clipping service," keeping files on trends your new career direction may demand that you watch closely. You can strengthen your ability to spot trends in your current or emerging fields by reading widely outside of those fields to capture the context of new events. This calls for reading such (perhaps unlikely) sources as *The Wall Street Journal, Advertising Age* or *Ad Week*, the *Newsletter on Newsletters*, the *Utne Reader*, and even *National Review*.

Hot Jobs

The following job titles are expected to grow by the largest percentages of their current numbers over the near term, based upon increases in the number of employers' requests for them.[14]

Job Title	*Predicted Growth*
1. Temporary executive	314%
2. Internet software architect	198%
3. Chief marketing officer	178%
4. Health-care CIO	121%
5. Internet executive	99%
6. CTO/chief technology officer	96%
7. Vice president–year 2000	83%
8. Start-up CEO	81%
9. Executive search consultant	76%
10. Security analyst	75%
11. Vice president—staffing	74%
12. Information technology consultant	68%
13. Vice president—call centers	51%

Not-So-Hot Jobs

The following job titles are expected to decline by the largest percentages of their current numbers, based upon employers' requests to fill a position.[15]

Job Title	*Predicted Decline*
1. Car sales manager	67%
2. Tobacco industry executive	59%
3. Advertising account executive	51%
4. Print advertising sales manager	46%
5. General manager, Semiconductor industry	39%
6. Political strategist	36%
7. Steel manufacturing executive	22%
8. Administrative assistant	15%
9. Switchboard operator	12%

The Too-Little-Too-Late Syndrome

Andrew Grove[16] defines a "strategic inflection point" (where the second derivative of a trend curve changes from negative to positive, from convex to concave) in the following terms. A group is on a hike in the woods and getting lost. One member says to the leader, "Are you sure you know where we're going? Aren't we lost?" The leader marches on, uneasy over the lack of trail markers. At some point (the strategic inflection point), he stops and says, "Hey, I think we're lost."

As an example, Grove cites a strategic inflection point in the trend lines and indicators during a metamorphosis in the computer industry. Between 1980 and 1995, the computer industry transformed itself from vertically organized (marketing systems by corporation) to horizontally organized (marketing by function). Unfortunately, many organizations, such as IBM, were not well positioned for this "paradigm shift." They thought that whatever had worked during their "championship season" would continue to work for them: "the inertia of success."

What applies to industries and large corporations applies to individual careers as well. Grove says, "I have never made a tough change . . . that I haven't wished I had made a year or so earlier."

"Careers" of New Companies

Between seven and eight hundred thousand new enterprises were started by individuals each year between 1985 and 1995. In 1995, about one in eight failed (defined as those companies that shut down owing money to creditors). The four biggest obstacles to success[17] of a new business start-up are:

1. *Poor concept.* Many new enterprises "have a product in search of a market instead of looking for a market in search of a product."

2. *Poor business plan.* New companies may not know how to make a product or have a realistic idea of how much money it will take to produce it. Many new business owners also know little about how to distribute their products successfully.

3. *Lack of capital.* A new business owner may be unable to raise enough money to survive a start-up. A new owner also may not know where to find money or may not understand the terms of a business loan.

4. *Inexperience.* Usually the biggest obstacle a new enterprises faces. Many people who have good ideas and find money to get themselves started, fail because they lack the day-to-day expertise needed to run a company.

Recast these as obstacles to success in career transitions.

1. If you are a *product* in search of a *market*, instead of searching for a market that's looking for you, you will slow your career transition (see Sections 2.07, 3.08, 3.17).

2. If you have no plan for the career transition, no "theory of victory," no detailed map and compass, you can get lost. Project scheduling and project management of a career transition are essential (see Section 3.17).

3. If you lack the emotional wherewithal, the "metaphysical capital," the energy and optimism, you are missing key search ingredients: fuel and oxygen (see Section 2.07).

4. If you lack the experience of small success in new career directions, or if you have difficulty distinguishing what you do know from what you don't, you must acquire these as needed (see Section 3.12).

Here's a man who was able to make a transition into an area of expanding opportunity. He readily reveals resilience and willingness to configure himself successively to emerging national trends in research (acoustics), nuclear test ban treaties (seismology), defense (intelligence and oceanography), industrial research, ecology, and environmental policy.

ROBERT FROSCH

••••••••••••••••••••••

Transition From Quantum Mechanic To
Federal Agency Administrator To GM
Research Lab Director

As I was finishing my doctorate at Columbia University in theoretical physics in 1951—I'm a "quantum mechanic," since I worked on the spectra of diatomic molecules in a magnetic field—I schlepped around talking to people so that I could find a job. The Office of Naval Research had started up funding at Columbia, the Hudson Labs, to find out what could be done in acoustic detection of submarines. I went to work there as a theoretician, but found myself in an underwater lab designing experiments and going to sea. I became a seagoing engineer, project managing big science oceanography.

The lab grew from 50 people to 350 by 1957 while I was its director. We did huge experiments. Suddenly, I was doing things I was not trained to do, which was to sit in a corner and do theory. I had a fine old time of it, nevertheless, even though it was not what I had in mind to do with my life, which was to teach and do research. I was good at it, and it was interesting.

In the spring of 1963, I was still doing these big projects, when I got a phone call asking me, "Why don't you come to Washington?" The limited test ban treaty had begun, and ARPA, in the office of the Secretary of Defense, needed a director, nuclear test detection, to run the R&D. I went to Washington to refuse the job, but Jack Ruina, who was leaving, sold me on taking it. So I had to learn about detecting weapons in the ocean, in space, and, by the way, underground. So I became a seismologist and project manager, contracting out projects. I knew nothing about management, and suddenly I was a Pentagon civil servant and all that jazz. Then I was asked, "Would you be deputy director of ARPA?" doing antiguerrilla, ballistic missile defense, intelligence, running an agency, testifying before Congress. I noticed that Harold Brown at Defense Department Research and Engineering, who preceded me at Columbia, Johnny Foster, and Bob Sproul are all former physicists. I think mathematics, which you learn while you're young, helps as a universal tool and language. An awful lot of physicists, economists, and others are wandering around in other professions because they can think abstractly: Structure sets and problems are really the same things.

In the middle of this, in July 1966, Johnny calls and asks, "Are you willing to be the Assistant Secretary of the Navy?" Paul Nitze then asked me to go to Vietnam. I knew about ships from ONR work, but I had to deal with admirals and Marine Corps generals. I stayed through the Johnson administration and continued with the Nixon administration with Mel Laird and David Packard, because they considered this a technical, not a political department. By 1972, I couldn't afford to stay, I didn't want to stay, but I didn't know what else to do.

I was to somebody talking on a plane going to the USSR, and he later suggested I might be interested in a job at the UN in environmental issues as assistant secretary general, a bureaucrat. It was interesting. We moved to Geneva, then Nairobi. But how do you now become a diplomat, and how do you survive the UN bureaucracy? I quit after two and a half years.

In 1975, I had to look for a job. I called friends (I had been offered, but declined, a job as dean of engineering at Columbia, since it was a Washington fund-raising job). I spoke to friends at Woods Hole Oceanographic Institution. An MIT job evaporated, and I became assistant director of applied oceanography. I helped invent the subject. Frank Press, the dean of seismologists, and the Carter nominee for science advisor, had a house in Falmouth, Mass., and there in the summer over drinks, he said, "Come to Washington and be the administrator of NOAA," but that did not happen, so he said, "How about NASA?" I seemed to fit the bill well enough. I was interviewed by the president and became administrator from 1977–1982. I presided over the space shuttle. As in many government agencies, you never start anything you finish, and you never finish anything you start. Carter was not reelected. I became the president of the American Association of Engineering Societies, which I failed after a year because engineering societies don't like to be associated.

A friend in underwater acoustics called me and asked if I'd like to work at GM, running the research lab. We moved there in 1982, and stayed for eleven years. I had to retire at 65. We came to Boston, where I'm a fellow at the Kennedy School. I do "industrial ecology," tracing the movement of metals through the metal-working industry.

In looking back, I think most of my transitions happened because someone called me. Also, I got bored. More people knew me because I had visibility in each of my positions, and I did not make a mess of things. Perhaps it's modest to say this, but modesty is very helpful, just as arrogance is.

If you're modest, people pay attention to what you say, they ask what you want them to do. You can't do everything yourself. If you want to take data at sea, you need two ships and a shore station, but the most important guy is the bosun's mate. The modesty comes in because I don't know how to be a bosun's mate. You do a lot of listening, and it's very valuable even if you don't do what they want.

The arrogance is, I know science and I know shit when I smell it. I would hear some management stuff at a meeting, and no one could explain how it worked. I'm arrogant enough to say, "The meeting is over" if no one can explain this management baloney.

I would say it's very important to pay attention to the problem. The question is not, "Are you a physicist?" The question is, "What's the question?" Follow the problem, not what you are. Some crystals are right-handed. If you want to see inherently interdisciplinary transitions, look at geophysics, look at environmental issues.

Also, as you go up higher in complexity, you get new phenomena because there are more parts. You don't violate the laws of physics as you move from chemistry to biology. Yet you cannot deduce biology from physics.

I once told someone starting a job: The last guy here tried to do all of this job, and they took him away; the next guy tried to do 10 percent of the job, and they took him away; your job is to do 1 percent of this job, and to find out which 1 percent.

Of course, in an expanding universe, it's easy to find jobs and to change careers. But now we inhabit a shrinking universe of jobs in many specialties. It's not obvious what you can transition to when we're contracting, but two invariants are: (1) know yourself and (2) know trends and niches.

A mathematician was the trailing spouse of her physician husband. Her career transitions were driven by her necessity to adapt to her husband's venues. She exemplifies resourcefulness combined with her knowledge of her best and favorite skills and the emerging trends for a field from her specialty: numerical analysis in differential equations.

After learning how to use computers in numerical analysis, she became interested in the delivery of health-care services. She started experiments in telemedicine, doing grand rounds by remote video, delivering health-care services nationally, getting specialized knowledge to geographically dispersed patients and physicians.

The private sector was interested in similar information-distribution capabilities, and so she found herself designing remote delivery systems for brokerage houses like Merrill Lynch and Paine Webber.

After being appointed to the board of a settlement house, she realized that the front-line workers in hospitals, brokerages, and settlement houses had similar information flow problems and management needs. She raised significant funds to implement the idea, trading on her knowledge of trends (information flow management) and her abilities to capture and use the similarities among the things she had done in many different venues.

Trends From A to Z

Venture capital firms are experiencing a boom, and their partners are so busy raising and investing billions that inexperienced associates and interns are learning the business as they help determine whether struggling new businesses get financed.[18] A number of venture capital firms participate in a fellowship program that selects and trains a small pool of people at an annual stipend of $80,000 for two years.

In monthly surveys of emerging firms with under 1,000 employees, technology manufacturing job growth by industry (monitored by CORPTECH) shows the sectors with the job growth (approximate projected growth per year):

Computer software	(10% per year)
Computer hardware	(5–8% per year)
Telecommunications	(6% per year)
Biotechnology	(4–6% per year)
Pharmaceuticals	(3–5% per year)
Defense-related	(3–5% per year)
Medical	(3–4% per year)
Transportation	(3% per year)
Environment	(3% per year)
Test and measurement	(3% per year)

"Adult care" and "zoning" are examples of trends outside of your specialties that bear watching because they may alter your search strategies. Increases in the elderly population will lead to a need for new facilities, new adult-care services, and new products like walkers, braces, and wheelchairs, for example. Personal and home-care aides are projected to increase from 1994 to 2005 by some 120 percent, or some 400,000 individuals. How does this affect your job search or career change? Think about it. Research it. Technology is extending our useful working lives. What can you do to serve that trend or to extend your career into an eighth decade?

Another example: As zoning gets tougher around the country, real estate people will have a tougher time getting projects approved, creating a need for zoning consultants. How does that affect your job search or career change? Think about it. Research it.

Probably the fastest-growing area in the United States is incarceration: prison cells, prison guards, and prison administration. One of the hallmarks of capitalism is that every problem is an opportunity, and often an opportunity to generate income.

Trend tracking is a learnable skill, and can be self-taught and improved by practice.

3.09 QUINTESSENTIAL INFORMATIONAL INTERVIEWS

Whether you are making a career change or planning the next career step in your present field, informational interviews are essential. Although they are *not* job interviews, you often discover job opportunities and career possibilities during or after an informational interview. Think of the informational interview as a way of creating several generations of contacts—not as a way of asking for or finding job openings.

Here is how an informational interview works. You arrange a meeting with someone (called a *target*) who works in a field or organization that you consider a possible career or job choice. *You* are the interviewer, and therefore *you* structure the interview—by asking *appropriate* questions that will provide you with important career-choice information. For appropriate questions, see below.

You may not be aware of all the people you know who could be targets or sources for informational interviews. Such sources for informational interviews are found in the list of categories that follows. Begin to make your own list of likely targets, and add names of leads, contacts, and targets as they occur to you. These are called your *first generation* leads, contacts, and targets. Each target is a potential source of *new* contacts, leads, and targets, called *second generation;* each of the latter is a source of *third-generation* contacts, and so on. They may be compared to the branches of a tree, to nuclear fission, or to successive layers of social acquaintances called a *network*. Using your social intelligence allows you to take advantage of the resources of others, in effect *amplifying the intelligence outside your brain*. Your research intelligence can reside in other people if you know how to ask them and how to mobilize their assets. This works *if and only if* others do not feel you are exploiting them. We will show you how to develop the necessary atmospherics and mood of reciprocal, mutual interests.

How do contacts help you get a job? You don't expect to get a *job* from an informational interview target, you expect to get *information*, including contacts. However, when you reach a certain stage in information gathering for one purpose (to get more contacts), you segue to information gathering for another purpose (to locate job openings). You can say, "I'm not asking you for a job. But you may lead me to someone else who knows another person who knows about a job opening."

Tom Lehrer, the mathematician-turned-humorous-song-writer/performer, has written about social competence in a song called "Lobachevsky." It's about how to plagiarize someone else's work. With apologies to Tom, who granted us permission, we have adapted his verse:

> *Socialize,*
> *Let no one evade your eyes.*
> *Remember why the good Lord made your eyes,*
> *So don't shade your eyes,*
> *But socialize, socialize, socialize...*
> *Only be sure always to call it, please, "research."*

Use the following list to generate as many names as possible of people you know who know others who can help you.

Categories of Contacts, Leads, and Targets

Articles (newspapers/magazines)

Athletics/sports/hobbies

Bankers

Business owners/merchants

Children's teachers/coaches/PTA

Clergy

Club/church/synagogue members

College/graduate school friends

College placement and alumni offices

Competitors

Consultants

Coworkers (past and present)

Customers/clients

Doctors/dentists/therapists

Family (parents/spouse/children)

Financial advisors

Fraternities/sororities

Friends/relatives/colleagues

Fund raisers

High school friends

Holiday card/party lists

Industrial business directories

Investment/real estate/insurance brokers

Lawyers/accountants

Local chamber of commerce

Military service

Neighbors/community

Newspaper editors/reporters

Other job seekers

People met at conventions/traveling

Pharmacists/opticians

Politicians/civic leaders

Professional/trade associations

Reference librarians

Retirees

Rolodex/address books

Secretaries/assistants   Travel agents

Social/politicial organizations   Volunteer associations

Teachers   (You can add categories).

Making Professional Contacts Systematically

You can generate dozens of informational, or "contact," interviews at the highest level in any organization if you use the proper approach to your target. These are *not* job interviews—*you* are asking most of the questions. You may call or write to each person, although telephone contact offers you the advantage of immediacy and directness, and—compared to a letter—usually improves your chance of securing an interview (see "Face-to-Face, Voice-Only, or On-line" in Section 3.11).

But if you feel uncomfortable making contact with strangers because you feel that your self-confidence (or other abilities) is not yet high, you should probably write first, then call.

If you send a letter first, mention that you will call; then always follow up with a phone call to schedule your meeting. (For an example, see Section 3.13, "Letters," especially Example 3. When you call, you may say to the secretary, "He/she is expecting my call"; if the secretary inquires further, you may say, "In my letter of (date), I mentioned that I would call.")

However, the secretaries of busy targets are usually instructed to screen their telephone calls. You can try different techniques, such as calling before nine in the morning or after five in the afternoon, when the target often answers the telephone personally. Moreover, if you perceive secretaries as a *link* to your target, rather than as an obstacle, you can often elicit their help to reach your target. Ask the secretary's name and remember it or make a note of it.

To elicit help, you need a very short version of the reason you are calling, which may include the phrase, "I am not seeking a job," or, better yet, "I wish to discuss his/her article in the 1989 *Biophysics Journal* [for example] on [subject] . . . I have some results that support/contradict [choose one] his/her results." In other words, you should somehow make it clear that you want to talk shop.

Once you have reached your target on the telephone, be brief, but include the following information:

1. Introduce yourself, telling how you obtained the target's name (another colleague, a mutual friend, a newspaper or journal article, a professional association, etc.).

2. Explain that you would like to *obtain the target's advice* about a career or job change because the target is a leader in his or her field (this

will acknowledge the target's role as an authority and his or her importance to you).

3. Provide a short (one- or two-sentence) summary description of your background to gain sufficient credibility so that the target will want to spend some time with you.

4. Ask for a short meeting, fifteen to twenty minutes, so that the target will know you are respectful of his or her time.

A possible script that covers these four points can be found on the following pages. Most people like to be helpful, and they will enjoy *advising* you—as long as they know that you are not specifically asking them for a *job*. (Most people hate to say no.) Try to arrange for a personal meeting. If this is not possible, ask for a short interview on the phone at the target's convenience.

Once you have reached your target on the telephone, be brief and show that you respect the fact that he or she is probably very busy. (Important people—those who have many contacts—usually are very busy, and they will feel more friendly toward you and better about you if you recognize this fact.) Identify yourself by name. You should almost always ask, "Have you received my letter?" "Is this a convenient time to talk?" "Have you had time to read my letter?" If the answers are all Yes, then you may proceed to the contact interview script.

How to Use Systematic Desensitization

If you are reluctant for any reason, especially shyness, to call or write a stranger who may have information and contacts that you are eager to obtain, consider the exercise/questionnaire that follows. This is a diagnostic paper-and-pencil tool developed to pinpoint the stage at which "reluctance," or shyness, begins to defeat your information-gathering goals.

Once you know the stage at which you begin to resist progress toward those goals, you will have an edge. You will know when the resistance begins, and you will be able to desensitize yourself accordingly. For example, if you know that picking up the telephone to call a stranger is the point at which you feel very uncomfortable, then try calling a friend, several friends, then an acquaintance, then several acquaintances, then someone you barely know, then several you barely know, and so on. If you practice this enough, you will find that it gets easier and easier. The same can be done if your resistance builds at any other level. Write down the steps (in your journal or diary) you intend to take to desensitize yourself before you begin to do them. Then begin. It's like exercising a muscle.

Systematic Desensitization: Graduated Networking Activities

What is your level of discomfort for each of the following graduated networking activities?

Mark your discomfort level for each step (A through M) by putting a mark in the appropriate box from 1 (low discomfort) through 9 (high discomfort). Look at the profile you develop on this chart. Those items with high numbers should be raised to your conscious attention. Is there some earlier step that is easier to do? Can it partially replace the one(s) that present difficulty? Can repetition of the imperfect movement surmount your discomfort—or perfect paralysis? Can you focus on the difficulty with a colleague, mentor, or counselor?

	Discomfort Level									
	Low									*High*
	0	**1**	**2**	**3**	**4**	**5**	**6**	**7**	**8**	**9**
A. Thinking about making a list of contacts										
B. Writing a list of contacts										
C. Writing to a professional contact: A friend										
An acquaintance										
A stranger										
D. Calling a primary contact on the phone (a good friend)										
E. Calling a primary contact on the phone (an acquaintance)										
F. Calling a primary contact on the phone (a stranger)										
G. Leaving a message with the contact's secretary										
H. Leaving a message with the contact's spouse										
I. Explaining to the contact why you are calling										
J. Explaining to the contact that you are asking for advice, information										
K. Saying, "I'm not looking for a job. . ."										
L. Asking for assistance										
M. Asking for the names of other contacts you might write to or speak with										

Once you have found the activity that induces stress, see if you can focus on practicing and rehearsing that activity until you have desensitized yourself. Then move on to the next. You may also practice with contacts or leads that are unimportant or irrelevant, so that you will be prepared properly for the truly important contacts.

∙∙∙

*C*ontact Interview Script

Your goal is to schedule an appointment for a contact interview (also called a focus meeting) with a target or professional contact.

1. "Hello. My name is _____ ."
2. "_____ suggested that I call you because I am a/an _____ and I am researching a career move into the field of _____ , and he/she thought you'd be a knowledgeable source of information and opinions."

or

"I am a/an _____ researching a career move into the field of _____ , and I was very impressed by your article/speech/book/accomplishments (or heard you were involved in a relevant professional organization), and I was hoping you might be able to offer me some advice."

or

"I wish to know what your field/job/career looks like from your vantage point."

3. "My professional background has been in the _____ field, where my areas of expertise included _____ ."

4. "I'm looking for *information and opinions only* at this point (to become familiar with the territory/to compare with the information I've read about/to help me in making some choices). If you could spare me a few minutes of your time, I would appreciate the opportunity to meet with you at your convenience."

∙∙∙

Additional pointers to help you:

The Telephone

- The phone is one of your most potent job-finding tools. It's the principal medium of communication of our times. But e-mail is catching up and requires a very terse writing style.
- Don't believe that letters must be written before phone calls are made. If you believe this, you will miss chances to beat your competition. You could also be procrastinating because cold calling makes you uncomfortable. (This is also known as "call reluctance".)

- Picking up the phone and asking for a meeting or interview is the cutting edge of any effective job-search campaign, but it can also be the greatest barrier.
- Making cold calls is probably the single most common fear of job seekers. The best way to minimize this anxiety is to *prepare yourself*.
- The phone can be your first oral contact with a potential employer; therefore, you need to come across as confident,competent, and credible.
- Good telephone technique is a skill learned through preparation, rehearsal, and practice (the same way you get to Carnegie Hall).

Telephone Advantages

- It is faster and more effective than letters, and therefore moves your campaign along.
- It saves you doing unnecessary paper work.
- You may see someone before your written credentials are evaluated in depth.
- You come across as a real person, rather than as a static image in a letter or résumé ("My résumé is not yet as good as I am").
- You can modify, emphasize, or personalize your message on the spot as you need to.

Telephone Techniques

- Phone only if you are *prepared*, so that you appear *focused* and *businesslike*.
- Be *organized*, *prepared*, and *thoroughly confident* in using the phone.
- Make a *script* with an introduction, body, and conclusion.
- Have a prepared opening statement (the first fifteen seconds are critical).
- Identify yourself up front (who are you?).
- Establish friendly rapport (smile over the phone).
- Ask if it's a good time to speak.
- Clearly state the purpose of your call (what do you want and why are you calling?)
- Tape-record your calls to see how you are coming across (listen to yourself critically).

- Work with your friends and advisors (or, if you need one, a career counselor) on telephone techniques.
- Making a series of calls at one sitting allows you to achieve greater confidence than making calls intermittently. So line up your calls and make them methodically (make them by Friday morning).
- Practice using the phone by starting with close friends and/or small firms or targets whose advice you may not need, until you feel comfortable and confident.
- Group your calls according to similar purposes.
- Speak to the right person and for the right purpose.
- Your manner will largely determine how you will be received.
- Speak at a normal speed. A friendly/conversational tone is best.
- Be businesslike and direct, and ask for what you need.
- The less information you give, the better. (Imagination may fill in.)
- You want an appointment for a contact or focus meeting *only*—not a job interview.
- Concerning appointment time: offer two alternatives (don't forget before or after work or for a meal).
- Keep your calendar handy.
- Always try to get other contacts to help *exponentiate* your network.
- Close by thanking the target and confirming the date, time, and location of the contact meeting.
- Get the complete name, correct spelling, and title. Write the name, phonetically if necessary, for future use.
- Don't be interviewed over the phone (if you can help it).
- Keep a complete record of all your calls.
- Secretaries can be an obstacle or enormously helpful, so build a relationship, be courteous, get their names and remember them.
- To get the name and title of a hiring manager, call the company receptionist and ask for the correct spelling, title, and mailing address. Then call back.
- If you got a name from a directory or other publication, check with the company to be sure the information is correct.
- Call early in the morning or after work.
- Call back if the target is out. Try not to ask to have her or him call you back. If you must leave a message, leave a "time window," a period when you will be available.

- The caller has the edge because of preparation; the target, or "callee," has no idea why you are calling and may assume the best. This is a major reason for you to call back if the target is out.
- Keep trying—*persistence* is the key.
- Always make calls when you feel "up." People can hear smiles on the phone, and can also sense when you are worried or feeling down.
- Write a letter first if cold calling is not for you.

Overcoming Objections

- Anticipate that the target will not agree to see you. (If you anticipate it, you can do something about it in a positive manner.)
- If the target objects to seeing you, acknowledge the objection by restating it in your own words (keep your purpose clear in your own mind).
- Then try to get around the objection politely at least three times. But listen and know when to quit (before you make a nuisance of yourself).

*T*elephone Planning Log *(Make photocopies)*

Telephone number _____ Date _____ Time _____

Name _____ Title _____

Company _____

Address _____

Secretary _____ Other names _____

_____

Reference material needed _____

_____

_____

Objcctivc of thc call _____

_____

_____

Referral _____

_____

Opening statement _____

_____

Questions _____

_____

_____

_____

Confirm/clarify information/next steps _____

_____

_____

_____

Close/thanks _____

_____

···

*E*xercise: *Preparing for Your Telephone Calls*

Write your own brief script below, including the above four points. (You can refer to this exercise, if necessary, when making your calls.)

_____

_____

_____

_____

_____

_____

_____

_____

_____

_____

_____

···

The Meeting

Because *you* are the interviewer, it is *your* responsibility to arrange the meeting, prepare your questions, and guide your target through the informational interview process. By doing so, you guarantee that you will obtain the information that is most helpful to you. Since this is *not* a job interview, there is very little pressure on you. The worst that can happen is that the target may refuse your request for a meeting. If this happens, ask if there is anyone else the target knows who might be helpful to you. If the target declines to give names thank him or her and move on to the next target.

Before your meeting, you must *prepare, rehearse,* and *practice* your opening and your questions. You must know the field, industry, or organization of the person you will be interviewing. Refer to the appropriate research topics in Section 3.12 to learn how to obtain such background information. You will learn where to find background information that shows the target that you have done your homework. Preparation always leaves a positive impression, so be ready with a list of eight to ten open-ended questions (those that start with "who," "what," "where," "when," "why," "which," or "how").

Since one purpose of an informational interview is to involve the target in a dialogue, refrain from asking questions that may elicit Yes or No answers.

Use the "Informational Interview Record" below. It is acceptable to write your questions out ahead of time so that you can take notes during the interview. Moreover, we recommend it.

Suggested Questions to Ask in an Informational Interview

Ask about the target's background. "Tell me, how did you get started here?" "What training did you have?" "What do you like most about your field or your position here?" "How do you spend your time (managing staff, doing research, selling)?"

Major issues in the firm, the work, and the industry. "What do you like about your job?" "What areas would you like to see improved?" "What skills are required?" "What type of personality works best in this kind of job, company, or field?"

Hiring practices. "What do others look for when you hire someone?" "What are the standard starting salaries in this field, and what is the earnings potential?"

Career paths in the field. "What different routes to careers in this field have you seen people take?" "Are there particular firms or organizations that you think I should contact?" If this person is not a scientist, engineer, or medical professional, ask if he or she knows scientists, engineers, or medical professionals who have made career transitions.

Be prepared to explain your own background in a *few sentences*. You can then ask, "How do I best fit into your field?" "Perhaps you can suggest where my skills could be used after I give you a brief summary of my background?" Use the results of your self-assessment process (Section 3.01, 3.02, 3.03, 3.07, and especially 3.04) to present key points about yourself with confidence. Assert the truths about yourself in the most positive, optimistic, and energetic terms you can summon.

Always thank your target orally (and again with a written follow-up note), and ask who else the target knows that you can speak to in order to learn more about your field of interest. Try to get as many names as possible—at least two or three. Try for more after you've gotten a few. Also, if you have a list of well-known targets in your desired career, you may wish to present this list to the target, who will *recognize* more names than he or she will *recall.* It's like "priming the pump." Most people recognize more names than they remember.

Thank the person for his or her time, suggestions, and referrals, and tell him or her of the next steps you plan to take in your career change, and that you will be keeping him or her informed of your progress. This is very important, since it prepares the person for later contact and "relationship development."

Never volunteer your résumé, since this gives the impression that you are asking for a *job* rather than for *information*. If you have an *appropriate* résumé with you, present it *only if asked*. An appropriate résumé is one that by research, in advance of the meeting, you have determined fits a specific opening like a key fits a lock. If you do not have a résumé, you may instead say that you are now doing informational interviewing, and will send one later. You may also consider sending a letter after the meeting (situation-specific) summarizing your most relevant experience.

We believe that a well-crafted biography (not a résumé) can represent you in narrative form to a professional colleague or contact, without implying (as a résumé does) that you are looking for a job. In fact you are *not* looking for a job (yet!—although you will be very soon), and you do not wish to even hint or suggest that you are by presenting a résumé, even if demanded by the best-intentioned contact or colleague. The résumé is virtually the last step in the lengthy process of gathering enough information in order to decide what about yourself you wish to tell. If you are an orange, and you wish to be perceived as an apple, you have to learn what apple-ness is before you attempt the metamorphosis.

A business card is better than a résumé at this stage for the following reasons:

1. It is shorter, and "less is more."

2. It has vital, nonextraneous information only.

3. It can appear in multiple incarnations (but know something about your target *before* you decide which one to part with).

Don't offer your card (especially at professional or social events) until it's asked for. Ask for the other person's card first, and you will likely be asked for yours.

Informational Interview Record (Make photocopies.)

Date _____

Person/title contacted _____

Referred by (name/title/company) _____

_____

Company name/address _____

_____

Telephone number _____ Note whether conversation was face-to-face [ ] or by telephone [ ].

Were letters exchanged? [ ] Dates: _____

Information on person/company/industry known prior to informational interview

_____   _____

_____

_____

_____

_____

_____

_____

_____

Questions for the target of the informational interview

1. _____

2. _____

3. _____

4. _____

5. _____

6. _____

7. _____

8. _____

9. _____

. . . .

$\mathcal{S}$*ummary of Informational Interview*

What you learned that moves your job search or career change forward to the next step:

1. _____
2. _____
3. _____
4. _____
5. _____
6. _____

Date sent and content of thank-you note:

_____

_____

_____

_____

_____

_____

Informational interview follow-up: When and how will you recontact the target?

_____

_____

_____

_____

_____

_____

When and how will you contact the target's contacts? Give yourself dates and appropriate follow-up steps.

_____

_____

_____

_____

. . . .

The geophysical engineer below worked on seismic and electromagnetic prospecting methods. After working in Texas, Iceland, and Germany, he decided to reassess his career. He started to investigate finance and trade, an early interest. His informational interview technique was rather unorthodox, but it was so successful that he accepted a job offer before he had gotten very high up the informational interview learning curve.

Transition From Geology/Mineralogy To International Finance

I started looking at *New York Times* ads in finance. A lot of those ads were from "headhunters," who would say, "Let's meet." I said, "Forget it," most of the time. They were just collecting résumés. This was a time when engineers, mathematicians, and physicists were flocking to Wall Street, doing derivatives while using mathematical methods, the Black-Scholes equation, Monte Carlo techniques.

I got better and better at talking to new people, to strangers, in these fields. I made contacts directly instead of through headhunters. I even started walking in off the street to companies without having an appointment. I would just start talking to the receptionist; if it was a temp, I'd ask, "Can I see a list of names of the people in such-and-such department?" Then I'd call from the reception area and say, "I'm right here. Can you spare a moment to meet with me?" This is how I got my first job offer in finance—by walking in at Lehman Brothers. I never spoke to human resources people; they were a dead end. The better I got at this, the more job offers I was getting. In fact, I got my first job too soon, before I really got good at these drop-ins.

He was also very resourceful in making contacts in a new field by speaking about it to anyone in the field. "I would read a journal or magazine, look at who was on the editorial board or whose names were on the masthead, then call these people and ask, 'Do you have a few minutes?' I would never ask for a job, but nine out of ten were helpful in telling me where to look."

3.10 BIOGRAPHIES ARE BETTER THAN RÉSUMÉS FOR CONTACT INTERVIEWS

Because a one-page *biography* is normally not asked for or offered during a job search or career change, it will not normally be viewed as a request for a job. This is extremely important. When a *résumé* is offered or asked for during an informational interview, the person reading it will almost reflexively assume that you are asking the reader (or the reader's contacts) for a job. This tends to evoke a no from the contact because (1) the contact has been approached for advice—not a job, and (2) the contact probably doesn't have a job for you. During an exponential, informational, or contact interview, a résumé will tend to extinguish your next generation of contacts via this target. Worse still, a well-intentioned contact might pass your résumé along in hopes of helping you out, but only one in a hundred or a thousand résumés are appropriate to an unresearched opening. Furthermore, "your résumé is not yet as good as you are." It never is, and you don't want it floating around where it is out of your control because it does not represent who you are in your new career identity or direction. That's the purpose of the informational or contact interview—to help you find out enough about the job market for your new career.

A one-page biography is a completely different matter. One-page biographies can be adjusted to fit almost any occasion—a contact interview to gather information and contacts for career direction A, or a second-contact interview to gather information and contacts for new career direction B, or to accompany a letter asking for advice, and so on. It will almost never be appropriate to forward a biography in response to an ad or to a request for a résumé or CV.

One-page biographies are often used by seasoned professionals in describing who they are and what they have done, and to lend support and credibility to a proposal, usually a business proposal, a foundation proposal, and so on. You can see biographies of many scientists, physicians, or engineers included in initial public offering (IPO) documents or business plans used to document a start-up. In these contexts, a one-page biography is an unself-conscious marketing document. Biographies are also used to introduce a speaker at conferences, especially professional and business conferences, at certain public lectures, and at after-dinner speeches. We have seen biographies of senior or managing partners of old-line management consulting firms, or white-shoe law firms. Biographies may also be referred to as profiles.

The advantage of creating several variants (or a range) of a one-page biography is that a biography can be a dignified way to present yourself with integrity without appearing to (because you're not going to!) ask for a job.

You can also emphasize different aspects or facets of your experience, displaying your most positive and true assets and experiences that are relevant to the contact or occasion.

Of all the facts about you that are true, only a very small fraction are not only true, but interesting and important to your contact target. It takes some practice and research in advance of any meeting to learn how to rewrite, to shape, and to pull up to the surface those intriguing elements about you that evoke the positive responses that will move you forward to the next tier or generation of contacts. In marketing terms, this is referred to as *positioning*. It resembles shaping a key to fit a lock.

Beware adjectives in a profile. Use facts about you that let the adjectives spring to the mind of the reader.

Biographical Metamorphoses: Themes and Variations

Here are some examples of one-page biographies, where the individual has "morphed" from one incarnation to another.

How a Scientist Presents Herself as a Researcher and Teacher

Margaret Morgan (not her real name) has performed research to test the effect of vitamin D on the tumorigenicity of human prostate cancer cells transplanted into immunodeficient mice. Positive results suggest that a range of nonhypercalcemic analogues inhibit tumor growth.

She initiated, directed, and organized a team of researchers at the Snyder Tumor Institute that obtained major NIH funding for this project. In addition, she led an effort to reorganize the lab for greater efficiency, to minimize waste, and to maximize the institute's research activities and focus.

Dr. Morgan was a key contributor to the five research papers and three presentations that resulted from this research, and is author or coauthor of fifteen publications, three book chapters, and twenty-one abstracts.

In a continuing collaboration with senior researchers at the School of Medicine, University of California at Los Angeles, she has explored the use of long-distance polymerase chain reaction to clone estrogen-binding proteins in opportunistic yeast *Candida albicans*.

She was awarded the New Investigator Award of the PCR Center, University of Michigan, NIH Post Doctoral Training Grant, University Fellow, the Molecular Biology Laboratory Fellowship, several Pilot and Feasibility Awards, and the Best Graduate Student Presentation at Cold Spring Harbor Conference on Genetic Exchange.

Her research on how the immune system regulates expression of fibrinogen showed that human heptoma cells could be stimulated with recombinant interleukin and by isolating nuclear proteins that interact with regulatory portions of the fibrinogen A, a gene.

She has taught Human Anatomy and Physiology, Cell Biology, and Nutrition. Her students were among the highest achievers in their program, some of whom won competitive scholarships, switched to premed, and achieved high scores on placement exams and MCAT .

How a Scientist Becomes Advisor to the President's Science Advisory Council

David Z. Robinson attended Harvard University, receiving a A.B. magna cum laude in Chemistry and Physics, an A.M., and a Ph.D. in Chemical Physics in 1950.

He joined Baird as research physicist and became Assistant Director of Research in 1951, developing commercial optical and electronic instruments and infrared detection devices for the Defense Department.

He joined the White House in 1961 as staff scientist in the Office of the President's Science Advisor, working on communications satellite policy, command and control, the hot line between the United States and the Soviet Union, science policy, and budgets.

In 1967 he was appointed Vice President for Academic Affairs of New York University, which at that time had two undergraduate campuses, sixteen schools, and 35,000 full and part-time students.

In 1970, Dr. Robinson was appointed Vice President of Carnegie Corporation of New York, an educational foundation; he became Executive Vice President and Treasurer in 1986. In addition to his administrative duties, he has worked closely with Carnegie programs in higher education, public broadcasting, college retirement, avoiding nuclear war, and science education.

In 1988, Carnegie Corporation established the Carnegie Commission on Science, Technology, and Government, and he became Executive Director. The Commission assessed how the federal and state governments incorporate scientific and technological knowledge in decision making, recommending changes to increase their effectiveness.

Dr. Robinson has been advisor to the President's Science Advisory Committee, the National Academy of Sciences, and The National Science Foundation, and member of the Naval Research Advisory Committee, the New York State Energy Research and Development Authority, the Governor's Advisory Committee on Education, and the Science and Law Committee of the Bar Association of the City of New York. He has also been a board member of the City University of New York, the Dalton School, Investors' Responsibility Research Corporation, the Citizen's Union Foundation, and the Santa Fe Institute.

He is a Fellow of the Optical Society of America, and a member of the Council on Foreign Relations, the New York Academy of Sciences, the Harvard Club, and the Century Association.

How a Scientist Looks Like a Management Consultant

Howard Ellis (not his real name) is a seasoned marketing strategist and market researcher for medical, health-care, science, and technology companies.

His consulting assignments include special projects for Johnson & Johnson, SmithKline, Xerox, IBM, Englehard, Federal Express, merchant and investment banking firms, and innovation-intensive entrepreneurial companies.

To plan the manufacturing capacity for a new pharmaceutical company, he determined the world market sizes for the healing of surgical and injury wounds, burns, fractures, cerebral and myocardial infarcts, and decubitus and duodenal ulcers, and the size of the research market for fine biochemicals and organ extracts.

To prepare the next generation of products for a large health-care products supplier, he developed ten-year forecasts of clinically significant forthcoming medical innovations, likely to become large revenue producers.

To specify new directions in research and development of a pharmaceutical giant compatible with technical and social trends, he helped conceptualize the long-range goals.

For a medical-imaging computer-graphics company start-up, he created market strategies to reach hospitals and researchers with a new optical recording product.

He determined the marketplace acceptability of an innovative low-emissions combustion technology, examining the reactions of industrial and residential consumers. He developed a database of forthcoming developments as suitable investment opportunities.

As a member of the senior professional staff at the Smithfield Institute of Policy Research at Abraham Lincoln University, Howard Ellis developed policy and position papers on the intersection of labor and technological issues, funded by the National Science Foundation, NIH, and other organizations. He has physics degrees from the University of Wisconsin and Harvard.

His consulting firm, Ellis Associates, prepares forecasts of new technologies and their market impacts, technoeconomic market sizing, analytic and strategic market research, options analysis for acquisition opportunities, and due diligence and investment-grade prospectuses for technology firms.

How a Scientist Presents Himself as a Career Consultant

Stephen Rosen specializes in helping scientists, physicians, and attorneys who are altering their careers. He has written articles on career versatility planning for *The Scientist, The Wall Street Journal, National Business Employment Weekly,* and *BioTechnology,* and articles about his career programs have appeared in The *New York Times* and *Science*, and on the Internet and the World Wide Web.[19]

Dr. Rosen is the Founder and Director of Scientific Career Transitions, a nonprofit program that pioneered the development of systematic methods, Internet access, and specialized techniques for guiding high-functioning professionals (and East European scientists) to successful resolutions of their career dilemmas. Supported in part by foundations, including the Alfred P. Sloan Foundation, over five hundred have participated, with half landing jobs within six months.

A dozen of his research articles in high-energy astrophysics appeared in *Nature, Astronomical Journal, Physical Review, Il Nuovo Cimento, Atomes, Science & Technology,* and *Proceeding of the 14th International Astrophysical Symposium in Liège, Belgium.* The research topics included antiproton intensities in primary galactic cosmic radiation, variations in the flare-ups of supernovae and galaxy cores, generation and diffusion of cosmic rays in space, nuclear pair formation in the upper atmosphere, the amount of interstellar matter traversed from cosmic ray sources to Earth, and models of galaxy explosions. Some of this work was published while he was on a joint C.N.R.S. appointment at the Institut d'Astrophysique, Paris, and the Centre d'Etudes Nucleaire de Saclay.

He has appeared as a speaker at MIT's annual Alumni Homecoming on how to use the capabilities of the Internet to advance your career, at the annual meeting of the American Association for the Advancement of Science on how Ph.D.s can avoid "Permanent Head Damage," and at the Fourth Annual International Professional Development Conference on "Recycling High-Level Scientists and Professionals."

3.11 EXPONENTIAL INTERVIEWS, MENTORS, RECRUITERS, AND CAREER COUNSELORS

You may reach a point in your informational interviewing when you have defined your goals and interviewed knowledgeable people in your chosen field, but you have not yet obtained a job. What you need are more contacts, that is, *people who know people* who may have a job for you.

Techniques involving personal contacts and professional colleagues are more successful than responding to ads, recruiters, or employment agencies, or simply sending résumés out to strangers. Studies at Harvard University by sociologist Mark Granovetter[20] examined professionals who successfully changed jobs. A substantial majority (others say as much as three-fourths) of the successful job seekers obtained their employment through their own initiative and through personal solicitations to contacts and potential employers found through contacts. (For comparison, each of the "standard" methods, such as use of ads, employment agencies, and recruiters, accounted for less than about 10 percent of total successful job landings. U.S. Department of Labor and other studies, including our own, confirm these findings. The successful "personal contact" methods include those described in this book.)

To learn how to create a *biography* that will get you contact interviews without turning off your potential contacts and destroying your potentially large exponentiated multigeneration contact pool, please see Section 3.10, "Biographies Are Better than Résumés for Conact."

The ways employers find employees are differently from the ways employees find employers.

How Employers Find Employees

Here are the most common methods by which employers find employees, in order of priority and success:

1. Asking trusted employees (least expensive to employer)
2. Asking friendly competitors or counterparts at other organizations
3. Employment agencies
4. Placing want ads
5. Hiring executive search firms (most expensive to employer)

But Here's How Most People Look for Jobs

Here are the ways most *people search for jobs:*

1. Responding to classified/want ads (easiest, most unproductive)
2. Sending out résumés unsolicited
3. Using recruiters, headhunters, and employment agencies
4. Using college placement offices
5. Asking friends and colleagues (most difficult, yet most productive)

Therefore, if you use personal contacts or professional colleagues, not only will you be using the most effective methods, but you will also have less competition from other job seekers who are using the standard methods.

In addition, the formal methods will screen you out rather than bring you in. See the comparison below.

Job Search Systems

Formal or Traditional (Published, Conventional, Public, Closed)

- Want ads
- Agencies and search firms
- Résumés/letters ahead of you
- Slower/hitchhike
- Passive/easy to apply for
- Their control/choice
- Less work for you
- Others doing it for you
- Intense competition
- Preset specifications
- "I hope somebody wants me"
- "Applicant"—Easy to apply for
- Recruited/drafted
- Personnel departments
- Known openings
- Job interviews
- Screens you out/in

Informal or Creative (Unpublished, Unconventional, Private, Open)

- Research/information/investigation
- Individual with power to hire
- Employer needs/creates your position
- Focus meetings/discussions
- You screen in/out
- May assist, but you must get offer
- Proposal (more value than you cost)
- Faster/your ideal target
- Active/you risk and need courage
- Your control/choice
- More work for you
- Your initiative and responsibility
- Little or no competition
- Flexible specifications
- "Who will be lucky enough to get me?"
- "Candidate"
- Volunteer
- You find them

A Few Generations of Contacts to a Job Interview

Informational interviews can lead you to jobs because the people that you meet provide social, business, or professional relationships to other people—whose constellation of relationships may include a person who has a job for you. Research shows that you are about three to five people away from the person you want to meet who is a key to your next job opportunity. For example, you may not realize that your own contacts or circle of acquaintances may include at least two hundred individuals. If each contact knows two hundred others, each of whom knows two hundred more, your "contact pool" of three generations is about eight million individuals.

You will therefore need to establish priorities, sorting your potential contacts or targets into the following three categories:

- *A or primary contacts:* A contacts are your current "inner circle" of family, friends, and colleagues—people with whom you already have a relationship and from whom you probably already have received referrals for subsequent-generation informational interviews.

- *B or bridge contacts:* B contacts are people who can provide you with information on the industry you are researching; hence, these are a rich category for informational interviews. They are likely to be experts in their fields, and have useful contacts of their own. B contacts may not have the authority to hire you, but they have industry knowledge that you need, and they can give you valuable advice and feedback. They can refer you to other B contacts or, in some cases, can lead you to the decision makers who can hire you for existing openings, or who can create or tailor new ones.

- *C or hiring contacts:* C contacts are the individuals in an organization with the authority to make you a job offer, or at least are close to those in decision-making roles. Once you have identified the field or industry that is right for you (one that lets you use your skills and interests; reflects your values, supports your long-term goals), you will want to identify specific C targets within the specific industries and organizations for which you want to work. As you become more comfortable in informational interviews, you will be able to refine and focus upon your discussions, in order to get referrals to job interviews. But you must differentiate between contacts you are gathering information from and C contacts who may lead you to job interviews.

Strictly speaking, all interviews are similar in that all provide useful information and provide windows on an expanding circles of B and C contacts.

An exponential interview is clearly aimed at providing you with access to any appropriate target, people that your contact knows. The purpose of an informational meeting with B or C contacts is to provide information about a particular field, industry, company, organization, or subject. It can and does allow you to identify new B and C contacts to expand your circle as well. Try to locate "gatekeepers"—people who can offer you multiple referrals related to your job objective.

Never misrepresent yourself to anyone that you are doing informational interviewing when you are really asking for a job. Do not attempt to convert a request for information into a request for a job—it will confuse or even irritate the contact.

Try to elicit as much active assistance as possible. The best possible outcome occurs if your contact sets up the meeting with a next-generation contact and attends it. It is almost as helpful if the contact calls to suggest the meeting; or if the contact writes a letter, and perhaps recommends meeting you. It may still be very useful to you if a contact allows you to use his or her name, but is not present at the meeting.

The Exponential Informational Interview

In planning an exponential interview, consider the following points:[21]

1. Focus on outcomes. What do you want to know? What do you want to reveal? Avoid vague or hidden expectations. The final outcome of each meeting should be help in the referral process to increase the scope of your relationships, and this should be specifically asked for once rapport is established.

2. Questions that are too specific or too general are likely to break the rapport in a exponential interview. Stay away from broad, naive, innocent queries at one extreme, and prying, confidential, proprietary, highly specific queries at the other.

3. Virtually any career obstacle or disadvantage you possess can be turned into an advantage by proper relationship building. You can find targets who share your disadvantage or disability. You can exploit your obstacle by seeking advice from a target who has already made a successful—but difficult—transition into your field of interest.

4. You can conduct your network campaign in a "wide-angle" mode, by asking those you already know for any referrals in a particular career activity, geographic area, or industry. Or, you can network in a closed-end or "telephoto" mode, by finding out who would know the important per-

son you need to meet. For example, if you wanted to meet the president of a company, you might scrutinize a list of his board of directors, staff, related professionals the firm does business with, and the firm's clients or customers to discover names that friends of yours might know.

5. Practice your exponential and informational interviewing skills in low-stress situations, and develop your confidence and style before doing an interview that counts. You must be able to explain your background very briefly—with energy, optimism, confidence, and poise—and then ask where your skills and background can best be utilized.

6. Use the exponential interviewing process to form a bridge into the job interview process. You may ask, "What sort of people does the industry look for?" "What kind of people, what sort of personality, does *your* organization look for when staffing up?"

A relationship of contacts resembles a spider's web: Touch one part of the web and the rest reverberates; push a little too hard, and the web snaps.

Social Intelligence, Emotional Competence

"People with high social intelligence are enormously qualified for life," said Howard Gardner, a psychologist at the Graduate School of Education at Harvard University. In his book,[22] he proposed that there are several other important kinds of intelligence beyond abilities for math or language, and this has been highly influential in the new appreciation of social intelligence, or what has been called "emotional competence."

Social intelligence, Dr. Gardner said, allows people to take maximum advantage of the resources of others. "We're finding that much of people's effective intelligence is, in a sense, outside the brain. Your intelligence can be in other people, if you know how to get them to help you. In life, that's the best strategy: mobilize other people."

He adds: "If you have social intelligence, you know that this only works if there's some kind of mutuality. If it's all one way, people will end up feeling you've exploited them."

Making professional contacts is an exchange of information, a *social transaction,* a form of learned behavior.

It is impossible to learn to play the violin, to swim, or to dance merely by reading a book. These skills—like contact or informational interviewing, contacting professional colleagues, contact development, job interviewing, and salary negotiation—all require practice, practice, and more practice. This is the same answer the Jewish grandmother gave to the stranger who asked her, "Can you give me directions to get to Carnegie Hall?"

You cannot learn all of the skills needed to find work in a social universe or community of employers by simply reading this or any other printed matter. You must be out there getting interviews (and even getting rejected) for these methods to work. It is the difference between theory and experiment. To put it another way: If you wish to create children, it's fine to study Freud, but eventually you have to make serious, practical contact with the opposite sex.

Desensitization to Contact Development

Contact development is an improvable skill, a learnable art, like emotional intelligence, which has such very high survival value in the marketplace that Daniel Goleman[23] calls it "the master aptitude."

But for those who are reluctant to call or write to strangers, to ask for advice, it is important to overcome your resistance. An aphorism that may be useful to remember is; "Imperfect movement is better than perfect paralysis."

The discomfort level at each stage in the necessary networking process can be clearly specified. Please refer back to the table entitled "Systematic Desensitization: Graduated Networking Activities" in Section 3.09, "Quintessential Informational Interviews."

Using the Telephone to Get Face-to-Face Meetings

Telephones bring order and organization to our lives. Yet they change the nature of how you communicate and exercise your social intelligence, and how you mobilize other people. (Please refer back to Section 3.09, "Quintessential Informational Interviews.")

However, for contacting purposes, if you are very shy, it probably makes sense to (1) write, (2) call, and (3) visit a target, in that order.

Your wisest policy is to present your truest and best natural self in any interview. When you see how you present yourself in an interview on videotape, you can make an objective analysis of how you are seen by others. This is a major benefit of videotape feedback in preparation and coaching for information and job interviews. It helps to have such rehearsals or practice sessions immediately prior to the interview. It also helps if your practice "coach" asks tough, and sometimes even hostile, questions (see Section 3.15, "Preparation for Job Interviews"). Make your mistakes in a practice setting that does not hurt your job search. Since everyone will make mistakes in the art of making contacts, it helps a great deal if you "make all your mistakes as quickly as possible."

Impression Management: Face-to-Face, Voice-Only, or On-line

Which type of conversation (face-to-face, voice-only, or on-line) would you expect to be most effective or favorable, if your purpose is to . . .

Check One	Face-To-Face	Voice-Only	On-Line
1. Successfully present yourself to others?			
2 Transfer information?			
3 Solve problems?			
4.. Reduce cooperation?			
5. Negotiate wages?			
6. Accurately estimate someone's opinion?			
7.. Change someone's opinion?			
8.. Detect lies?			
9. Deceive someone?			
10 Have a discussion?			
11. Sell something?			
12.. Come to an agreement?			
13.. Talk freely if you're shy?			
14. Control your behavior?			

The key to the conversation modes of communication (or "impression management") is the number of dots to the right of each question's number. One dot indicates that column one is the most favorable channel to produce the desired effect. Successfully representing yourself to others—for example, negotiating wages, deceiving someone (counterintuitive result), or controlling your behavior—is best done face-to-face. An accomplished actor or magician can use visual cues to misdirect your attention in order to deceive. Detecting lies, therefore, is easier on the telephone, since visual misdirection is absent and the careful listener may be able to hear the vocal tension that often accompanies a lie. Two dots after a number refer to the second column.

If you are shy, you may be able to communicate most readily on-line—transferring information, solving technical (but not necessarily human relations) problems, and having a discussion.

. . . .

Voice and Personality

If you want to be perceived as *intelligent,* you should talk . . .

   a) softly   b) fast   c) slowly   d) a normal rate   e) loudly

Answers: softly and fast

If you want to be perceived as *honest,* you should talk in a voice that is . . .

   a) low-pitched   b) high-pitched   c) soft

and at the same time . . .

   1) fast   2) slow   3) normal in rate

Answers: low pitched and slow

. . . .

What Attracts Worthy Mentors?

What attracts worthy mentors? A certain level of autonomy and independence? Maybe the appearance of potential capability in a new field? The appreciation of a younger version of oneself? Human chemistry? Mutual respect? Bonding?

Is a mentor-protégé relationship similar to friendship (or even "love")—just as mysterious and unfathomable? Perhaps it is also a desire on the part of the mentor to be well remembered and appreciated, respected and cared about. A mentor can be a teacher/coach, a sponsor/advocate, a sounding board/guide, or someone important at a career crossroads.

Few have studied the process of acquiring a mentor. Few of us know how we become mentors or become protégés. We can watch the protégés of other mentors and try to model our behavior on theirs, but they have different chemistry. Perhaps useful advice is to simply be yourself.

As a senior scientist said: "Even at age 65, I still need a mentor (who is 84 years old) to guide me, since I am 'still tempted by reckless idealism.'"

Protégés gain acceptance and confirmation of their abilities from mentors. They gain role models, get challenging assignments, and build long-lived attachments.

Any successful career transition resembles altering the original direction of an ocean liner with the help of many small tugboats, each one producing small impulses. Mentors can be those tiny impulses. "Sponsorship" (or "reflected power") is the most frequently observed career function in mentoring. In fact, very few career transitions occur without help from mentors as "coaches."

If you have worthy mentors, you will have access to more contacts and generations of contacts (see the first part of this section). If you have more contacts, you'll have access to more up-to-date job market information. According to Bonnie Oglensky,[24] "social credit is extended to the protégé because there appears to be a more powerful set of resources in the distance. The protégé gains recognition from important people in some field or organization by being connected to an influential figure and de facto having the stamp of approval." Also, mentors assign responsible positions to their protégés so that their competence and performance can stand out to those higher up in the hierarchy.[25]

"Coaching enhances a junior person's knowledge and understanding of how to navigate effectively in the [professional] world. Much like the athletic coach, senior colleagues suggest specific strategies for accomplishing work objectives, for achieving recognition, and [for attaining] career aspirations."[26]

Oglensky says that individuals are likely to get more mileage out of "weak ties" in furthering careers than out of close, intense relationships such as mentoring. Weak ties have the advantage of creating a diffusion of contacts, permitting exposure to a broader spectrum of opportunities. Mark Granovetter[27] does not consider the wider range of assistance and the high quality of career leads and opportunities that closer contacts are likely to render.

Consider the closeness of the following transitioners to their mentors. David Nash developed a lifelong mentor relationship that began when he was in high school.

DAVID NASH
••••••••••••••••••••••

*Transition From Economics To Physician
To Clinical Scholar In Business*

As a senior in high school, I wanted to combine my two interests, business and medicine, into one career. My father, a civil engineer by training, and a Sloan Fellow at MIT Sloan School of Management in the 1950s, a classmate of Paul Samuelson, heavily influenced my interests. He built his own business manufacturing language laboratories, called Educational Technology. As a kid I used to read *Business Week* and *Fortune*. My parents wanted me to be a doctor.

In the spring of 1973, I read an article in the *New York Times* about nonpracticing physicians who were presidents of major hospitals. In a now-famous quote, a professor of medicine and business, Samuel P. Martin III, who was running the Robert Wood Johnson Clinical Scholars Program at the University of Pennsylvania's Wharton Business School said that in the future there will be two types of doctors: managing doctors and practicing doctors. I wrote him a letter, and he called me at my parents' home. He said, "Come to Philadelphia." So I got on a train, and went to visit him, and to ask what he would suggest I do to prepare for my career in medicine and business. This began a lifelong mentoring relationship (he died twenty years later) of correspondence, advice giving, and suggesting what courses I should choose and what schools to apply to, and he took on a role of influence equal to that of my father.

He wrote letters of recommendation for me to Rochester Medical School, which was strong in community medicine and research. After I finished my B.S. in economics, I started there; I survived my first two years there, and only blossomed in my third year when we had patient contact.

I graduated in 1981 and my wife and I moved to Philadelphia, so that I could be close to Sam Martin and because she came from this area. We had gotten a hospital to allow us to be on call together. While an intern at the U of P hospital, I applied two years in advance for early admission to the Robert Wood Johnson Clinical Scholars Program, which I had sought for nine years. In 1982 I was accepted for deferred admission in 1984. I finished residency on a Friday and began as a Clinical Scholar at Wharton the following Monday. I received my MBA two years later, in 1986.

From 1973 to 1985, I had a single goal—from high school through college, medical school, residency, the Scholars Program—but I was still formulating a vision of my life. I thought there must be a way to combine medicine and business.

For the next four years I split my time between being deputy editor of the *Annals of Internal Medicine* (the third largest journal) and being medical director of a nine-physician group practice associated with the University of Pennsylvania. I had dual loyalties—to the American College of Physicians (about 40 percent of my time) and to my practice. In the fall of 1989, there was a palace putsch, and I left to find a way to operationalize what I had learned. I came to Thomas Jefferson University to credibly teach cost-effective medical care, quality improvement, and community health business issues, and I satisfied their requirements.

My assignment was to create a credible academic institution that would combine business and medicine, and have a measurable impact. We started with me and an assistant; now we have eighteen people. I didn't foresee the rise of Bill Clinton and the managed-care debate, but we were here at the right time. We helped create a locus of academic interests discussing with (and for) medical school faculty the issues of the day. Our output is intangible: We have helped to sensitize doctors to the inevitable changes in the economics of the health-care environment. It's been like turning an aircraft carrier in the Panama Canal.

I'm one of the most optimistic doctors I know. And I am especially proud of my mentoring role to young physicians, modeled after my mentors—especially Sam Martin, whose portrait looks down on me at work.

David Nash's lifelong mentorship is remarkable for its intensity. Walter Massey moved along a traditional career path, acquiring mentors along the way who knew what his next transition should be.

WALTER MASSEY
• •
Transition From Low Temperature Liquid
Helium To Director Of Lab, NSF, And
College President

The patterns of transition have depended on the period in my life in which a transition was made; a lot of change is age-related. The common threads are (1) I wanted to be in science policy rather than research, and to be in a position to have an influence on a national level; (2) to help create the inner-city science teaching program, I had to discover my abilities to administer, and (3) my most recent transition to Morehouse College allowed me to go back to my early roots.

I have some advice, based on my own transitions. First, seek advice broadly. It's extremely important at every point in your career and transition. What made a big difference for me was having people who really knew about my next move, who were older mentors to me. How do you find mentors? In my case, I took people at their face value. I assumed that they really wanted to help. I have found that other cohorts and peers can be so distrustful that they take offers of help too skeptically. Maybe it's "life" that does this to them. I always risked asking advice, and assumed that a mentor had my best interests at heart.

Second, the skills you gain in the study of science are much more transferable than most people realize. Also, taking risks to change careers is necessary, as is self-discipline and willingness to work hard, and of course intelligence. These attributes allow you to compete very effectively.

I have found that I was happy at each point in my career, no matter what its stage or transition.

I did a theoretical dissertation on low-temperature liquid helium at Washington University in St. Louis, finishing in 1966. I moved along on a traditional route of postdoc at Argonne National Lab, then the University of Illinois at Urbana, and Brown University, assistant professor to associate professor. The changes are fairly structured in that my interests evolved out of what I was doing.

I started an interdisciplinary program to bring up the quality of science teaching in the university schools, funded by NSF, with five other departments. I co-directed the program, starting in 1972, with an education professor. It ran for ten years. But the program led me to believe that I might enjoy, and have talent for, leadership. I was concerned about the poor quality and preparation of black students for science.

The American Council on Education had an academic administration fellowship for faculty who think they want to go into administration but are not yet ready to make that break. So in 1974, I went to do a year at the University of California in Santa Cruz. I found out that I did enjoy it, so when I came back to Brown, I was made dean of the college, although I still taught courses.

In 1979, I moved to Argonne as a full-time administrator. I liked it, I enjoyed it, I saw I had some talent for it. I knew people liked working with me. I felt I could make a bigger difference running an organization than teaching in a classroom. I wasn't sure I could manage 5,000 people and a $300 million budget, but I stayed on for five years.

In 1983, Argonne was reorganized by the University of Chicago, and we created a position of vice president for research at the University. It was a promotion; the director of the lab reported to me. It was a natural move for me. I became fairly well known in science circles. I was on the President's Council for Science and Technology, and in 1991 President Bush appointed me to be director of the National Science Foundation.

The staff was about 1,100 people, the operating budget was about $200 million, and our grant-making ability was about $3 billion. I found the transition fairly easy; learning how government worked was new. In 1995 I was made president of Morehouse College.

Asking for advice may be a low-risk strategy to acquire mentors. It also worked for Peter Fiske.

PETER FISKE
....
Transition From Geology And Civil Engineering To Research

I majored in geology and civil engineering at Princeton (1988). I knew, I really knew that I wanted to be a researcher and professor. I was absolutely certain. My professors affirmed my abilities, and an NSF graduate fellowship confirmed my desire to go straight to graduate school. My doctoral dissertation at Stanford (1993) was on high-temperature nuclear magnetic resonance spectroscopy of silicate crystals and glasses. Going straight to graduate school seemed inevitable; I had done this with very little inspection of the real work environment. It was based, in part, on the fact that my father is a geologist who leads a wonderful, wonderful life. Summers, my father had field research trips to the High Sierras, and the family went along. It was just a wonderful time. I knew I loved being in the mountains. It seemed so simple, right?

Then you go off to graduate school, and it's not what you thought it was going to be. It's solitary. It's isolating. It's unfriendly.

At the end of my fourth year, a friend in applied physics got two offers: one in industrial research and development, and the other from a management consulting company (McKinsey). I just happened to be in an office when he was talking about the offers. I was absolutely astounded by the consulting job offer: $85,000 plus $15,000 signing bonus plus benefits worth about $60,000. This was a tremendous wake-up call to me. I wondered, what does this guy know that I don't? He's making so much money. The gears began to grind. I was left feeling that I wouldn't get a faculty job, and I wouldn't get to pick my location—my wife and I didn't want to live in Idaho. These geographical constraints were very strong. We had lifestyle issues. There were only a few areas of the country where we would live.

So I went to the career planning and placement office on campus, to sit down and talk about this with a counselor there, Al Levin. He said, "What's going on in geology? You're the fifth one here this week!" I told him my goals. He introduced me to some assessment tools: the Meyers-Briggs and the Strong Interest Inventory. What came out loud and clear was that I had skills and interests very different from those of my science peers. I *knew* I was an oddball. I explored careers in management consulting. (By the way, the friend who started me thinking about this was let go by McKinsey and now works for a technical company.) I did not get an offer in management consulting, but I did get an offer to go to Lawrence Livermore Lab for a three-year postdoc. I still think management consulting is a very interesting profession—not all are like McKinsey. I had a great introduction to it by interviewing. Besides McKinsey there are Anderson, Boston Consulting, Booz-Allen and Arthur D. Little, plus there's investment banking as well. I'm still exploring these nontraditional careers for someone with my training, but not with my interests and values.

My three years in Livermore were a wonderful reward. They reawakened in me my love for doing research, and made me reconsider a career in science.

At the end of the postdoc, I was thinking of science policy fellowships. I applied to seven and was offered three, and accepted the White House Fellowship. It's really a remarkable project. Twelve to eighteen early- to midcareer people become special assistants to the president, the vice president, and the cabinet secretaries.

I had a meeting with Al Levin, and we discussed the commonalities we'd seen in graduate students, how they're approaching their job or career, making the same mistakes. I organized an American Geophysical Union panel that Al and I gave together; in two hours we summarized the method of modern career planning. We tried to tailor this material to the backgrounds and careers of pre- and postdocs. We had very limited cooperation from the society. I arrived and the room was packed to standing room only, spilling out into the hallways. The feelings I had were quite pervasive. I ran the program alone at the next society meetings at Stanford. I had amassed a lot of material by then.

(By the way, I came to the AGU with this material to see if they wanted to publish a book, and they thought it a silly idea. But one person from the society saw my handout materials, and I had photocopied some copyrighted things without permission. Well, it turned out that the AGU had just won a copyright infringement suit against Texaco. So he said, "You have to stop doing this," and I said, "You have to start doing this right." So my book, *To Boldly Go*, was published.)

What's fun as a scientist is that you make a research contribution; but these contributions go out there, one after another, and very little happens. But the career work allowed me to do things directly for people, a real audience, and I really believe I was helping somebody. It was a very different experience. I really enjoyed it. This made me realize that I really dig the difference and I should really do different things myself.

I am currently exploring my next career. It's very interesting to me that although I have been talking a good game about others' careers, I can really appreciate how difficult it is to take advice. In my patterns I see a lot of serendipity and rolling dice. If I hadn't been in my office when the guy with the McKinsey offer came in, I wouldn't have thought to reevaluate my career directions. If I hadn't gone to see Al Levin, I don't know where I'd be now.

Good and bad career changes may not happen on their merits. Each of us must have a ration of good and missed opportunities linked to that great cosmic wheel.

Good career habits are very important in exploring changes and job hunting. An industrial researcher told me that 80 percent of her week she spends doing the best job she can; 10 percent of her week she is just exploring, looking in new directions where her wide interests take her; and the other 10 percent of her time is taken up telling as many people as she can about the other 80 percent. So it's a pattern that successful people spend time investing in potential payoffs, and aren't afraid to project what they're doing to other people. Graduate students have to learn this—not only in the office, with their advisor, but in their neighborhood and the community.

What started out as a career counseling relationship ended up fulfilling Peter's "people" interests.

What attracts worthy mentors? Authentic interest and curiosity in the mentor's life work. Risk taking. Need for guidance. All these and more, including a desire to have validation that one's interests and skills are compatible.

Recruiters

The *recruiter always represents the employer* (their client) because recruiters are always compensated by the employer—not by you. The recruiter's objective is to find a candidate who fills their client's specifications, *not* to find you a suitable job. This is clearly demonstrated by the statistic that recruiters place only 10 to 15 percent of all candidates who contact them. One of the best indications of a high-quality recruiter is that he or she is very clear to all parties about this financial relationship with the client, the employer.

A recruiter is *not* hired by an employer to find candidates who want a new career or a different specialty. Employers always want the best-fit candidate for their opening, and that candidate is often working for the employer's competitor. Thus, the recruiter acts as an intermediary.

Once you recognize and fully appreciate this, you can decide *if, when,* and *how* to use recruiters in your search.

How to Use Recruiters

- *Be selective.* Work with ethical, honest recruiters that you trust. Be clear about what type of employer they represent. Use your network to find recruiters whom colleagues and contacts have found reliable and effective.

- *Be clear about the job you want.* Don't allow the recruiter to pressure you into looking at jobs that are not right. If the recruiter tries to persuade you to look at jobs that don't interest you, analyze the situation for yourself. Perhaps the recruiter doesn't represent clients with the type of job you want; this means you need a different recruiter. Another reason could be that the recruiter doesn't believe you are qualified for the job you want. It is useful for you to explore this second reason. You may need to improve your presentation, or possibly there are significant objections you must overcome. Remember, using a recruiter is not the most effective search strategy when your background is not a good match for the job. (This is especially true when you are changing career directions.)

Through competent exponential interviewing, you can gather high-quality information about the market for your skills, and your need for new skills. You should understand that the recruiter's knowledge of the job market can be extremely valuable to you. The problem is, the recruiter is not working for you. In most cases, recruiters will be friendly to you. However, often they are merely collecting archival or file résumés for future employer assignments. Also note that many display ads, often with box numbers only (called "blind" ads), are placed by recruiting firms who are looking for a needle in the haystack. The recruiter may be paid on a contingency basis, meaning that he or she receives compensation (some 10 to 30 percent of the first year's salary) only if he or she finds the right candidate, or the recruiter may be paid on a monthly basis (on retainer).

- *Sell yourself to the recruiter as if you are interviewing for the actual position.* The recruiter is a gatekeeper whose job is to prevent unqualified applicants from reaching the employer. Don't share information that is potentially damaging. Your job is to persuade the recruiter that you are right for the position. Both sides are looking for information on which to base a very important decision. The best recruiters have developed close relationships with their clients (your potential employer!) that are based on trust. They are experienced, skillful interviewers, and you should talk to them only when you are thoroughly prepared to present accurate information in a positive way (see Section 3.15, "Preparation for the Job Interviews").

- *Manage the relationship* Make sure the recruiter gets your authorization before contacting a potential employer. Ask the recruiter to give you a list of the people and organizations your résumé was sent to. Keep good notes so that you are clear and avoid duplications. This is particularly important if you use more than one résumé. If you change your résumé, make sure the recruiter destroys the old résumé and is using the new one. If you decide not to work with a recruiter who has your résumé, inform the recruiter in writing, and ask that no more of your résumés be sent out.

Since recruiters fill about 10 to 15 percent of job openings, an efficient search strategy is to spend no more than 15 percent of your total job-hunting time with recruiters. Devote most of your effort to exponential interviewing and other effective job-searching techniques discussed in this book. Note that most recruiters are hired by employers to fill jobs that the employer could not fill by (1) word of mouth or (2) classified or display ads; therefore, usually the hardest-to-fill jobs are assigned to recruiters, and these jobs are usually at a very high level (and high compensation).

Here are some pointers from a recruiter.[28]

How to Ace a Meeting with a Headhunter

Headhunters are often the keys to job opportunities. Don't underestimate your need to impress them. While you may deliver what headhunters call "a great piece of paper"—fabulous credentials and job experience—the personal encounter can determine whether or not you get your foot in their client's door. Here are some tips on how to make an effective presentation:

1. *No torn socks. No wimpy handshakes.* Think of headhunters as prospective employers. Appear at your physical best. Remember, the initial encounter forges a lasting impression. For men: wear black, blue, or dark grey suits. For women: don't overdo the make-up or fingernails. Keep skirts at an appropriate length. A firm handshake and eye contact throughout the meeting will bring you high marks. Exhibit winning behavior: Be self-confident, upbeat, enthusiastic, and personable.

2. *No berating the boss.* Focus on the business reasons why you want to leave your current employer—to learn new skills or add to your background. If you have been asked to leave or your department has been downsized, don't be afraid to be candid. Be ready to explain the circumstances. Ask the headhunter how you can best be marketed. Under such circumstances, offer to include references right on your résumé. Inform a headhunter of any conflicts with others in your office, using diplomatic language. What you say is not as important as how you say it.

3. *Anticipate trick questions.* Don't be caught by these minefields: What are your strengths? What is your greatest accomplishment? What is your worst flaw? Where do you want to be in five years? Give a big picture response to questions about your abilities by listing results of your efforts; don't give a laundry list of your responsibilities. Emphasize what you have done to turn weakness around rather than state the weakness itself—for example, "I often worked unnecessarily late, but I have since learned to delegate responsibility." In today's market, no one can know where he or she will be in five years. Give a short-term goal in answer to this question.

4. *Anticipate gender-biased questions.* Headhunters cannot legally ask about marriage or children, but they frequently ask women if they will travel or work overtime. Unless you want the job under any circumstances, be up-front about your needs—family or lifestyle.

5. *Be specific: Define your goals.* List your current compensation and salary threshold, geographic preferences, and the type of culture you are looking for. Don't waste each other's time.

How to Find Recruiters

- *Directory of Members of NAPS (National Association of Personnel Services).* By specialty and geographic location. 3133 Mt. Vernon Avenue, Alexandria, VA 22305.

- *Directory of Executive Recruiters.* Kennedy Publications, Templeton Road, Fitzwilliam, NH 03447. (603) 585-6544. 1996. (800) 531-0007. Kennedy maintains a searchable database of 8,000 executive recruiters,

50,000 management consultants (often a euphemism for recruiters), and 3,600 major recruiting firms.

- *Crain's NY Business: Executive Search Issue*. This annual issue features the twenty-five largest executive recruiting firms. This is an example of a regional business publication that may have counterparts in your region.

- Colleagues and contacts who may have employed or been placed by recruiters.

- College, university or other placement offices.

- The Job Bank Series, e.g., *The Metropolitan New York Job Bank 1995: The Job Hunter's Guide to New York*, Adams Publishing, Holbrook, MA; (617) 767-8100. This Job Bank Series is also available for other large cities, including Atlanta, Boston, Chicago, Dallas, Denver, Los Angeles, Seattle, Washington, D.C., and other areas. Covers recruiters and potential employers in various industries in these cities (7215 Oak Avenue, River Forest, IL 60305, (800) 829-5220).

Career Counselors

Who can use career counselors?

If, after you have read some of the hundreds of book titles on career management, you are confused, you probably can benefit by seeking a high-quality career counselor locally or on-line who has experience working with scientists, engineers, physicians, technologists, and other credentialed professionals.

If, after years of dithering, or months of reading career management books, you still have difficulty in deciding what to do next in your job search or career change, you may benefit by seeing a high-quality career counselor.

If you cannot push yourself forward to what you believe to be the next step in your job search or career change, you will definitely benefit by seeing a high-quality career counselor.

If you are stuck in a job or career in which you are unhappy, and have been frustrated at your inability to move on, you will benefit by seeing a high-quality career counselor.

What are the hallmarks of high-quality career counseling?

One set of answers to this question may be found in what is perhaps the best book on career counseling—the venerable warhorse *What Color Is Your Parachute?* by Richard Bolles.[29] The answers are in the form of searching questions that the reader is urged to ask each career counselor, and to compare the answers.

Here are some questions Bolles suggests you ask a career counselor before you proceed: (1) What is your Program? (2) What types of individuals do you usually help (salary, profession, etc.)? How many credentialed professionals have you worked with over what time period? (3) Who will be doing the counseling, and how long has that person been doing it? What characteristics does that person have that suggest competence, empathy, emotional intelligence? (4) What is the cost of your services? Is it an hourly rate or flat fee? Are there any extra fees for testing, research, resumes or cover letters?

Career counselors should inform you of their experience relevant to you, and that no guarantees, miracles, or magic are realistic. If they charge a fixed fee and help you land a new job or career, they are worth their weight in gold. Advantages of a fixed fee to you are somewhat counterintuitive: (1) you get a full-term program of unlimited time (hours or months) until you land safely, which must include ready access to the counselor on demand; (2) your career counselor will move you effectively and rapidly through the assessment, options and strategy phases since it is in his or her financial interest to see you land quickly, and the counselor will concentrate on the prompt job landing acceptable to you; (3) the counselor does not have to interrupt the counseling process to persuade you of the (virtually universal!) need for additional counseling, strategy, modules, résumés, or contact hours: (4) you get the emotional support when you need it most—as you approach job interviews, when "the squeaky wheel (you) gets the grease (the counselor's full attention)."

The following career-transition narrative explains what was useful in the counseling process.

DONNA FERRANDINO
Transition From Nutritionist To Dean

I would like to summarize for you my experiences with Scientific Career Transitions (SCT). As you are aware, your organization was partly responsible for my obtaining a great job in a very short time. I will be dean of health technologies, public services, and natural sciences at Jefferson Community College in Steubenville, Ohio.

Before I started working with SCT, I began my job-hunting endeavors in late January 1995. I put together the best résumé I could, and by July I had received only one phone interview, for a job I really did not want. After finding out about SCT, and briefly speaking with you and Dan White (an SCT counselor), I decided to make some personal contacts, but those did not lead to employment either.

After joining SCT, I completed the skills inventory and the focus and values exercises. I found these to be incredibly valuable. With Dan's help, in one conversation, I pinned down my most valuable skills as interpersonal skills, writing, organization, and project management. I had used all of these skills in the past, but doing the exercises, and having one conversation with Dan, helped me to identify these skills and thus emphasize and relate to them in a new skills résumé, in cover letters, and especially in the one successful interview I had with Jefferson.

Completing the focus and values exercises helped me to really think about what I wanted from my job, and what I was and was not willing to endure. I realized that what had been missing from my last few jobs, and being in graduate school for six years, was high earnings potential, regular and predictable hours, and creativity. I had been applying mostly for positions as assistant professor of nutrition, gerontology, or health science, and I realized that I really did not want to be assistant professor of anything, since I would not have any of the three values that were important to me. Thus, I stopped wasting my time applying for assistant professor jobs.

The specific circumstances regarding Jefferson were interesting. I had first applied for the job last April or May, and received a letter that indicated that Jefferson did not consider me to be one of the more suitable candidates. In August, I saw the job readvertised in the *Chronicle of Higher Education*, so I sent an updated cover letter, emphasizing the new skills I had learned I needed to focus on, and saying that I had completed my Ph.D. Jefferson soon called to schedule an interview, and gave me the choice of traveling to Ohio at my own expense or doing it by phone. I chose to go in person.

For the two weeks before the interview, which I was told would be conducted with eight administrators and faculty members, as well as the person who would be the dean's assistant, I prepared furiously. I spent hours speaking with the associate dean at Virginia Tech, for whom I had worked for five years; with my major professor, who was dean emeritus of our college; and with a person who held a similar position at our local community college. All gave me suggestions, talked about the philosophy and mission of community colleges, and proposed sample questions that I would be asked and that I could ask the panel. Finally, I spoke with Dan the day before I left, and he helped me again focus in on what we felt were my four major skills, all four of which he believed would be very important in this position. He also advised me on some questions to ask and not to ask, how to maintain eye contact with one person at a time, and how to smile and appear approachable and friendly; and he advised me not to dress like a banker.

I went to the interview with ten pages of typed notes I had compiled over the previous two weeks, including the names of the people on the interview panel, sample questions, and examples of how I had used my four strongest skills in the past. I wrote down statements to convince the panel that I was a perfect fit for the job. On top of my ten pages, most of which I committed to memory, I had one page to which I could refer during the interview, which contained the names of the panel members, my four skills, and questions for me to ask to make me seem prepared (which I was).

I was a little nervous at first when I was confronted with eight people asking questions, and trying to respond intelligently to each of them. However, after about five minutes, I was really comfortable. I felt that all nine of us had established a rapport, and we started making jokes, and I threw some humor into my answers. We seemed to be compatible, and were on a first-name basis. I left the interview feeling that I had prepared as much as I could have (which was about forty hours), glad I had chosen to do it in person, and confident that, if they already did not have an internal candidate in mind, I had a good shot at the job. I was told that they were considering five people, and I was the fourth they had interviewed. This occurred on Friday, December 8. On the following Wednesday, I received a call to informally offer me the position, and was told a letter was being drafted. This was two days before graduation, and I was ecstatic.

I really cannot say that any one item was the reason I got the job after trying so hard and fruitlessly for almost a year. It was a combination of identifying my skills and what I liked and wanted to do in a job, of preparing for many hours, and of receiving input from several people, including Dan. All these things together contributed to my success, and helped me to achieve a level of self-confidence when I walked into the interview, and the knowledge that I had done my most and my best when I walked out the door. The SCT exercises for skills, focus, and values were of tremendous help, and Dan White's advice and support were right on the mark. I would have no hesitation about recommending your services to others. I also give you permission to use any part of what I have written here as testimony to the effectiveness of SCT. Thank you, Steve, and thanks to Dan and Victoria, for all of your help and advice. I will keep in touch from time to time, and will seek you out when I get ready for a promotion. I wish you all the best of luck with the SCT program. Know that you are truly providing a much needed service in a competent and effective manner.

Scientific Career Transitions welcomes your inquiries regarding private or group career counseling, and is prepared to answer questions, and to help you select the best career counselor for you (1776 Broadway, Suite 1806, New York, NY 10019-2002, Tel: (212) 397-1021, Fax: (212) 397-1022, e-mail: srosen@ix.netcom.com, www.toa-services.net/sct001.html

Career Counseling Pros and Cons

Our alumni, career counseling clients, have analyzed what they achieved from working with a career counselor, and others have explained why they did not retain such outside counsel. Here are the pros and cons from their vantage point as consumers or nonconsumers of the service.

Whether it is called urging, inducing, pushing, inspiring, cajoling, luring, nagging, shoving, or kicking, alumni of the process feel that they need the *imposition of structure* that an outsider (almost any outsider) can bring to the career-transition process. Guidance is not easy to self-program.

Furthermore, it is not always easy to see one's own mistakes. This is especially true in interviews. A videotape can feed back to you what you look like under the stress of a mock interview. Most feel that this is invaluable ("to see ourselves as others see us"). We know of no one who has done videotape feedback alone. An outsider also can differentiate clearly between what's internal and what's external that may be stalling or obscuring the transition. Virtually every candidate who sees their playback says, "Do I really look like that?"

Those who intellectually understand the principles and necessity of expanding their circles of contacts and professional acquaintances are not always able to do so easily. The counselor can show the candidate techniques and strategies that will facilitate the process and tailor them specifically for the candidate.

A career evaluation can clarify career paths, reduce confusion, and help the individual move forward. Clients felt that the Meyers-Briggs, when interpreted by a career professional, was among the most helpful assessment instruments. This standard personality test is taken by some two million people annually. A new use for this test: to help accountants identify the kinds of clients to pursue.[30]

Among the reasons given for not seeking a career counselor: the cost, and a belief (often justified) that "I can do it myself." Our career-change champions certainly confirm and justify their own self-confidence. A compromise is to try it yourself for a while (several months) and see how far you get; when you get stuck, ask for help on the sticking points.

Temporary Work for Scientists

One advantage of temporary work for both you and the employer is that you get to know each other, as if you are on an extended job interview. This may last weeks, months, or longer. You discover if you're good at or enjoy the new work, and the employer discovers if you're employable.

For changing careers, you stretch your skills and learn new skills, using the temporary job as a stepping-stone to a new transition.

How to Find Temporary Work

On Assignment. Arranges work for B.S. and M.S. chemists, neurobiologists, and others; mainly in the Western United States, including Phoenix, Seattle, Orange County. (800) 998-3411.

Advanced Science Professionals. Provides lab support, environmental scientists, and others to employers; mainly on the East Coast. Located in New Jersey. (908) 981-1404.

Manpower Technical Division, Manpower, Inc. Has made agreements with the American Institute of Physics and other professional societies to provide access to temporary work. URL: htttp://www.manpower.com. Located in Milwaukee, Wisconsin. (800) 262-4314.

Kelly Scientific Resources, Kelly Technical Services. Headquarters in Troy, Michigan. (800) 535-5917. (810) 362-4444. URL: http://www.kellyservices.com.

Here's an example of how the "master aptitude," social intelligence, pays off. See if you can read between the lines of the following career-transition narrative. What does the narrator do that illustrates his emotional competence?

Transition From Economics To Law To Microbiology To Journalism

I majored in economics, finished college in three years and had a year off, then I went to law school for a year, took a leave of absence from there, and then became a microbiologist. I get restless, I guess. I came down to Birmingham as a microbiologist, as a postdoc, then I joined the faculty and began to not be excited by the science I was doing. I thought about it and talked about it with my wife, and I thought I was more interested in writing.

I've read newspapers all my life; I've always been a reader. I thought, "Gee, a newspaper might be a good place to start," and so I thought I'd take a course in journalism. I called up a journalism teacher I knew and said, "Here's where I am, who I am, and what I'm doing. What should I do?" He suggested I take the second-level course because the first level was remedial; I could just read the textbook. I was able to do all of this while I continued my work. The course turned out to be taught by the managing editor of the paper, and I realized that all I had to do was impress him and I'd have a chance for something. So I talked to him after the course and said I was interested in exploring things, and we set up something where I would work part time. I went in and talked to the chairman of the microbiology department and said I was going to do that, too, because I thought there shouldn't be any confusion.

So I spent about four or five months working part time, and that gave them a chance to see me. They really didn't believe that a scientist could write regular newspaper style. At the end of that "work-in" period, I told the editor that I was interested in making a switch, and he said fine. The one fortuitous thing was that the paper was starting a health and science section, and so I fit into the content that was needed. We had two other health reporters; one of the others was a chemical engineer. He knew he didn't want to be a chemical engineer in his junior year, and the university said, "Oh, just finish your degree," which is what you hear from a lot of people when you're in school. He then went and got a master's in journalism.

I didn't stay in health and science. Probably the juiciest thing I've done was a year-long exposé of the Birmingham Housing Authority, which was straightforward investigative reporting. I was general assignment and then I did business reporting, and then we were having trouble in the health section and needed some warm bodies, so I'm doing health. I branched out and do other kinds of writing from time to time.

I like writing. In terms of career path, I would have gone to a different city at some point, but my wife is a lawyer here; we're tied to Birmingham. We also, in the middle of this, had a baby that we didn't expect, so that kind of changed our direction.

Other people see you as a risk taker when you do something like this, they come out of the walls and say "Hey, I've always wanted to open a restaurant." or "Would you like to read my poetry?" or things like that. I think many people have an alternative idea of what they want to be doing. It's probably healthy. Most of the time it's probably just fantasy. I've always been somebody who, if I tried to do something, did it well. I applied myself. It didn't become a real emotional kind of thing; you do it and try it and see what happens.

Having support was kind of important. There are financial implications that are important. You have to not really care about stepping back a few steps on money.

I've had probably five or six people call me up and say, I'm interested in this, and I'll sit with them and have lunch and tell them a little of what I know. The freelance route is a difficult one. Journalism can be hard. I happened to join the largest paper in the state, which is very different from starting somewhere else. I think the hardest thing for people is deciding what it is that they actually want to do. I think often we say, "well, it seems like it's attractive to have something else" because we're dissatisfied with what we're doing, but I don't think people end up committed to that. If it's what they really want to do, I say, well, do this and this and this and this. It'll be satisfying, but it takes commitment. I think most people think about it as an escape in some way, from something, rather than something they really want to do. I don't think my path is easily replicated. But I think if you read things about how people get jobs, the entire networking thing, there are many elements of chance or timing that work out for people as they go into something. I also didn't end up burning bridges. I didn't quit and do this and starve. I did it as an add-on so I could try it.

I really think that people who have a clear idea of what they want to do, then go out and work that plan, are not very common. I'm not holding myself up as someone who's done that, but . . . I did it.

Notice how he was friendly to others who were doing informational interviews. Does this imply that he was replicating informational interview behavior that he had benefited from? And what sort of behavior on his part evoked such informational generosity towards him?

Social competence and emotional generosity pay off. Companies' abilities to foster employee morale and loyalty, to attract talented people, to practice emotionally intelligent policies towards their employees are quantifiable. A study of 275 portfolio managers suggests that investor decisions are some 35 percent driven by nonfinancial factors. Balance sheet factors account for only 60 percent of the average company's stock valuation.[31]

How do "rainmakers" make rain? Here's what one consummate rainmaker does. He has a prodigious network of contacts he calls "the daisy chain," lovingly maintained with an elaborate 3×5 index card system, which he stockpiles in his car, near his bed, and even in the bathroom. He jots down a name or an idea or a task on each, organized by date. He says it earns him productivity as well as free time to enjoy life.[32]

3.12 JOB SEARCH RESEARCH: GET REAL BEFORE YOU GO VIRTUAL

Employer Research

Now that you have worked on the career options exploration research (Section 3.08) and the informational interview (Section 3.09), you should have an idea of which career or job options interest you most. (If you have had difficulty or have not yet accomplished this goal, this may be another occasion to consider professional guidance.)

You will be gathering information from people and paper contacts concurrently, and this will amplify and supplement your career options research. (People contacts are face-to-face; paper contacts are by fax, snail mail, or e-mail. You will probably develop a professional or cordial relationship more readily by face-to-face contact, since the most effective communication for this purpose is nonverbal.)

Your next step is to identify prospective employers within the *actual activities* and *industries* that interest you. You will identify some through exponential interviewing (as described in Section 3.11), and some through job-search research as described here.

As with career options research, do not try to research too many options at a time, or you will become overwhelmed. You should be seeking to answer the question: "Specifically, which organizations or companies will be most likely to be able to use my (most enjoyable) skills?" For example, if you have quantitative skills you enjoy using, you may wish to investigate financial analysis (actual activities) in the investment banking field (industry), at Merrill Lynch (company) and/or the Financial Analysts Society (organization).

In order to complete your employer research, you will need to consult directories, databases, and other resources. You will find directories for al-

most all industries in a business library. As a first step, use the *Encyclopedia of Business Information Sources*[33] to help you identify specific sources related to the field(s) you are exploring. Consult the librarian for expert assistance. The following resource list will provide you with sources on paper, on-line, and on CD-ROM. We have marked with an asterisk (*) materials that we know are available on CD-ROM and with a plus sign (+) those that are on-line, but some of those not indicated may be updated electronically, so you should check with the library or the company publishing that directory.

If the directories provide too many names, decide on screening criteria, such as geographical location, size, options research results, your predilections or preferences, input from contacts, and so on. You may wish to photocopy portions of the directories to simplify record keeping. *Don't forget to enter salient information into your job-search diary or career-change journal.* Enter the most promising items for further research, detailed examination, and follow-up. Look in the appendix for checklists of specific industries, sizes, and locations and use this as a guide.

Business publications and trade journals have special issues dedicated to certain companies in their industry, to "Industry Outlook," to "The Year Ahead," etc. See *Special Issues Index* and Special Libraries Association's *Guide to Special Issues and Indexes of Periodicals* to find the appropriate periodical. Examples are the "500 List" issues of Fortune, Forbes, and Business Week.

Another rich source of information about companies and industries is the indexes to business periodical literature that are available on-line and on CD-ROM. Most business libraries of any size and many public libraries have either ABI/INFORM or Infotrac/General Business File. These indexes provide abstracts of articles along with many of the citations, so you can get an idea about the article and decide if you want to look up the full text in the periodical. You can search these indexes by name of company, product or service, or SIC code as well as by subject.

You may also use the *Encyclopedia of Associations.*[34] Find the professional associations related to your fields of interest and call them. There is also an international version of this encyclopedia. Ask for the names of officers, a copy of the association's newsletter or magazine, and listings of its member organizations or companies, if these are available to the public. If you know you are interested in a field, it may be worthwhile to join the organizations (if necessary) to obtain their lists and even bulletins or job postings or openings. (Their job openings, like all posted job openings, will be sought after by others, and so your positive response rate will be about 1 percent or less—unless your résumé is the key that fits the lock).

Here are some observations from a specialist in optics who earned both a Ph.D. and an MBA. His early exposure to an industrial environment led him to the insight that best opportunities for scientists and engineers were in management. This lesson was critical to his decision to get a B.S. in physics and an MBA, but a job at Thiokol showed him how limited his career options were in a technical company.

Transition From Physics To Industry

Because the goal of being a scientist had always been in my mind, I had started work on a Ph.D. at the University of Arizona in physics on an in absentia basis at the same time I started work at Thiokol. After two years at Thiokol, I returned to my academic studies full time. There were many reasons to do so, and, additionally, I expected the time I was in school to coincide with the tough times I could see coming for the defense/aerospace industry. I always assumed I could return to Thiokol.

After three years at the University of Arizona, I earned my Ph.D. in physics with a minor in optical science. I was still very interested in an industrial position, although I was looking for a research position. To some extent I had narrowed myself to those types of work that a physicist ought to do. I remember giving lectures near the end of my Ph.D.; my work was well received, and I felt that I could consider myself a professional scientist, an important feeling.

Jobs were very hard to find. I applied for academic and industrial positions (I tried to avoid postdocs) of the kind advertised in *Physics Today*. Thiokol was not hiring, and I finally accepted a temporary teaching position. Although I tried hard, I was frustrated and quickly dissatisfied by the academic environment, and particularly the lack of resources offered by the small university where I was teaching. I also realized that I could never make a decent living at that university. I accepted a postdoc at Argonne; it offered better potential—work at a national lab, interaction with industry, and the prospect of a permanent position.

Work at Argonne was challenging and enjoyable. I was quickly offered a permanent position at the expiration of my postdoc contract. I was delighted; my family could settle down and live a "normal" existence. But budgets were tough at the lab, and two contract cycles later the permanent position had not materialized. Although the work had been enjoyable at first, the challenge had begun to disappear. All of these things resulted in enough discomfort that I began to consider my options.

I came to a number of realizations as I considered my work, my career, and my goals. First, I realized that I did not enjoy being a bench scientist as much as I once had. Second, I realized that there was already a significant administrative/project management component to the work I was doing (and I enjoyed it). Third, and most importantly, I changed my definition of myself. I was no longer a professional scientist, I was a well-educated, versatile professional. Although it may seen simply a matter of semantics, the change was equivalent to a paradigm shift. As a professional, there were more options open to me. I could do anything I like without being a failure. If I was a scientist, not doing science was failure and a waste of talent. As a professional, I could do science, management, politics, or anything else that seemed worthwhile.

I considered different options. Some were too far from the technology and science I loved for me to enjoy, such as management consulting. I thought about this a lot, and finally decided that what I wanted was a job that combined technical and managerial skills. I found such a job and am challenged, excited, and having fun. I also ran across a once-in-a-lifetime opportunity by going to work for a small, rapidly growing company. Parenthetically, the promise of a position at Argonne did materialize; I turned it down.

I can only encourage other scientists to use the "profession" paradigm; it removed the feeling of failure. Pick an industry you are interested in and determine what skills are needed. In my case, optics was the industry of choice. I determined what skills were of value in this industry and worked hard to see that I added those skills to my repertoire. The reason that I said that I did and did not make a career transition is that optics is a field in which many Ph.D.s are employed in industry. That and the fact that I am heavily involved in technical/engineering issues means that the change is more subtle than entering management consulting or financial analysis.

Once the decision is made, it is important to make sure that the résumé helps industry see the skills they are looking for (rather than general brilliance); *the résumé has to sell you*. My rude shock concerning this came when a recruiter's client decided that I looked too academic; the client doubted that I could work in industry. I asked a nontechnical friend to examine the résumé; he did not think it sounded like the person he knew. I made changes. Here's a summary of what I learned.

1. The APS News jobs insert says that using the Internet is useful to maintain a presence. I have found that it is more than useful. It is a gold mine! Specifically, I have found posting a résumé to the Online Career Center (www.occ.com) and IPA (www.ipa.com) to be the most useful. They are also easy places to see current openings. Many companies have on-line postings, so you can see what they have (and send something to personnel that will not be filed away).

I have had many interested recruiters call from these sources. (They are still calling.) Incidentally, a good recruiter will prepare you for the phone and on-site interviews.

2. The job market seems better now than in 1993—Either that or the two years of postdoc at Argonne made a world of difference. I think that the answer is a combination of both factors.

3. In my case, I found that prospective employers were really impressed by breadth. About half the time, the positions offered were ones that could put the breadth to use. The other half were technical positions that might have been advertised in traditional venues.

4. Finally, although the numbers were fewer, responding to companies who came recruiting at my university (obtained by calling the department) yielded interviews.

5. The job I accepted came from contacts made while working at Argonne. The company's need coincided with my availability—a perfect match. So, it is possible to have a postdoc really lead to an industrial job.

6. The hardest part of the process was the résumé. Although there is a strong urge to have a broad career objective, I think it helped to decide "what I wanted to be when I grew up" and what kind of position would help me get there, and then make it clear in the objective.

7. For an industrial position, do not write the résumé to read like a scientist's CV. *Sell yourself.* Tell prospective employers what you do well. My biggest help was getting some outside advice from someone in industry who could offer the critique to make this happen.

The epiphany "it is possible to have a postdoc lead to an industrial job" can apply to other venues and search strategies. The unspoken part here, which we refer to in Sections 3.09 and 3.11, has to do with social readiness to speak to virtually anyone to learn what he or she knows. You can amplify your contacts exponentially by approaching unlikely sources, not only on-line, but also face to face and by telephone. Job-market research is essential to find what fits who you are, rather than to bend yourself into an unnatural shape.

Answer the following questions for each industry you are researching. Make copies of these forms if necessary.

Research (Investigation)

Doing adequate research is critical to a successful job-search campaign. You've done this before anytime you've purchased a "big-ticket item," such as a house, car, or major appliance. Now you will do it for something equally as important to you—finding the job of your choice. Doing this research well takes time, energy, and focus. You can locate just about anything you want, but only when you are *clear* about your *objective*.

Why Do Research?

- It gives you a strong competitive edge (most people can't be bothered).
- It helps you specifically to
  1. Get appointments.
  2. Conduct those meetings/interviews.
  3. Uncover unpublished job leads.
  4. Gain self-confidence by your preparation.
  5. Obtain job offers.

There are two main reasons for doing research yourself (as opposed to having someone else do it for you or not doing it at all):

1. To develop background about your objective or to clarify your target
2. To develop information about specific organizations of interest to you

There are two major sources of information:

1. Secondary sources: printed material; the Internet
2. Primary sources: direct in-person meetings
   - Your contacts
   - Your information meetings

A Digression on Search Strategies

There are as many search strategies as there are people who search. The following list is intended to suggest of the rich variety of methods, of ways of looking and styles of seeing, of theories of discovering, of ways of knowing. (A friend tells us that he is responsible for "knowing," and his wife is responsible for "remembering" everything.) It would be ideal to separate the data acquisition function from the data storage function in your search. Many of the following people are scientists whose names you will recognize.

Many of their ideas or styles are those you will recognize.[35] How about your own style?

Strategies for Discovering

Young's principle: One cannot possess a useless talent or skill.

Kettering's principle: Action creates results.

Disraeli's principle: Court serendipity by being eccentric.

Truesdell's advice: Learn from the masters.

Pauling's principle: Try many things.

Salk's advice: Do what makes your heart leap!

The problem-choice principle: Think big.

Thomson's principle: Importance does not correlate with difficulty.

The problem-formulation principle: The formulation of a problem is often more essential than its solution.

The lost key conundrum: Dare to explore where there is no light.

The pioneering urge: The frontiers are the richest source of novelty.

Szent-Gyorgyi's advice: Renew old knowledge.

Medawar's advice: Challenge expectations.

Pasteur's method: Find a contradiction between theory and data.

Bacon's principle: Truth comes out of error more rapidly than from confusion.

Delbruck's principle: Be sloppy enough that something unexpected happens, but not so sloppy that you can't tell what happened.

Lord Dainton's advice: Cherchez le paradoxe.

Bernard's principle: All data are valid.

Imp's first principle: Play contradictions.

Imp's second principle: Play implications.

MacFarlane's law: When a number of conflicting theories coexist, any point on where they all agree is the one most likely to be wrong.

Kuhn's principle: Revolutions follow the recognition of anomalies.

Fermi's admonition: Never try to solve a problem until you can guess the answer.

Darwin's option: Without speculation, there is no good and original observation.

Grimm's law: Any rough-and-ready rule will be aggrandized automatically into a law ideal and perfect completeness.

Huxley's principle: Every day, some beautiful theory is destroyed by cruel, harsh reality.

Arrhenius's principle: Things that are said to be impossible are the most important for the progress of science.

Bohr's principle: We all agree your theory is crazy; what divides us is whether it is crazy enough to be correct.

Monod's principle: Precision encourages imagination.

Thomson's advice: Demonstrate, don't measure.

George's strategy: Vary the conditions over the widest possible range.

Langmuir's principle: Turn it on its head.

Taton's principle: Synthetic discoveries are made by those whose research is diversified.

The novice effect: Ignorance is bliss.

Burnet's advice: Do as large a proportion as possible of your experiments with your own hands.

Planck's principle: Only when I have convinced myself.

Occam's razor: Seek simplicity.

Szent-Gyorgyi's principle: Nature is parsimonious.

Dirac's principle: Seek beauty.

Maier's law: If the data don't fit the theory, ignore the data.

Agassi's law: Not all data supporting a theory are to be believed.

Richter's rule: A new theory must account for all existing data as fact or artifact.

Rosen's recollections: (1) Where does it hurt? (2) The conscious flashlight

We highlight several search strategies in boldface for emphasis. The "lost key conundrum" is familiar to many of us: Should you look for the key where the light is best, or where the key was lost? Grimm's law is a general alert, a "heads up," a primer on the abuse of oversimplification. Applied here: There is no universal law for job search or career change; that is one reason we have included so many disparate career-change narratives, so many voices, so many points of view, Rashomon style. In a country and an economy as large and diverse as ours, "everything is true and so is its opposite."

The last item on the list is common search biases. The patient was asked by the physician, "Where does it hurt?" The patient said, "It hurts here (points to head). It hurts here (points to stomach). It hurts here (points to foot)." The doctor's diagnosis: "You have a broken finger."

Suppose a flashlight were to cast its narrow beam in a darkened room. Suppose, further, that the flashlight has a "consciousness," and is asked, "In which direction do you see light?" The flashlight would have to answer, "In every direction." Victor Weisskopf said that science illuminates a part of our experience with such brilliant intensity that the rest remains in even deeper darkness.

Reflect upon how your search strategies may bias you toward or away from certain career or job directions. Notice how your information gathering is a function of your hidden assumptions, your latent premises, exercising your favorite muscles. End of digression. Now let's get practical.

I. IDENTIFY THE TARGETED EMPLOYERS.

A. Select twenty-five organizations/companies in the industries or actual activities you have chosen as a result of your career exploration research.

_____

_____

_____

_____

_____

_____

B. What are key issues/problems facing the activity, industry, specialty, or field that these targeted employers are part of? How are changes in other activities, industries, or parts of the economy affecting your target? Which of the companies/organizations you have chosen are financially successful? Which of the organizations are growing? Eliminate or practice interviewing those that are not. In a business library, seek the target's most recent annual report (foundations and other nonprofits have annual reports as well), or its 10K filing if it's a public corporation. *Standard & Poor's Register of Corporations* is useful for large corporations; *Corptech Corporate Technology Directory* is useful for small to medium-size technology companies. Look at college or university catalogs. Use periodical indexes like ABI/INFORM to get industry and company information. In *Standard & Poor's Corporate Directory,* you'll find an alphabetized list of SIC codes, mainly of products and services for all industries. Look up those products, services, or industries you wish to know more about. Using the four-digit SIC codes, you can search in the *F&S Index of Corporations and Industries* to find recent news articles from over 750 publications, arranged by SIC code and company name.

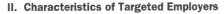

_____

_____

_____

_____

_____

_____

II. Characteristics of Targeted Employers

Now you need to find out detailed information about the companies and organizations that you have chosen. Answer the following questions for each of the ten to twenty-five most desirable organizations/companies you have identified above. Use a separate page for each. Some resources for this research can be found in the appendix.

A. What are the major products and/or services that the organization/company provides?

_____

_____

_____

B. What are its major successes? Its major problems or failures? Other issues of interest to this company or type of work?

_____

_____

_____

C. What areas of the organization/company might be able to use your skill/expertise? Who heads these areas? What information can you find out about these targeted individuals that would be useful in approaching them?

_____

_____

_____

_____

_____

_____

Don't "Go Virtual" Until You "Get Real"

You can search for employers on the Internet. Several of our career-change narrators have mentioned how they used this method.

But caveat emptor. If you don't know what you are looking for, you won't find it. (You may find something else.) So it's important to keep focused on your career options (see Section 3.08) to remind yourself in detail of what you are seeking.

The following reasons against and for using on-line search are collected to help you keep a tight focus on your job search or career-change goals.

Cons

Among the reasons _not_ to cruise the information highway for job search or career change are the following:

- Some 90 percent of useful human communication is nonverbal, and the information highway is crowded with words.

- The Net is filled with excessive or trivial information, much of it irrelevant to the career needs of many candidates.
- Sturgeons's law applies: 98 percent of *everything* is uninteresting, trivial, or useless (not the four-letter word he used).
- Life on the information highway is infinitely distracting.
- Vitally important ingredients of a successful career can be found off-line, elsewhere, face-to-face—by exercising emotional intelligence and other social skills that are essential to survival in the Darwinian job-market jungle.
- Those who develop fulfilling careers succeed because they know themselves. They've learned processes that enable them to discover how their favorite skills will dovetail with marketplace niches, and to discover how their strategies fit out there in the real world. They've adopted a fitting "theory of victory" to get where they want to be, not collected *data* and *information* when what they need is *knowledge* and *wisdom*.
- Therefore, it's necessary to "get real" before you "go virtual."

Pros

Rationales that *favor* using the Internet for career-change or job-search help include:
- On-line search for professional contacts, especially in technical and professional fields, can be done quickly and efficiently twenty-four hours a day, if you know even approximately where on the Net to look, or how to search with keywords.
- On-line search about specific geographically dispersed industries, market sectors, employers, universities, companies, and job openings can be done quickly.
- New career counseling services are becoming more readily available on-line, with new features, at increasing quality.
- Even self-assessment and other tests that answer the question, "Who are you?" can now be found on the Net (check out "Career Well-Being Inventory" for example, or Myers-Briggs, Strong Campbell, and others).
- You can easily and inexpensively learn to access and use the Internet, adding new marketable skills to your repertoire.
- On-line news groups, databases, bulletin boards, and chat groups may encourage you to post your résumé—especially useful at entry level, but see Section 3.10 first.

How-Tos

How would you (a candidate for on-line searching) proceed if you are inclined to do it? The following suggestions will make the process reasonable, practical, and fast. See the appendix for a list of practical Web sites, and an actual on-line session by a real scientist undergoing a real career transition.

1. Decide who you are (skills, interests, values, skills you most enjoy), what this implies about your career options and paths, and what strategies to adopt to reach career goals based on these options and paths, and objectify these sequential steps before you "go virtual" (Sections 3.01 to 3.08)

2. Focus the on-line activity narrowly for each step in the sequence; don't get ahead of yourself; "stay real." Use the information in Sections 3.08 and 3.09 to structure the process just as if you were doing paper, face-to-face, or phone contact research.

3. Remember, "If you don't know where you're going, you'll end up somewhere else."

4. Don't get distracted by interesting sidebars; make note of them and set aside time to explore them later.

5. Dare to search where it's hard to see, "outside the beam," not where the light is best (the lost key conundrum, the conscious flashlight).

6. The Internet illuminates part of our universe and our experience with such intensity that the remainder and most important parts may be left in even deeper—or total—darkness.

7. During the search, your predilections can bias you and your search strategies to habitual decision patterns (what you *think* you need) rather than leading to careers that appear inevitable based on your interests, (most enjoyable) skills, values, and fit. "Each of us must find and obey the demon that holds the very fiber of our being."

3.13 LETTERS: COVER, CONTACT, THANK-YOU, AND UNORTHODOX

Letters and E-Mail

Invest considerable time and thought in writing good *contact* (or "broadcast"), *cover*, and *thank-you* letters to use in your job search, because they are important marketing tools, and they represent you. *Never send form letters*; studies show their response rate is extremely low.

A contact should receive a *contact* (or "broadcast") letter *without a résumé*. If a résumé is included, the recipient or target will assume that you are asking for a job, which the target is unlikely to have. A contact letter is designed to establish contact, a prelude to a relationship. It is usually sent (or broadcast) to many technical, scientific, and engineering experts—your professional counterparts or peers—and to employers to interest them in meeting you. You do not have to include all of your résumé information in the contact letter, so you can select the material that sells you the best to that specific recipient. See example letters below, sent by a mathematician/statistician seeking an informational or contact interview about market research and a coal mining engineer looking for contacts.

A cover letter accompanies ("covers") your résumé, and is sent in response to an advertisement or other specific request for your résumé. Though shorter than the contact letter, it should not be trivial or perfunctory, and it must contain salient features of your background. Remember that your biography may be more suitable than your résumé under many information-gathering circumstances (see Section 3.10).

A thank-you letter is sent after an informational interview or a job interview. It can be a simple note or an elucidation, elaboration, or correction of some of the points raised during the interview.

A remember-me letter is sent to remind a contact that you are interested in a continuing exchange, or cultivating a relationship.

Letters have an introduction, a body, and a close. Open your letter with:

The Introduction

1. The "reference" introduction. If you have a living, breathing mutual acquaintance, mention the name, since it links you and your target instantly. See Letters 3 and 5 below.

2. The "research" introduction. If you can find a point of mutual interest (like an article written by the target or an article by you cited by the target and found by you in the *Science Citation Index*), use it to open your letter. See Letter 2 below.

3. An "accomplishment" introduction. If you have achievements from your P.A.R. (Problem, Action, Result) statements (Section 3.14) that will apply to employers (or contacts), use them. If you can prove that you are worth more to the employer than you will cost, you are hireable.

The Body

The body should support your request for a meeting.

- Emphasize your accomplishments with *measurable* quantitative results, as you did in your résumé.

- You can repeat important points from your résumé in your letter. Some employers will focus on the letter, some on the résumé.
- Limit the length of your points. (This letter is not a dissertation!)
- Say no more than is necessary to interest the target in seeing you.
- Use the "bullet" format for your accomplishments.

The Close

Use an active close to your letter. Request a meeting in a cover or broadcast letter. Tell the target when *you* will call to follow up, if possible—and then follow up at the appropriate time. Keep the ball in your court.

*L*etter 1: A Cover Letter for Answering Ads

(Résumé Enclosed)

Situation: Technical Project Leader

Dear _____ :

I found myself challenged by your advertisement inviting talented engineers to apply for your position of project leader. In addition, my qualifications match your stated preference for experience in x-ray engineering.

For the last 13 years, I have worked for General Electric. When I first joined in 1965, they were just starting up the x-ray design and application division. In the course of our growth, I have been given increasingly responsible positions, and presently enjoy a senior project leadership role.

Among my recent accomplishments have been:

- Initiated a make/buy evaluation involving a high-speed rotor controller. *Results:* Improved performance at $500,000 savings annually.
- Reevaluated a high current x-ray tube program against changing market demands. *Results:* The program was cut, saving $600,000 in development and start-up costs.

Throughout my career of 20 years, my superiors have recognized my personal commitment, creative talents, and ability to meet whatever objectives were assigned.

I am now interested in utilizing my expertise for a company that can provide new challenges and opportunity.

Enclosed you will find a résumé that provides a comprehensive summary of my experience and achievements. Realizing that a written biography cannot adequately communicate the benefits I can provide Westinghouse, I would appreciate the opportunity to speak with you personally.

Yours Truly,

[signature]

Typed Name

Enclosure

• •

Comment: Be careful. Only about 1 percent (or less) of ads responded to bring an interview, mainly because (other things being equal) hundreds of others will also respond. Also, once your résumé is circulating, that version of you is the only one recipients will believe. Your résumé is not yet as good as you are! It's *never* as good as you are.

• •

*L*etter 2: No-Resume Request for Informational Interview Letter 1

Bertram Hill
169 West 11th Street
Brooklyn, NY 10248
(718) 345-6789

September 6, 1994

Dr. George Statler
Senior Statistician
Johnson & Johnson Company
New Brunswick, NJ 07567

Dear Dr. Statler:

Your article on nonlinear statistical sampling of focus groups in the *Journal of Applied Market Research* (January 17, 1990, Vol. 6, No. 9, pp. 73–81) was extremely interesting for several reasons.

I have done similar work at Procter & Gamble, using multivariate and factor analysis, cluster techniques, and analysis of variance, with SPSS. First, I would be delighted to discuss with you the areas where our work overlaps and is similar. Second, I would like to point out that there are technical differences in the kinds of results that your methods and mine are capable of producing.

I am in the process of exploring several options and alternatives. Before I make any crucial decisions about career directions, I would like to have the benefit of expert advice like yours. Your journal article mentioned above, and others I have seen written by you, demonstrates clearly that you are an extremely knowledgeable authority in the field I have specialized in for twelve years. Therefore, I would welcome your ideas and suggestions about how my statistical skills may be applied elsewhere, and in which market research applications.

I know you must be very busy, so I will call you in the next week to see if you have a few moments to discuss these questions briefly on the phone. I look forward to our conversation.

Sincerely,

[signature]

Bertram Hill

. . . .

. . . .

*L*etter 3: No-Résumé Request for Informational Interview Letter 2

Neil Almond
Address
Address
Phone Number/Fax/E-mail

July 1, 1997

Mr. Harry Martin
Longwall Product Management
Meco International Inc.
177 Thorn Hill Road
Warrendale, PA 15086

Dear Mr. Martin:

It was a great pleasure to meet you recently at the Longwall Conference in Pittsburgh.

I regret that we had so little time to talk. I would have liked to ask your advice about which direction I should follow to offer my 25 years of experience in research and development of new longwall layouts, loading capacity calculations, ground control, stability of gate entries, general mine design, operational research, mining process optimization, and field performance testing.

Should it be in an operating company, a consulting firm, or some other possibility? I could sense from our brief conversation that you are very familiar with these matters, and that you know many other important people in the longwall mining community, especially in operating and consulting firms.

Since I am an academic, I do not have a clear idea of job descriptions, salary ranges, and the criteria used by mining and consulting companies to hire longwall R & D specialists. It is my feeling, however, that salary is secondary to the growth opportunity, and despite my extensive experience, I would accept an entry-level position in order to gain hands-on experience.

You suggested that I write to you to arrange a telephone conversation. Would it be convenient if I called you in a few weeks? If not, could you leave word with your secretary about when would be the best time?

It was a special pleasure to meet you, and I look forward to speaking with you again very soon.

Very truly yours,

[signature]

Neil Almond

P.S. My résumé is not enclosed as you asked, since it is not yet as good as I am.

• •

• •

*L*etter 4: A *"Remember-Me" Letter*

Harlow Jones
8 Center Street
Bronx, NY 13456
(718) 234-5678

December 3, 1996

Mr. John Elston
Vice President, Engineering
Royal Industries, Inc.
3456 Fordham Road
Bronx, NY 10389

Dear Mr. Elston:

Thank you very much for taking the time from your busy schedule yesterday to meet with me, and to review my job options and my job-search plans.

Your insightful comments were extremely useful. I especially appreciated your interest in me, and your willingness to let me contact other electrical engineering professionals that you know to assist me in my job search. George Smith at General Electric and Arnold Schwartz at Westinghouse sound very promising.

As we discussed, I will call you at the end of next week to see if you have been able to reach Andy Hartigan at the Excel Corporation. Andy's position and Excel's reputation make him a potentially significant professional contact for me.

Thanks again for your encouragement. I will keep you informed of my progress.

Cordially,

[signature]

Harlow Jones

• •

Note: The last sentence in the body of this letter is a presumption that the target will be interested enough in your progress to want to know more. It is one way of letting him or her know that you wish to speak regularly. Its purpose is to cement your budding relationship.

• •

*L*etter 5: A Nonorthodox Response to nn Administrative Academic Post

Ty Woodhouse
Address
Address
Phone Number/Fax/E-mail

Date

Dr. Malcolm Abramson
Associate Provost
University of Connecticut
Storrs, CT 06269

Re: Application for Position of Dean for International Affairs (Search No. 9X168**)**

Dear Provost Abramson:

I am writing to apply for the newly created position of dean for international affairs. I have had an interest in international affairs throughout my career. In addition, I am the kind of "bridge builder" you will need, as my qualifications, set forth below, will indicate.

Responsibilities of Position	My Qualifications
Carry out the responsibilities of this newly created position.	Over the years I have filled a number of newly created positions; among them, I was a founding partner of the first private law firm of women attorneys in Connecticut, and was the first director of public relations at a Ford Foundation/BOCES school for gifted students.
Supervise and coordinate a wide range of research programs involving faculty, staff, and students.	Trained and experienced in research as practicing lawyer for eight years. As law firm partner, I supervised and coordinated caseloads of many different legal matters, which required extensive research.
Serve on university's Council of Deans, report to the Provost, and make presentations to the Board of Trustees, the news media, and potential donors.	Experienced as member of significant bar association committees in metropolitan New York, Stamford, and State of Connecticut professional ethics committees. Promoted research and external funding for these programs. Prepared and delivered more than fifty speeches on topics of interest to foundations and other potential donors. Originated, wrote the scripts for, and moderated a series of local television programs; secured TV time for the series.
Supervise all contractual agreements involving foreign travel, student and faculty exchanges, and international centers.	As a supervising attorney, experienced in preparing, reviewing, revising and updating wide-ranging contractual agreements.

I hope the above will provide you with some indication of the ways in which I can carry out the responsibilities of the newly created position of dean for international affairs. As requested, my résumé is enclosed, together with references.

I would be most pleased to come to meet with you to discuss further my qualifications and the requirements of the University of Connecticut with respect to this position. I look forward to hearing from you.

Sincerely,

[signature]

Ty Woodhouse

Enclosures (2):   1. Résumé
                   2. Reference List

● ●

● ●

Letter 6: Example of a Thank-You Letter for a Job Interview

Louis Grossi
Address
Address
Phone Number/Fax/E-mail

Date

Ms. Helen Trent
Vice President
Asset Management, Inc.
553 Fifth Avenue
New York, NY 10036

Dear Helen:

Thank you for taking time from your busy schedule to meet last week. I enjoyed our discussion on Boeing's debt financing matter, and the *Barron's* article on the so-called artificial demand for airplanes. I noticed in the *Wall Street Journal* today that Boeing's latest long-term forecast predicted a 25 percent greater demand for aircraft through 2005 than Boeing foresaw last year. If that is correct, the future certainly looks bright for the company.

During our conversation, you asked me why I wanted to become a security analyst. I see it as a logical extension of my work in high-technology management. Certainly, I have enjoyed the financial and strategic aspects of my work, and would like to move into security analysis so that I could deal exclusively with those issues. An evening course gave me a solid grounding in credit analysis and public offerings. I recognize, nonetheless, that I need some training in quantitative areas and feel that Asset Management would be an excellent place to acquire that training.

My practical experience and analytical skills would be useful to AMI in evaluating companies and their strategies. Through my work, I have studied many companies' strengths. From my experience at General Motors, I understand how major corporate decisions are made. On an extracurricular basis, I have studied the stock market profitably for several years. This background would enable me to absorb AMI's training quickly and become an effective member of your team.

Thank you very much for your time and your interest.

Sincerely,

[signature]

Louis Grossi

··

··

Letter 7: Request for Informational Interview with Résumé

Casie Carmichael

Address

Address

Phone

Date

Mr. Sol Smith, Director
New York State Department of Health
88 East 44th Street
New York, NY 10016

Dear Mr. Smith:

I understand that Bud Hawkins contacted you about me, and that you are expecting this letter and the attached résumé.

As Bud told you, **I am seeking to make a career change out of corporate research and development to an administrative position, shifting from the private to the public or public-interest sector.** I had already arranged to speak with Bud about employment possibilities with health-care organizations when I saw the article in the *New York Times* about your appointment as Chairman of the Research Consortium. Bud suggested that I talk to you as well.

While my proposed career change is fairly dramatic on the surface, you will see from my résumé that I have been continuously involved as an active volunteer for public-interest organizations for the past six years.

I am looking for a job that would allow me to apply skills that I have developed primarily through my extraprofessional public-sector activities. These include designing and implementing organizational structures and strategies, helping to resolve conflicting interests at the individual and institutional levels, and making written and oral presentations. I have enjoyed applying these skills to research and development, too frequently. I am also seeking to apply those skills to a purpose that I find personally more fulfilling than corporate goals.

I would appreciate meeting with you to discuss job opportunities at the Research Consortium—or elsewhere—that you think might be appropriate for me. I will be out of town December 21 through December 28, but will call your secretary on January 4 to arrange a convenient time.

Sincerely,

[signature]

Casie Carmichael

Attachment: Résumé

• •

Note: Please observe that the boldface is a bridge from her skills, interests, and values exercises. She makes it clear why she is changing and why she will be successful at it. Mark Twain said, "Always tell the truth: You will please some people and astound the rest."

• •

*L*etter 8: "Remember-Me" Letter, Computer Support Opening

December 8, 1996

Dr. Stanley Burt
Head, Scientific Applications Group
NCI-FCRDC
P.O. Box B, Building 430
Frederick, MD 21702

Dear Dr. Burt:

Thank you for taking time from your busy schedule to talk to me about the computer support position. It was a pleasure talking to you about the position, and especially about your research. I hope you and your experimentalist colleagues are able to resolve the "flap vibration" issue in short order. I have some further thoughts that occurred to me after our meeting that may avoid the problem.

As a research scientist and a computer consultant, I have experience communicating with everyone from secretaries with a high-school education to Ph.D. researchers. Your job opening attracts me because I like working with both people and computers. I am particularly drawn to it because I see it leading to a career helping scientists get the most from their computer resources, and giving them more time to devote to research. It makes equipment and people efficient.

If you have any questions about my abilities or background, feel free to call at either phone number above. Please keep me in mind for other openings at Bethesda if this one doesn't pan out.

Sincerely,

[signature]

Typed Name

• •

• •

Letter 9: "Remember-Me" Letter, Government Affairs Position

December 8, 1996

Robert Mauro
Vice President
Technology Transition Corporation
1800 M Street, NW, Suite 300
Washington, DC 20036

Dear Mr. Mauro:

Thank you for taking time from your busy schedule to discuss Technology Transfer Corporation's (TTC's) structure and the range of possible responsibilities associated with the government affairs position. It was interesting to get a glimpse of the wide range of issues TTC must track.

Our continued reliance on fossil fuels is simply not sustainable. The silent energy crisis that is brewing will impose hefty environmental and economic costs on all countries. Although it will take decades to move to sustainable energy sources, bringing renewable energy on-line as soon as possible will substantially reduce the damage.

I would be delighted to assist TTC in bringing renewable energy sources to market by applying my writing, research, and policy skills where needed. In particular, providing government affairs services to TTC's diverse clients and affiliates will be an exciting challenge. If you need further information about my abilities or background, feel free to call me at either phone number above.

Sincerely,

[signature]

Typed Name

3.14 THE LENGTHY PROCESS OF RÉSUMÉ RESEARCH AND DEVELOPMENT

A Liability?

Your résumé can be a great *liability* in gathering contacts and persuading them to introduce you to second-, third-, and fourth-generation contacts. The reason? Most recipients of a résumé assume that the person whose résumé they are scrutinizing is asking for a job! You are going to foreclose four generations of contacts and exponentiation if your résumé scrutinizers think you are asking them for a job—simply because he or she is unlikely to have a job, and will tend to believe that any contact he or she forwards you to is unlikely to have a job. The person may also have been looking for a job, and so he or she knows, or says, that there are no jobs in his or her universe out to fourth-generation contacts. But see Section 3.10 to learn how to create a *biography* that will get you contact interviews without turning off your potential contacts and without destroying your potentially large exponentiated multigeneration contact pool.

Résumés: What Are They and How Do They Work?

Your résumé is a written communication that clearly demonstrates your ability to produce results in an area of concern, need, or demand to a potential employer—in a way that motivates him or her to want to meet you face to face. A successful résumé is defined as one that gets you an interview.

Your résumé should be a professional and accurate presentation of your work history and you at your "truest best," with a focus on your next position. Think of it as a key customized to fit a lock, and your self as a locksmith who must analyze the lock before you insert the key.

Rewrite your résumé in the vernacular of the person you want to hire you. Don't get caught up in the details. A lot of people I speak to are caught up in the fact that they're doing their Ph.D. on the DNA repair mechanism of some little mutant bacteria. They're locked into that role, as opposed to looking at what their skills are and what they like and don't like about what they're doing. Did you ever train a technician? Well, that shows you can manage people. Did you ever write a grant or help your advisor write one? That's something to put down. I translate my biochemistry in graduate school into something that sounds more environmentally related.

You always have to think from the point of view from someone who's going to be looking at you.

Employer's Résumé?

Most large corporations maintain personnel or human resource departments with a responsibility to sort through résumés looking for appropriate applicants. (We'd say they're looking for the right *keys* to fit—and open—their *locks*.) In effect, though, from our vantage point, their job is to exclude or *reject* most résumés. Now let's look at their sales or marketing departments. Their job is to include, welcome, gather, and bring in likely new clients—figuratively "embracing" potential customers.

We urge you to contact the sales or marketing department (or better yet, have someone else do so) and ask for sales literature: brochures, pamphlets, corporate annual reports, press releases, and so on. This information has been developed, usually at great expense, to help the firm generate business. It's really the corporation's "résumé," its qualifications for creating revenue.

We urge you to study the company's résumé and to select those true personal work experiences and portions of your training that are appropriate. With only slight exaggeration, the company's literature has outlined your customized new résumé for you—if you choose to design the right key that will fit into that lock. In other words, if you could write a new résumé for each job you apply for, your chances of acceptance for a job interview would be vastly increased. Of course, with modern word-processing technology you can alter your résumé and even create new ones. We would urge this résumé re-creation as an ideal goal, as a process near the end of your search when you know enough to make it as good as you are.

The Résumé: Purpose and Benefits

1. The purpose of writing your résumé is to effectively organize your work history, contributions, and key skills or abilities so that their selection and presentation are clear and concise, and support both your job objective and the employers' need.
2. It allows you to identify, articulate, and build upon your work history and achievements.
3. This written information serves as support for your job campaign and presentations. It is not a substitute for an active search.
4. A résumé is basically a written description of your work experiences, contributions, achievements, capabilities, and education.
5. An excellent résumé is like a personal advertisement.
6. It says enough about you to interest an employer—and no more.
7. It is a one- or two-page showcase for your contribution statements.
8. It is designed to help generate an interview (not a job offer) with employers you want to see.
9. The content of your résumé must arouse the curiosity of the reader and make the reader want to meet you.
10. It should communicate to others what you want to do, what you have done, and how well you have done it.
11. It may serve many purposes during your campaign:

    May be passed along to others

    Acts as an outline that helps you prepare for job interviews

    Acts as a detailed calling card

    Introduces you to potential employers who want to see it before they see you

    Gives you greater insight, self-knowledge, and self-understanding

    Acts as documentation for third parties such as search firms and agencies

    Reaffirms your positive qualities, strengths, and qualifications

    Serves as a summary that you leave behind after a job interview

12. It is often the first impression a prospective employer has of you, even though you try to use it to follow personal meetings.

13. It is essential to understand the relative importance of the résumé in your overall job search campaign. It is primarily a *supplement* to your use of personal contacts (phone calls and focus meetings), *not a substitute.*

14. It informs the reader how you have successfully contributed to other organizations' success, especially financial success. (This is why your accomplishment statements should include specific accomplishments in quantitative form.)

15. In fact, *if you can prove to any employer that you will generate more in revenue than the employer will compensate you in wages, benefits, and bonuses, you will have a job offer.*

16. As a general rule of thumb, you should avoid sending your résumé to anyone in lieu of a personal meeting.

17. Your résumé should not reveal everything about you; it should tempt and tantalize the reader, leaving much (or most) for the face-to-face meeting.

18. It provokes questions to be asked during interviews, and does *not* give all the answers.

19. Résumés that say too much allow others to make adverse judgements prior to meeting you in person.

20. Streamline "extras" such as honors, awards, professional memberships, military, community involvement, languages, hobbies, publications, and the like, to include only those that support your objective and the employer's need.

21. You can always bring up "extras" during the interview, if appropriate, and at your discretion.

22. Simply summarize any work history that goes back ten years or more under the heading "Early Experience."

23. There are no rigid rules for designing and composing a résumé; it is an *art,* not a *science.*

Résumé Do's

1. Do keep it simple, clear, and easy to read.

2. Do use short, concise sentences.

3. Do start with a first draft and expect to do several, maybe many, revisions.

4. Do state the most important information at the beginning.

5. Do focus on your special abilities.

6. Do rank-order (prioritize) and inventory your accomplishment and contribution statements.

7. Do tell the truth.

8. Do state your objective—if you have one.

9. Do be consistent in punctuation and capitalization.

10. Do use past tense throughout.

11. Do start every sentence with action verbs.

12. Do use words for numbers from one to nine.

13. Do use numerals for numbers from 10 and above.

14. Do write out complete dollar amounts: $5,700,000.

15. Do make it visually appealing.

16. Do use white (or buff) high-quality paper.

17. Do have it critiqued and proofread by *others* (spelling, grammar, and punctuation).

18. Do have a tailored or customized résumé for each employer. Remember, each résumé is like a different key that opens a unique lock and a unique door to the unique needs of a specific job opening.

19. Spend sufficient time to develop a résumé that is truly representative of your highest-level skills, a résumé that is as good as you are.

Résumé Don'ts

1. Don't use the mailing of hundreds of résumés as a substitute for an active job campaign.
2. Don't include extraneous information:
   Age, sex, national origin, race, religion, or political affiliation
   Height, weight, health, or marital status
   Hobbies or personal interests (unless related to your job objective)
   References or the phrase, "References will be furnished upon request"
   Salary history or requirements
   Reasons for leaving previous position(s)
3. Don't leave gaps between employment dates without stating a good reason for the gap.
4. Don't overemphasize your educational background (if you have been out of school for over five years, you are selling your work experience rather than your academic record).
5. Don't be modest (use your contribution statements).
6. Don't include negative information.
7. Don't use abbreviations (make it a formal document).
8. Don't include salary.
9. Don't include your photograph.
10. Don't use the phrase "responsible for . . ."
11. Don't volunteer your résumé during an informational interview. You may offer your biography. (See Section 3.10.)
12. Don't allow anyone else to write your résumé.
13. Don't use "cute" formats.
14. Don't highlight skills you no longer wish to use or have outgrown.

The Chronological Format Résumé

You outline your employment history by beginning with your most recent position and working backwards, and include your education at the end. In fact, this is "reverse chronological."

Advantages

1. This is the most widely used and accepted format.
2. It is preferred by employers who wish to have a complete and detailed account of a candidate's work experience.

3. It is logical and easy to follow.

4. It presents your background in a straightforward and clear-cut manner, thus enabling the reader to quickly size up your background.

5. It emphasizes career growth and continuity.

6. It highlights names of employers or companies (especially if they are prestigious).

7. Use it if you are staying in the same or a related field.

8. Use it if you have a stable work history with no unexplainable gaps.

Disadvantages

1. It may not play up your major contributions if they did not occur in your most recent job.

2. It presents you as an X when the employer may need a Y, especially if you are changing fields.

3. It is not useful when your work history is spotty.

4. It highlights frequent changes of employers or unexplainable employment gaps.

5. It draws the reader's attention *to*, rather than *away from*, your lack of experience.

Elements to Include in Each Variant or Version of Your Chronological Resume

1. Name: full and formal (no nicknames).

2. Home address.

3. Telephone number(s): home, office (if still appropriate), or message center.

4. Job objective: one sentence (only if you have a specific one).

5. Summary statement: two or three sentences (optional).

6. Work experience.

Start with the name of the most recent firm, company, or organization, and its city and state (then work backwards)

Dates employed (usually years without months)

Job title or function (their words or yours)

Major contribution statements (rank-ordered and appropriate job title)

7. Education (highest level attained first, such as graduate school; include education below college only if it supports your job objective).

Name of institution

Degree

Major (optional)

Location (optional)

Year of graduation (optional)

8. Other (all optional).

Personal

Hobbies/interests

Professional memberships

Awards/honors

Publications (separate page) and presentations

You may mention the number of publications you have on the one-page résumé, and on separate additional pages present a list of all of your presentations and publications, or a list of selected ones if the list is too long. (A CV may include all publications, presentations, and honors.)

PAR Statements

Each résumé has a specific *objective*, or purpose—to fit a specific job opening—and that objective must be supported by *facts*: facts about your education, training, and experience; facts about your accomplishments:

- **Problem** presented to you by a prior employer, a research challenge, a mentor's assignment, and so on
- **Action** you decided to take to solve the problem, what you did
- **Results** and benefits to the employer, especially *financial* benefits that are clear, specific, and quantitative, if possible; publication of an article is of less interest to a for-profit organization than saving money, reducing staff, improving a process's efficiency, and so on.

So each résumé resembles, conceptually, a pyramid, where the objective is supported by the facts. (See the résumé examples, at the end of this section.)

The best way to present your accomplishments is the following:

Try to quantify your results, indicating time or labor saved, percentage (of something tangible) increased, and so on. Begin with an action verb (see the list that follows). Below are some examples.

- Saved division over $1.37 million in production costs by developing new technical improvements to a chemical process plant.

- Developed mathematical software that automated the presentation of algebraic equations.

- Invented a method to cut titanium at triple the previous rate while extending the life of the cutting tools to weeks from hours.

- Reorganized research laboratory procedures so that overall productivity increased by 17 percent annually.

- Persuaded a granting agency to fund a critical research project at a level of $185,000 per year for three years.

- Developed special workshops that increased the number of students who secured competitive scholarships by 18 percent.

- Proved that human heptoma cells could be stimulated with recombinant interleukin.

*A*ction Verbs for Résumés and PAR Statements

Created	Obtained	Served
Instructed	Purchased	Compounded
Corresponded	Oversaw	Rendered
Negotiated	Installed	Counseled
Planned	Reduced (losses)	Received
Sold	Routed	Built
Completed	Audited	Detected
Designed	Coordinated	Selected
Consulted	Researched	Recommended
Evaluated	Implemented	Distributed
Calculated	Presented	Arranged
Identified	Instituted	Disproved
Performed	Directed	Developed
Constructed	Managed	Edited
Controlled	Eliminated	Wrote
Dispensed	Provided	Analyzed
Formulated	Solved	Produced
Improved	Determined	Conducted
Tested	Collected	Delivered
Protected	Referred	Founded

Assisted	Organized	Reviewed
Obtained	Increased	Established
Studied	Expanded	Scheduled
Consolidated	Trained	Systematized
Ordered	Devised	Guided
Invented	Supplied	Recruited
Diagnosed	Prepared	Conceived
Examined	Maintained	Catalogued
Lectured	Interpreted	Reshaped
Processed	Administered	Moderated
Reviewed	Interviewed	Expanded
Translated	Advised	Enlarged
Prescribed	Discovered	Contracted
Charted	Restored	Straightened
Represented	Conserved	Approved
Promoted	Arbitrated	Investigated
Recorded	Criticized	Originated
Operated	Assembled	Governed
Supervised	Realized	Presided
Drew up	Navigated	Rectified

For your current job, produce at least three "PAR" statements here:

....

PAR STATEMENT NUMBER 1

Problem: _____

Action: _____

Result: _____

PAR STATEMENT NUMBER 2

Problem: _____

Action: _____

Result: _____

PAR STATEMENT NUMBER 3

Problem: _____

Action: _____

Result: _____

• •

Using a separate sheet, write at least three PAR statements for each of your two prior jobs.

Follow the same format for each job. If you are finding it difficult to write the PAR statement, go through this exercise with a friend, colleague, or career counselor (one who can often offer an objective view) to help you form your PAR statements.

You now have the most difficult part of your résumé completed. Which of your PAR statements most closely match the requirements of the jobs you are seeking? Develop a detailed list of a job's specifications based upon your informational interviews (Section 3.09) and job-search research (Section 3.12). Call this *characteristics of the job you will be applying for*. Now, rank-order the PAR statements (for each job you have had) according to how well they match the characteristics. Place them on the résumé outline below in the order you have selected. You can eliminate some if they do not fit well into the characteristics of the prospective position. Also fill in the dates of employment, job title, company name, address.

A short statement of your employment experience may also enhance your résumé by summarizing the most salient aspects of your background and integrating your experience. This is most easily written *after* you have completed all the other parts of your résumé. (See résumé outline for placement.) For an example of summary statement, see Résumé Example 1 (Kevin Aylesworth). An objective may also be useful if the type of job you are seeking is not obvious from your background. See Résumé Examples 4, 5, and 6.

Review all your résumé outline sheets. Ask yourself, "Does my presentation market what I have to offer most effectively for the type of jobs I want?" Since there is no rigid format for a résumé, feel free to adjust, alter, or fine-tune your presentation to meet your needs. Because everyone has weaknesses, it is advisable to rearrange your résumé to emphasize your strengths, as has been done on all the example résumés. For instance in Résumé 4, experience appears before education to highlight people and business skills.

Notice how Kevin Aylesworth's three examples (Résumés 1, 2, and 3) show different strengths. Example #1 is Kevin as a computer consultant, emphasizing his technical expertise: design, administering, and installation experience, operating systems, software, and hardware capabilities. He does not even mention his Ph.D. in this version of his "best and truest self." Example 2 shows Kevin as a science policy person, featuring his work as a Congressional Fellow, and his testimony, book, and articles on the training and employment of scientists. He barely mentions his metamorphosis from computer person to policy expert. Example 3 shows Kevin's CV in more or less standard form, with all of his activities, including offices, committees, policy publications, invited talks, selected papers presented at meetings, and technical publications truncated. In a short version of the CV, one would list salient publications only.

The method of résumé development we use has been found to be very effective because its focus on your accomplishments shows the potential employer how you can meet his or her needs.

. . . .

R*ésumé Outline* (Make Photocopies)

Name _____

Address _____
            City   State   Zip Code

Home (   ) _____

Business/messages (optional) (   ) _____

Objective (optional)

_____

_____

Summary (optional)

_____

_____

1993–Present

_____

Company   City/state   Dates employed

_____

Dates   Job title

One-sentence description of job:

_____

_____

_____

_____

Contribution (PAR) statements (rank-ordered):

• _____

   _____

• _____

   _____

• _____

   _____

1989–1993

_____

Company   City/state   Dates employed

Dates   Job title

One-sentence description of job:

_____

_____

_____

_____

_____

Contribution (PAR) statements (rank-ordered):

• _____

  _____

• _____

  _____

• _____

  _____

1981–1989

Company   City/state   Dates employed

Dates   Job title

One-sentence description of job:

_____

_____

_____

_____

Contribution (PAR) statements (rank-ordered):

• _____

  _____

• _____

  _____

• _____

  _____

Education

Graduate school   Diploma/degree

Location   Year of graduation

College/university   Diploma/degree

Location   Major (optional)   Year of graduation

Other education, if relevant

Memberships (include societies)

_____

_____

_____

_____

_____

Personal/hobbies (optional)

_____

_____

_____

_____

_____

Awards/honors

_____

_____

_____

_____

_____

_____

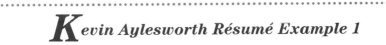

K*evin Aylesworth Résumé Example 1*

(My Computer Résumé)

KEVIN DONALD AYLESWORTH
myaccount@myprovider.com
100 My Street
My City, MS 11111
(999) 555-1234 (home)
(999) 555-3456 (work)

SUMMARY A versatile professional with a graduate science degree and self-developed techni cal expertise. Proven self-starter with excellent communication and customer service skills and an aptitude for learning quickly.

SELECTED EXPERIENCE

Networking

- Designed and administered an eight-node (5 PC and 3 Macintosh clients) Novell NetWare 3.12 network with ISDN and standard dial-in remote connections.
- Administered a three-node NetWare 3.11 network.
- Installed and supported a two-node Personal NetWare network and a two-node Windows for Workgroups network.
- Installed and configured SLIP and PPP Internet dial-up software and Internet tools, including Trumpet Winsock Netscape Web Browser, Mosaic Web Browser, Pegasus Mail, Eudora, CCMail, Trumpet Tel.

Operating Systems

MS-DOS	Windows 3.X	Macintosh
Windows95	OS/2	VMS
RT-11	RSX-11M	

Software

WordPerfect 5.X for DOS	Access 2.0	LapLink
WordPerfect 5.X for Windows	WinFax 4.0	PCAnywhere
WordPerfect 6.X for DOS	Paradox	Ascend
WordPerfect 6.X for Windows	MS-Works	Corel Draw
Excel 5.0	Close-Up	Quicken

Hardware

Laptop PCs	Desktop PCs	Printers
Modems	Scanners	Memory
Video boards	Monitors	CD-ROMs
Math coprocessors	Hard disks	Sound Cards
Network interface cards	Backup devices	Pointing Devices

EMPLOYMENT HISTORY

September 1995 to present   **American Physical Society Congressional Science Fellow**
Office of Senator Tom Harkin, Washington, DC

September 1992 to September 1995   **Owner/Operator**
Aylesworth Technical Services, Cambridge, MA

January 1990 to September 1992   **National Research Council Postdoctoral Fellow**
Naval Research Laboratory, Washington, DC

*K*evin Aylesworth Resume Example 2

(My Policy Résumé)

KEVIN DONALD AYLESWORTH
myaccount@myprovider.com
100 My Street
My City, MS 11111
(999) 555-1234 (home)
(999) 555-3456 (work)

EXPERIENCE

Developed policy on energy, disarmament, defense, and veterans' issues for Senator Tom Harkin. Wrote legislation and briefing papers. Interacted with constituents and interest groups.

Testified before two House committees and participated in five panel discussions on the issues of employment and training of scientists.

Co-authored a book and authored three articles on the need to develop a career spectrum for scientists. Founded the Young Scientists' Network to alert the physics community to the deteriorating basic research job market. Authored numerous published letters on the job market for scientists.

Advised the lead counsel for Daubert in the 1992 Supreme Court case Daubert v. Merrell Dow Pharmaceuticals.

POLICY PUBLICATIONS

Kevin Aylesworth, "Is 'Science Policy' an Oxymoron? Science's Next Wave, http://sci.aaas.org/nextwave/oldforums/training/aylesworth/ayleswo rth.html (October 1995).

Sheila Tobias, Daryl E. Chubin, and Kevin Aylesworth, "Rethinking Science as a Career: Perceptions and Realities in the Physical Sciences," Research Corporation, Tucson, AZ (1995).

Kevin Aylesworth, "What Scientist Shortage?" *Connection,* 9, 31 (1994).

Kevin Aylesworth, "The Shortage Myth," *APS News,* 2, 17 (1993).

Kevin Aylesworth, "'The Myth' vs. The Truth," *Newsweek* Focus, 8 (August 16, 1993).

EMPLOYMENT HISTORY

September 1995 to present   **American Physical Society Congressional Fellow**   Office of Senator Tom Harkin (D-Iowa), Washington, DC

December 1993 to September 1995   **Owner/Operator**
Aylesworth Technical Services, Cambridge, MA

September 1992 to December 1993   **Technical Consultant/Paralegal**
Kenneth J. Chesebro, Esq., Cambridge, MA

January 1990 to September 1992   **National Research Council Postdoctoral Associate**
Naval Research Lab, Washington, DC

AFFILIATIONS	American Physical Society
	Commission on Professionals in Science and Technology
	American Institute of Physics
AWARDS AND HONORS	American Physical Society Forum Award, 1996
	American Physical Society Congressional Fellowship, 1995
	National Research Council—Naval Research Lab Postdoctoral Associateship, 1990

EDUCATION

University of Nebraska	1989	Ph.D.	Physics
	1986	M.S.	Physics
University of Wisconsin—Stevens Point	1983	B.S.	Physics and Chemistry

•••

•••

K*evin Aylesworth CV Example 3*

(My CV)

KEVIN DONALD AYLESWORTH
myaccount@myprovider.com
100 My Street
My City, MS 11111
(999) 555-1234 (home)
(999) 555-3456 (work)

Education	**Ph.D. Physics, University of Nebraska** **1989**
	Dissertation: Magnetic and Structural Properties of Cosputtered Rare Earth-Iron-Boron Permanent Magnet Films
	M.S. Physics, University of Nebraska **1986**
	Thesis: Electronic Properties of Sputtered Ta-Cu Thin Films
	B.S. Physics and Chemistry, Math Minor, University of Wisconsin—Stevens Point **1983**
Summary of Qualification:	Diverse use of physics-related skills in government, law, computer consulting, and research. Strong networking and marketing skills. Excellent working relationships with clients and coworkers. Able to work independently and as part of a team.
Experience	Co-authored "Rethinking Science as a Career: Perceptions and Realities in the Physical Sciences." Wrote articles for *Newsweek, APS News,* and *Connection* on the need to develop a career spectrum for scientists. Founded the Young Scientists' Network to alert the physics community to the deteriorating basic research job market. Testified before two House committees and participated in four panel discussions on the issues of employment and training of scientists. Developed policy on defense, disarmament,

energy, and veterans' issues for Senator Tom Harkin. Wrote legislation and briefing papers. Interacted with constituents and interest groups. Ran a computer and network consulting business for three years. Analyzed customers' needs based on interviews, and designed computer systems and software procedures to meet their needs. Advised the lead counsel for Daubert in the 1992 Supreme Court case Daubert v. Merrell Dow Pharmaceuticals. Conducted basic and applied research in magnetic thin films and multilayers. Designed, constructed, and operated a variety of vacuum, cryogenic, mechanical and electronic devices. Authored or co-authored 17 papers published in peer-reviewed journals and presented 12 talks on the research.

Professional Memberships   American Association for the Advancement of Science
American Physical Society
Sigma Pi Sigma

Awards and Honors   American Physical Society Forum Award   1996
American Physical Society Congressional Fellowship   1995
National Research Council—Naval Research Lab
    Postdoctoral Associateship   1990
UNL Physics Department Distinguished Teaching Assistant   1986
UWSP Physics Student of the Year   1983
Bendix Award for Undergraduate Research in Physics   1982

Employment History

September 1995 to present   **American Physical Society Congressional Fellow**
                                                                Office of Senator Tom Harkin (D-Iowa), Washington, DC

December 1993 to September 1995   **Owner/Operator**
                                                                Aylesworth Technical Services, Cambridge, MA

September 1992 to December 1993   **Technical Consultant/Paralegal**
                                                                Kenneth J. Chesebro, Esq., Cambridge, MA

January 1990 to September 1992   **National Research Council Postdoctoral Associate**
                                                                Naval Research Lab, Washington, DC

Offices and Committees

Member, American Physical Society Executive Board   1996
General Councillor, American Physical Society   1994–Present
Member, American Institute of Physics Advisory Committee of the Career
    Planning and Placement Division   1994–Present
Member, External Advisory Group, Commission on Professionals in Science
    and Technology Project on the S&E Job Market for Recent Doctoral Graduates 1996
Student Member, UNL Graduate Council   1988
Graduate Representative, UNL Student Activities Board   1988
Graduate Student Member, UNL Physics Department Program Review Team   1988
Student Member, UNL Physics Department Graduate Committee   1987–1988
Associate Councillor, Zone 8 of the Society of Physics Students   1983
President, UWSP chapter of the Society of Physics Students   1982–1983

Policy Publications

1. Kevin Aylesworth, "Is 'Science Policy' an Oxymoron? Science's Next Wave," http://
    sci.aaas.org/nextwave/oldforums/training/aylesworth/aylesworth.html (October 1995).

2. Sheila Tobias, Daryl E. Chubin, and Kevin Aylesworth, "Rethinking Science as a Career: Perceptions and Realities in the Physical Sciences," Research Corporation, Tucson, AZ (1995).
3. Kevin Aylesworth, "What Scientist Shortage?" *Connection,* 9, 31 (1994).
4. Kevin Aylesworth, "The Shortage Myth," *APS News,* 2, 17 (1993).
5. Kevin Aylesworth, " 'The Myth' vs. The Truth," *Newsweek* Focus, 8 (August 16, 1993).

Selected Research Publications

1. J. E. Oh, J. A. Woollam, K. D. Aylesworth, D. J. Sellmyer, and J. J. Pouch, Thermal and Structural Stability of Cosputtered Amorphous Taxcu1-X Alloy Thin Films on Gas, *J. Appl. Phys.* 60, 4281 (1986).
2. K. D. Aylesworth, S. S. Jaswal, M. A. Engelhardt, Z. R. Zhao, and D. J. Sellmyer, Electronic Structure and Properties of Sputtered Ta-Cu Films, *Phys. Rev.* B 37, 2426 (1988).
3. J. Strzeszewski, A. Nazareth, G. C. Hadjipanayis, K. Aylesworth, Z. R. Zhao, and D. J. Sellmyer, Microstructure Studies in Nd2(Fe0.9Co0.1)14B Thin Films, *Mat. Sci. Eng.* 99, 153 (1988).
4. Z. R. Zhao, Y. G. Ren, K. D. Aylesworth, D. J. Sellmyer, E. Singleton, J. Strzeszewski, and G. C. Hadjipanayis, Magnetic Properties of Rapidly Quenched and Annealed Fe10RTi and Related Alloys, *J. Appl. Phys.* 63, 3699 (1988).

Invited Talks

1. K. D. Aylesworth, D. J. Sellmyer, and G. C. Hadjipanayis, Magnetization Reversal in Pr2Fe14B:Pr Cosputtered Films, Naval Research Lab, Washington, DC (1989).
2. K. D. Aylesworth, Magnetic and Structural Properties of Sputtered Films and Multi Layers, University of Wisconsin—Stevens Point, Stevens Point, WI (1991).
3. N. C. Koon, K. D. Aylesworth, V. G. Harris, and B. N. Das, Magnetic Properties of Amorphous Antiferromagnetic Superlattice Films, 19th Rare Earth Research Conference, Lexington, KY (1991).
4. V. G. Harris, K. D. Aylesworth, W. T. Elam, and N. C. Koon, Correlation Between Structure and Magnetic an Isotropy of Amorphous Fe-Tb Films, 19th Rare Earth Research Conference, Lexington, KY (1991).
5. K. D. Aylesworth, Magnetic and Structural Properties of Sputtered Films and Multi Layers, Miami University, Oxford, OH (1992).
6. K. D. Aylesworth, V. G. Harris, N. C. Koon, W. T. Elam, Magnetic Properties of Exchange-Coupled Multi Layers, 3M Optical Recording Department, Vadnais Heights, MN (1992).

Selected Papers Presented at Meetings

1. K. D. Aylesworth, D. J. Sellmyer, J. E. Oh, J. A. Woollam, Z. Zhao, and K. Xie, Electronic and Structural Properties of Cosputtered TaxCu1-x Films, *Bull. Am. Phys. Soc.* 31, 488 (1986), A.P.S. Meeting, Las Vegas, NV.
2. J. E. Oh, J. A. Woollam, K. D. Aylesworth, D. J. Sellmyer, and J. Pouch, Annealing Effects on Electrical Resistivities and Microstructures of Sputter-Deposited TaxCu1-x Alloys, *Bull. Am. Phys. Soc.* 31, 489 (1986), A.P.S. Meeting, Las Vegas, NV.
3. J. E. Oh, J. A. Woollam, K. D. Aylesworth, D. J. Sellmyer, and J. Pouch, High-Temperature Stability of Amorphous TaxCu1-x Diffusion Barriers on Gas, Materials Res. Soc. Meeting, Boston, MA (1986).
4. K. D. Aylesworth, D. J. Sellmyer, Z. R. Zhao, and S. S. Jaswal, Electron Localization and Electronic Structure of Sputtered TaCu Films, *Bull. Am. Phys. Soc.* 32, 690 (1987); A.P.S. Meeting, New York, NY.

• •

*R*ésumé Example 4

ROY G. BIV
5 Riverside Court
New York, NY 10025
Tel: xxx-xxx-xxxx   Fax: xxx-xxx-xxxx
E: RGB@aol.com

Seeking a position with opportunities to lead the profitable advancement and commercialization of technology, to bring people to their fullest potential, and to develop global business ventures.

CAREER SUMMARY

Self-motivated, Ph.D.-level Leader and Technologist with well-developed people and business-development skills and accomplished in the following areas:

• Troubleshoot manufacturing problems and technology issues to save time and millions of dollars
• Formed pro-active Customer-Supplier Partnerships and technical liaisons to create new products and resolve quality issues
• Provide critical support to numerous successful business and technology initiatives involving polymers, composites and their base raw materials
• Leadership through community service and adult education

EMPLOYMENT HISTORY

ATHENS MOLDING AND DIE, INC., Athens, GA   **1994–Present**
A Tier-One supplier of prototypes, tools and plastic automotive components to Toyota Motor Company
Testing Laboratory Coordinator 1997–Present   **Senior Materials Engineer 1994–1996**

• Conceived, designed and built first corporate material science laboratory ($140,000 project)
• Administered corporate testing laboratory with $1,200,000 in annual sales and eight technicians
• Organized in-house training classes for technicians and other employees
• Improved usage and prevented material price increases for photopolymer used in rapid-prototyping ($100,000+ in cost-savings)
• Interfaced with non-performing suppliers to reduce quality-related raw material issues ($400,000+ in cost-savings)
• Arranged cost-free access to major scientific instrumentation at Toyota Scientific Research Laboratories ($3,000 cost-savings per day of use)
• Conducted $200,000+ R&D program to make car parts from post-consumer recyclate materials
• Conducted $170,000 State of Ohio-funded R&D program to develop workable adhesives for hard-to-bond plastics like polypropylene and polyethylene
• Eliminated unsightly tarnishing problem on the brass cladding of newly-installed tempered glass doors ($400,000+ in cost-savings for external customer)

OWENS-CORNING FIBERGLAS, Athens, GA   **1986–1994**
A major producer of insulation, construction products, fiberglass reinforcements and polyesters.
Senior Scientist

• Resolved multiple complex issues dealing with industrial hygiene, manufacture, curing and shelf-life of phenolic resins ($2,000,000+ in total savings)
• Related cracking and poor cure in tub-shower units and boat hulls ($1,000,000+ in total savings)
• Solved insulation manufacturing problem involving oil-water emulsions ($100,000 in savings)
• Identified a catalyst critical to the development of alternative polymer binder systems for fiberglass mats and insulation

- Identified novel urethane-based materials with enhanced durability for use in cutters for glass fibers ($50,000+ in annual savings)

DOW CORNING CORPORATION, Corning, NY   **1980–1986**
A leading producer of silicone rubbers, sealants, adhesives, resins and organosilicon intermediates.
Analytical Specialist 1983–1986   **Project Chemist 1980–1983**

- Resolved customer acceptance issues for materials used in anti-freeze and adhesive formulations
- Established Dow Corning's first multi-nuclear NMR laboratory ($250,000+ project)

INTERNATIONAL EXPERIENCE

Working Knowledge of Spanish, German and French
- US Citizen willing to relocate overseas

Widely-Traveled with the Following as Countries of Experience:
- Netherlands, Belgium, England, France, Germany, Scotland, Colombia, Hong Kong, Puerto Rico, Bahamas, Martinique, French and English-speaking Canada.

Consultant, Rapid Design Service, Inc., Dayton, OH   **1994–1995**
- Translated German-language technical (automotive) documents into English

Excel Program, Junior Chamber International, San Juan, PR   **1990**
- Attained Certified National Trainer status through intensive training in the methods of adult education

Research Associate, University of Nijmegen, Nijmegen, The Netherlands   **1979–1980**
- Performed research in solid-phase P-31 NMR in the Department of Molecular Spectroscopy

ACCOMPLISHMENTS IN COMMUNITY AND PROFESSIONAL LEADERSHIP

Junior Chamber of Commerce

- Organized charity fund-raising and distribution programs for Christmas food baskets to over 200 needy families and relief supplies to Mississippi flood victims
- Increased overall fund-raising for Local Chapter by $100,000+ through creative initiatives; including large-scale Haunted Houses and entertainment events
- Received numerous awards for contributions; including Senator status, life-time membership and the Seiji Horiuchi Award
- Held multiple offices; including Local Chapter President and State Organization Vice-President, Program Manager and Training Director

Educational and Training Activities

- Taught leadership and human relationship skills to high school and college students and prison inmates through various Junior Chamber programs
- Taught basic business practices to fifth-graders via the Junior Achievement organization
- Coordinated seminars on subjects like doing business in the former Soviet Union, food science and medical imaging as Local Program Chairman for the American Chemical Society
- Taught in evening classes in Introductory Chemistry for Saginaw Valley State University

Received Other Recognition for Technical, Educational and Service Accomplishments, Including:
- O. F. Stambaugh Alumni Award from Elizabethtown College, Elizabethtown, PA
- Technical Achievement Award from Dow Corning Corporation, Corning, NY

Co-author of Five Publications and Invited Guest Speaker

EDUCATION

Executive MBA, University of Athens, Athens, GA   **1998**
- Program emphasizes creation of new business ventures, global competitiveness and management of technology

Ph.D., Chemistry, MIT   **1980**
Ms., Chemistry, MIT   **1977**
Bs., Chemistry, Harvard College   **1975**

··

··

R *ésumé Example 5 For Job 1*

VICTOR RELS
20 Calvin Court
Brooklyn, NY 11214
(800) 555-1212

OBJECTIVE   To apply and develop mathematical methods of operations research and data processing for increased efficiency of technical systems.

FIELD OF EXPERTISE Operation research, random processes, data processing, programming languages FORTRAN, PL/1, BASIC.

EXPERIENCE

1986–1989   **Associate Professor, Department of Mathematics, Purdue University,** West Lafayette, IN.
- Taught operations research, applied statistical methods, theory of reliability.
- Investigated methods of optimization for technical systems.

1979–1986   **Senior Research Associate, Electronics R&D Center,** Pittsburgh, PA.
- Managed research group for development and application of optimal systems of control and data processing for industrial manufacturing.
- Designed and implemented the interaction between research group and plants.
- Supervised the research lab of 11 graduate mathematicians and programmers.
- Performed research on optimal rank procedures for data processing and control systems.

1974–1979   **Junior Research Associate, Electronics R&D Center,** Pittsburgh, PA.
- Performed research and development of optimal algorithms of data processing for rapid testing of technical systems.

EDUCATION

1974–1979   **Ph.D., Purdue University,** West Lafayette, IN.
Degree in Cybernetics and Theory of Information.

1969–1974   **M.S., University of Pittsburgh,** Pittsburgh, PA.
Degree in Applied Mathematics.

PUBLICATIONS   Over twenty articles in the fields listed above.

LANGUAGES   English, Russian

Résumé Example 6 For Job 2

VICTOR RELS
20 Calvin Court
Brooklyn, NY 11214
(800) 555-1212

OBJECTIVE　　Application of statistical analysis, implementation of data management, and development of statistical software for enhancing the efficiency of technical and manufacturing systems.

FIELD OF EXPERTISE　　Statistical data processing, stochastic processes, applied statistics, theory of reliability.
Hardware: ES1040 (similar to IBM/360), SM2 (similar to PDP/7).
Software: FORTRAN, PL/1 (environment OS/MVS), C, UNIX.

EXPERIENCE

1986–1989　　**Senior Research Associate, College of Civil Engineering, Purdue University,** West Lafayette, IN.
Activities: Conducted several contract research projects for the Railroad Division:
– Application of the statistical algorithms for the data processing of railroad traffic.
– Implementation of the statistical analysis for the forecasting of the railroad track conditions.

1974–1986　　**Senior Research Associate, Electronics R&D Center,** Pittsburgh, PA.
Activities: Managed the research team for development and application of software for control systems and data processing.
– Conducted several contract projects for the electronics industry.
– Development of the statistical software for the data processing for rapid testing of microcircuits at the electronics plant.
– Implementation of the software for the quality control system of electronic apparatus at the electronics plant.
– Development and implementation of the software for data processing for testing microcircuits at the radio engineering plant.

Research
– Invention of statistical rank procedures for measurement and classification of microcircuit parameters.
– Investigation and probability modeling of the operation of the microcircuit groups.

EDUCATION

1974　　**University of Pittsburgh,** Pittsburgh, PA.
M.S. Thesis: "Development of Algorithms and Computer Programs for Testing of Statistical Hypotheses." Degree conferred with departmental honors. Five years of intensive training in Computer Science.

PUBLICATIONS　　Six articles in the above-mentioned areas published and available upon request.

*R*ésumé Example 7 For Job 3

GEORGE ESSLER, Ph.D.
2424 Benson Avenue
Brooklyn, NY 11214
(718) 714-4301

STATISTICIAN—INDUSTRIAL RESEARCH

A Ph.D. Applied Statistician with strong mathematical background and 15 years of consulting and teaching experience in an industrial and educational environment. Experience includes research and development of the algorithms and programs for data processing and quality control systems software. Major technical expertise is in statistical analysis, probability modeling, stochastic processes, theory of reliability, FORTRAN, PL/I.

EDUCATION

Baruch College, CUNY, New York, New York, 1990. Study of Statistical Analyses Software (SAS package) with practical application.

Ph.D. in Applied Statistics from Purdue University, West Lafayette, IN, 1979. *Dissertation:* "Nonparametric Methods of Estimation for Quality Control of Microcircuits."

M.S. in Applied Mathematics from University of Pittsburgh, Pittsburgh, PA, 1974. *Thesis:* "Spline-approximation of Probability Distributions for Hypotheses Testing." Degree conferred with departmental honors.

EXPERIENCE

Associate Professor, Civil Engineering, Purdue University, West Lafayette, IN, 1986 to 1989.

> *Consulting activities:* Designed and analyzed conditions of railroad tracks for the North West Railroad Division utilizing analysis of time series. Developed the mathematical models for the replacement of the railroad device units, applying theory of stochastic processes. Provided guidance on statistical methods for two civil engineering Ph.D. candidates.
> *Teaching activities:* Carried a full teaching load in Applied Statistics and Probability Modeling courses.

Senior Research Associate, Electronics R&D Center, Pittsburgh, PA, 1974 to 1986.

> *Activities:* Managed the research team of 11 graduate mathematicians and programmers for development and application of software for data processing and quality control systems. The trading of this software resulted in annual profit of $67,000. Conducted three R&D contract projects for the electronics industry on implementation of the statistical software leading, to a savings of six man-years of effort. Developed the mathematical model for the rapid testing of microcircuits, which reduced the testing duration by an average of 25% and resulted in an annual savings of $45,000.

ADDITIONAL INFORMATION

Publications: Over twenty papers:
- 2 papers on various aspects of nonparametric estimation.
- 3 papers on stochastic models of the elements' group behavior.
- 1 paper on probability modeling.

Activities: Executive director of "Student Research and Business Group."

*R*ésumé Example 8

ROBERT RICH

1740 Lexington Avenue
El Cerrito, CA 94530

(510) 215-8393
basset@fire.cchem.berkeley.edu

OBJECTIVE: An entry-level postdoctoral organic chemistry research position at a pharmaceutical or biotechnical firm.

SUMMARY OF QUALIFICATIONS

- Can plan and execute complex multistep syntheses of organic compounds.
- Familiar with NMR, IR, and UV-Visible spectroscopic techniques.
- Experienced in HPLC, GC, TLC, ionexchange, and silica chromatography.
- Strong background in computer-aided drug design, enzymology, and combinatorial chemistry.
- Leadership experience and team-oriented approach to large projects.

EDUCATION

Ph.D., Chemistry, *University of California, Berkeley,* 1995

Research Director: Professor Paul A. Bartlett.
Thesis Title: "Synthesis and Evaluation of 2-Haloshikimic Acid Derivatives as Substrate Analogs for the Enzymes of the Shikimate Pathway."

Graduate Student Researcher, 1991–1995
Graduate Student Instructor, 1991–1993

M.A., Chemistry, *Harvard University,* 1991

Research Director: Professor Jeremy R. Knowles.
Research Topic: Enzymes of the shikimic acid pathway.

Teaching Assistant, 1990
National Institutes of Health Biomedical Research Training Grant, 1991

S.B., Chemistry, *Massachusetts Institute of Technology,* 1990

Research Directors: Professor Steven R. Tannenbaum & Dr. Dagmar Ringe.
Research Topic: Chemical analysis of dilute carcinogenic metabolites in the bloodstream.

Undergraduate Teaching Assistant, 1990
Research Assistant, 1988–1990
Undergraduate Researcher, 1988

ACADEMIC AWARDS & HONORS

Received Department of Chemistry **Alpha Chi Sigma Award** in recognition of outstanding achievement in research, scholarship & service (M.I.T., 1990).

Elected to Sigma Xi and Phi Lambda Upsilon **scientific honor societies.**

SCIENTIFIC PUBLICATIONS

"Synthesis of (–)-2-Chloroshikimic Acid"
R.H. Rich, B. M. Lawrence, P. A. Bartlett
J. Org. Chem. **59,** 693–4 (1994).

"Human Serum Albumin-Benzo[a]pyrene *anti*-Diol Epoxide Adduct Structure Elucidation by Fluorescence Line Narrowing Spectroscopy"
B. W. Day, M. M. Doxtader, R. H. Rich, P. L. Skipper, R. R. Dasari, S. R. Tannenbaum *Chem. Res. Toxicol.* **5,** 71–6 (1992).

"Conversion of a Hemoglobin ∝ Chain Asparate (47) Ester to N-(2,3-Dihydroxypropyl)asparagine as a Method for Identification of the Principal Binding Site for Benzo[a]pyrene *anti*-Diol Epoxide"
B. W. Day, P. L. Skipper, R. H. Rich, S. Naylor, S. R. Tannenbaum
Chem. Res. Toxicol. **4,** 359–63 (1991).

EXTRACURRICULAR HIGHLIGHTS

Board of Directors, *Jewish Federation of the Greater East Bay,* 1994–1995

- Represents regional Jewish community as fiduciary of multi-million-dollar nonprofit philanthropic organization.

Mentor, *McNair Scholars Program,* 1993–1994

- Provided daily supervision of undergraduate minority student pursuing an independent research project and academic enrichment work.

Chair, *The Jewish Renaissance: Revitalizing Our Community,* 1993–1994

- Conceived, organized, planned, and executed day-long conference for 250 young adults. Convened and chaired organizing committee for the conference and supervised all aspects of preparation.

Founder & Coordinator, *M.I.T. Chemistry Magic Show,* 1988–1990

- Successfully led a group of undergraduate students to initiate a science outreach program directed at elementary students.
- Generated an exciting program of demonstrations, appropriate explanations, and follow-up materials to enrich the scientific content of local schools.

Coordinator, *Transfer Student Residence/Orientation Week, M.I.T.,* 1988

- Created week-long orientation program for 100 incoming transfer students at M.I.T. as a part of the overall Residence/Orientation committee.

The Functional Format Résumé

In the functional format résumé, you organize your work experience by "functional activity" or topical headings—finance, administrative, communication, data processing, etc—starting with either your strongest accomplishment or function, or the one you want to use in changing fields. Your contribution statements are placed under the appropriate functional heading to support that function without specifying when or where they occurred. You should have two to five functional headings. After the functional section, you may list employers, positions, and dates in reverse chronological order. Place all educational information at the end of the résumé.

Advantages:

1. This format is particularly effective if you want transfer your strengths from one specific occupation to another.
2. It's very effective if your work history is nontraditional or spotty.
3. It's useful if your recent contributions will not support your next preferred career move.
4. It emphasizes selected areas of strength and contributions.
5. It's more personal than the chronological format.
6. You can deemphasize work experience you don't wish to highlight.
7. It can distract from or camouflage a spotty employment history or inappropriate jobs .
8. It may be the best format if you are concerned about your age or background.
9. It gives you a great deal of flexibility.
10. You can organize your experience according to your new or future interests.

Disadvantages:

1. It is less commonly used and not as accepted by employers.
2. Some employers think you are trying to hide something.
3. Your specific accomplishments or contributions are not clearly linked to a specific employer.

*D*eveloping Your Functional Résumé

Heading:

Select the format you feel best suits you. It should include name, address, city, state, Zip code, telephone number, and a telephone number where you can receive and retrieve messages if you are not available at your home telephone during business hours.

Job Objective:

Your stated position, industry, skills, and what you can do for the organization.

Position _____ Industry _____ Skills _____

_____

What you can do for the organization: _____

_____

Qualifying Experience:

List skills you have developed through life/job experience. State them in such a way that you identify your specific involvement; the problem(s) presented to you, and what you did; the result(s), and their specific numerical benefit to the employer.

Skills: _____

Experience: _____

_____

_____

_____

_____

Problem presented to you by the employer: _____

_____

What you did (action taken): _____

_____

_____

_____

Result(s) and benefit (especially economic or financial) to the employer. How much revenue did you generate, or costs did you eliminate? _____

_____

_____

_____

Try to state results in percent of savings to company, increased sales, improved procedure, or recognition of experience by organization. For examples, see the PAR statements earlier in this section.

Continue with each skill and accomplishment you wish to stress.

Educational History:

List reverse chronologically, starting with your highest and most recent degree, certification, or appropriate education.

Degree _____ Major _____ Major _____ Minor _____

Cum. average (if appropriate) _____ Honors _____

Recognition _____

_____

Name of institution _____

Location _____ Year of graduation _____

For uncompleted degree, list the total number of credits earned _____

Continue with all degrees or special educational experiences _____

_____

Other business or professional seminars, workshops, courses _____

_____

Do not list high schools if other degrees are started or completed.

Work History (Experience):

Title _____ Company _____

Years or months and year employed _____

Professional Organizations:

List all organizations, offices, special considerations, and years involved. Controversial organizations should be weighed before you decide whether you want to include them.

_____

_____

_____

Special considerations: Licenses, willing to travel, relocate, etc.

_____

_____

Salient published articles and presentations:

_____

_____

_____

_____

Writing Rules for Résumés: Final Details

A résumé must be easy to read. Pay special attention to the following points when preparing your final copy:

1. Limit yourself to two pages. The extent of your work experience or accomplishments will determine whether you will need one or two pages.

2. Use a word processor for your résumé. Have your original reproduced commercially, or use a photocopier that makes sharp, clean copies.

3. Print or type the original on 8.5 × 11 inch white (or off-white) bond paper. Margins should be approximately one inch at the sides, top, and bottom of the page. Use double or triple spacing between sections.

4. *There must be no errors.* Check and recheck your spelling, grammar, and punctuation. Use copy editor.

5. Use clear and concise statements to describe your experience. You need not use complete sentences; however, *your phrases and/or clauses must be grammatically parallel.* Use copy editor.

6. When describing your experiences, use skill words and action verbs.

7. Use a heading at the beginning of each section. Set the heading off by typing it in solid capital letters and/or underlining it.

8. The subsections under each heading will stand out if you indent them a few spaces or if you double-space between them.

9. Have someone review your résumé before you place it in final form.

10. Make sure that the final copy is neat, accurate, errorless, and visually attractive before having it reproduced.

11. If you have multiple copies of your résumé printed or photocopied commercially, you may choose to have it reproduced on ivory paper. Slightly off-white is acceptable. Matching letter paper and envelopes are generally available. Avoid pastel colors; they are distracting and unprofessional.

· ·

*F*unctional Format, Example 1

ALEXANDER KELLY
135 West 238th Street, Apt. 3C
Bronx, NY 10463
Tel: (718) 796-8758

OBJECTIVE   A challenging position in biotechnology and biomedicine.

SUMMARY   Physical Chemist specialized in investigating vitamins and related molecules and implementation of quality control techniques in vitamin production.

AREAS OF MAJOR EXPERIENCE

Investigation of vitamins and related molecules
- Investigated catalytic action of vitamin B_{12} and proposed mechanism of process.
- Studied electron transfer in quinine-porphyrin systems (photosynthesis).
- Investigated chemical reactions followed by electron transfer.

Applied research

- Studied cyclization stage in production of vitamin B_2 (riboflavin) and raised the yield of product by 7%.
- Studied conductivity of polyanilinic films (nonmetallic conductors) and determined optimal conditions for polymerization.
- Elaborated polarographic methods for quality control in production of vitamins and intermediate products.

Technical expertise

- HPLC, GC, UV-, visible- and ESR-spectroscopies, photochemistry, electrochemistry (classical and pulse polarography), PC computer skills.

Other experience

- Taught General Physics classes in Medical University.
- Compiled abstracts for *Chemical Abstracts*.

WORK HISTORY	**Vitamin Research Institute,** Seattle, WA
1986–1992	Research Scientist
1981–1986	Junior Research Chemist
1977–1981	Research Associate
EDUCATION	**Institute of Physics and Technology,** San Francisco, CA
1975–1977	M.S. in Physical Chemistry of biological processes
1970–1975	B.S. in Physical Chemistry

• •

• •

*F*unctional Format, Example 2

LARRY GILROY
361 95th Street, #2B
Brooklyn, NY 11209
(718) 921-6043

Summary

HVAC Engineer with experience in design, maintenance, and control of HVAC systems for commercial, residential, and industrial buildings.

Skills

- Coordinating design of construction and maintenance.
- Estimating, checking, and balancing HVAC systems.
- Supervising and inspecting construction.
- Interpreting mechanical and electrical diagrams, and blueprints.
- Troubleshooting and servicing HVAC systems.
- Designing ductworks and control systems.
- Drafting complete HVAC systems.
- Calculating heating and cooling loads.
- Selecting heating and cooling units.

— Conducting site inspections and field surveys and measurements.
— Assuring compliance with codes and client requirements.

Experience

1990–1991   ASTRA CONSTRUCTION Co., Bayside, NY
             Assistant Engineer

1986–1989   HOTEL ASTORIA, New York, NY
             HVAC Engineer

1979–1986   PETERS DESIGN Co., Peterville, OH
             Engineer/Designer

1976–1979   CONSTRUCTION Co., Nashville, TN
             HVAC Construction Supervisor

Education

1990–1992   A.O.S. in HVAC/Refrigeration Technology,
             Technical Career Institute, New York, NY

1970–1976   Bachelor of Science in Mechanical Engineering with specialization in HVAC
             College of Civil Engineering, Polytechnic University, Brooklyn, NY

*F*unctional Format, Example 3

GLENDA DANIELS
1558 East 19th St., Apt. #1K
Brooklyn, NY 11230
(718) 375-3230

OBJECTIVE: To obtain a position as a Chemist in the research and development field in agricultural chemical production.

PROFESSIONAL HIGHLIGHTS:

- Investigated surface properties (hydroscopicity, adhesion) of powder and crystalline substances.
- Developed special method and created vacuum equipment to examine hygroscopic properties by vapor water adsorption in a vacuum.
- Studied correlation between hygroscopic properties of systems and individual components. Predicted hygroscopicity of salt systems.
- Discovered how hygroscopic properties of perchlorate salts and salt systems determined their safety.
- Found effective stabilizers and method to increase safe use of perchlorates to fatten farm animals. Using such weight stimulators resulted in a 12–15% average daily weight gain and feed saving of 8–20%.
- Implemented the technology to mass-produce these preparations that was consumed by a million farm animals per year to increase their weight.

PUBLICATIONS: Ten articles, eleven U.S. and nine international patents.

PROFESSIONAL HISTORY:

CHLORINE RESEARCH INSTITUTE, Fayette, KS

1985–1992   Scientist-researcher

1971–1985   Junior Scientist-researcher

EDUCATION:

1981–1985   MINERAL FERTILIZERS UNIVERSITY, Fayette, KS
Degree: Ph.D. in Chemistry
Dissertation: "Getting Safe Bio-active Preparations Based on Perchlorates for Intensified Fattening of Farm Animals"

1965–1971   COLLEGE OF CHEMICAL TECHNOLOGY, Dallas, TX
Degree: M.S. in Chemical Engineering

1961–1965   IOWA STATE UNIVERSITY, Ames, IA
Degree: B.A. in Agriculture

....

Here's a man whose arduous résumé research paid off.

Transition From Medicine To Basic Research To Management Consulting

For me there were two turning points; the first was when I decided to leave medicine. I had an M.D. and I decided to get a Ph.D. So the first turning point was when I went from medicine to basic research. The rationale there was that medicine was fun and very exciting, but I didn't see myself doing the same thing every day for the next thirty or forty years. Even though there's a lot in medicine that's exciting, really 95 percent of what you do is the same thing every day, no matter what specialty you're in. My dad's a cardiologist—many of the really bright people I knew got their intellectual kicks doing something else, something other than the pure practice of medicine. This applies to physicians, not surgeons specifically. I decided research would be the best thing to do, and I enjoyed it, but again, in research, 95 percent the same every day drops only to 90 percent. That was the first thing. Second, there was the uncertainty. I didn't think it was the right situation. You train for so many years doing a lot of bench work, you're trading off—you're already taking a lower salary than you otherwise would be able to get, et cetera.

On top of that, when you add the huge uncertainty there is currently, it was just unacceptable.

So from research to McKinsey involved two factors. One was that I was not totally happy with what I'd be doing. Basically, bench research was not that exciting—there's the intellectual part of research, but you have to do bench research. The second factor was that I thought the way the funding system was set up was not acceptable. Having to do two or three postdocs and work for seven or eight years before you potentially have a slot as an assistant professor, then you worry about it for the next ten years—that just didn't work for me.

So I decided I wanted to do something else. There was both a pull and a push: a pull because I thought there would be other things that would be fun, and a push because I didn't really want to stay given the current conditions.

I looked into a whole bunch of different things. You name the career and I investigated it, ranging from science writing to public policy, technology transfer to anything to do with business. I just sent out résumés. It was a seven- or eight-month process for me, in which I found out various things. In that seven or eight months, I must have sent out 300 to 400 résumés, all of them in completely different areas. I started talking to people. I invested an awful lot of time and effort trying to find out about different opportunities, trying to find a good fit because I didn't want to have to do this a third time.

I started off by going to the library, saying, OK, if you look at your skill base, what are the other things you could potentially do? Then from there I called around and asked friends if they knew people in that area. I went to some meetings, like there's a venture capital meeting in Baltimore, which I showed up at one fine day. But a lot of places, you call a friend who knows someone who knows someone else. You know, in a medical school, I spoke to a lot of professors, administrators, the dean whom I knew, and many of them were able to put me onto friends and from there to other people. I talked to probably seventy or eighty people in different areas. And one of the résumés that I sent out happened to be to McKinsey. I got a call back, I found out more about McKinsey, and I realized this was pretty much what I wanted to do. But not from a career point of view—I realized at that point that I still didn't know what I wanted to do long term. Anyway, I kind of see it, and I think most of us see it, as like a postdoc, except that they pay you better and it's a different area. Most people come to McKinsey, learn a bunch of skills and techniques, develop the credentials to go on to work in the corporate world, and move on. It's what I decided made sense for me. One of the options I'd been thinking about was also getting an MBA. I'd started to study for my GMAT and things. But with McKinsey, I don't need to do that. Why and how I joined McKinsey was purely happenstance.

I know that if I decide to stay in business, I'm very well equipped to do so. I don't think there's much potential for me to go back to bench research, but that's probably not what I want to do anyway. But eventually, I probably would like to find a way to use what I've learned in medicine and research and business.

I can see myself in five to ten years getting tired from jumping around so much. The biggest problem with McKinsey for me is the travel. The lifestyle can sometimes get tiring, so I don't know if I have the stamina to do this for the rest of my life. But for now, in retrospect, I think this was a perfect job in terms of what I was looking for at the time. It was just luck that it happened to me.

I think if something is important to you, it's worth spending quite some time and effort trying to get it, and it is important not to be discouraged. The single pattern that I think is important is to try many different things and keep trying them.

Don't be fooled by the conventionsl wisdom that you are trained to be a scientist and that's all you can do. I think that many people get the feeling that they don't have choices. I think that's the single biggest thing that holds people back: the feeling that they don't have choices. Recognize that most of us have a lot more choices than we realize. I didn't realize how many choices I had until I started looking. It's important that you believe there are choices and go out and find them. It's just like any other optimization process: You always run the risk of going down a fork and getting stuck in a local minimum. There are plenty of other global things out there. But I don't think I would have been able to do it if I hadn't had so much support all through this. In this switch, my wife was extremely supportive.

You can find other career transition narratives and résumé samples at our Web site.

3.15 PREPARATION FOR JOB INTERVIEWS, NEGOTIATIONS, AND DECISIONS

The Job Interview: a Conversation

Be yourself; nobody else is qualified. —John C. Crystal

Be yourself unless you're a jerk, in which case you should be somebody else. —Rabbi Mark Dissick

Your career options research (Section 3.08) will lead you to (1) professional contacts, who in turn become (2) sources for referral to second-generation contacts, who in turn become (3) sources of third- and fourth-generation contacts.

These lead you to (4) information about jobs, (5) job openings, and (6) job interviews—if you speak to a sufficient number. What is that number? One solid-state materials scientist, a crystallo-chemist changing careers, created some three hundred contacts in his several specialties; this resulted in ten job openings and four job offers. Generally, most people will need at least twenty to fifty or more contacts in each career direction searched.

How do contacts help you get a job? You don't expect to get a *job* from an informational interview target, you expect to get *information*, including contacts. However, when you reach a certain stage in information gathering for one purpose (to get more contacts), you segue to information gathering for another purpose (to locate job openings). You can say, "I'm not asking you for a job. But you may lead me to someone else who knows another person who knows about a job opening."

What Is a Job Interview?

The job interview is a dialogue that leads to two decisions. You, the candidate, make one decision; the interviewer makes another.

The dialogue is controlled by both participants. In this section we address the extent and degree to which you control the interview.

Your stance in any interview is simply this: "I am exploring *many* job options, *one* of which may develop out of the current interview." This stance may be difficult to adopt—especially if you feel desperate—but a goal of what follows is to show you how to develop and achieve this attitude.

The following diagram is meant to suggest that if you merely respond to the interviewer's questions, you will lose control of the interview by participating in a one-directional dialogue or KGB interrogation.

Interrogation Model of the Job Interview

INTERVIEWER ASKS	Q. $\longrightarrow$	CANDIDATE ANSWERS
QUESTION	$\longleftarrow$ A.	QUESTION

and then

INTERVIEWER ASKS	Q. $\longrightarrow$	CANDIDATE ANSWERS
ANOTHER QUESTION	$\longleftarrow$ A.	ANOTHER QUESTION

In this interrogation process, you are on the hot seat. You have to answer one question after another without getting to know the interviewer and gaining information about his or her needs.

Instead, we urge you to consider a model of the dialogue in which you answer a question, then immediately follow your answer with a question of your own. This creates a *two-directional* dialogue, which allows you more control of the process than the KGB interrogation does.

Dialogue Model of the Job Interview

STEP 1		**STEP 2**
INTERVIEWER ASKS	Q.1 $\longrightarrow$	CANDIDATE ANSWERS
ONE QUESTION	$\longleftarrow$ A.1	ONE QUESTION

and then

STEP 3		**STEP 4**
INTERVIEWER ASKS NEW	A.1 $\longrightarrow$	INTERVIEWER ANSWERS
QUESTION BASED UPON	Q.2 $\longrightarrow$	CANDIDATE'S QUESTION
ANSWER TO PREVIOUS	$\longleftarrow$ A.2	AND ASKS NEXT
QUESTION	$\longleftarrow$ Q.3	QUESTION AS IN STEP 1.
		PROCESS CONTINUES
		THROUGH STEPS 2, 3, 4,
		AND 1 UNTIL DIALOGUE
		PATTERN IS
		ESTABLISHED

Thus, you keep the conversation flowing in a nonthreatening way and, furthermore, obtain a great deal of information that will help you develop and create a field-tested résumé.

The advantages of a two-directional dialogue are the following:

- It allows you to find out more about the interviewer, the job opportunities, and the environment. Consequently, you can restrict your answers to those areas of particular interest to the interviewer. By eliciting such information, you uncover the aspects of your background that you should emphasize and "sell," and you can then focus the interviewer's attention on the most salient parts of your background.

- It keeps the interview natural and conversational, and allows you to feel comfortable and show your best attributes. *You can prevent the job interview from becoming a KGB interrogation!*

- It reinforces the idea that you are choosing a place to work as much as the interviewer is choosing a new professional for the organization. The interviewer then sells you on his or her firm or company. This gives you power in the interview process, and later on in the negotiation process

- And, most important, the quality, direction, and level of your questions reveal a great deal about you and your knowledge of the interviewer's organization ("I see your firm grew by X% last year; what do you anticipate next year?") Your questions can guide the interviewer into conversational topics and subject areas where you can most confidently present your experience, skills, and interests.

Preparing for the Job Interview

In order to create a fluent two-directional dialogue, you must prepare for it *before* the interview by (1) learning key facts about the organization, and (2) analyzing what you can bring to the available position. To focus your interview-preparation research, answer the following:

- What is the typical work of the organization? Who are its major clients?

- What type of service or product does it sell? What markets does it compete in?

- Who are the key figures in the firm? Where did they go to school? What are their achievements? Their personalities?

- Who are the people you will be seeing? Are they in a position to hire you directly, or will they be deciding whether you should be seen by others?

- Who are this firm's major competitors? How does this organization differ from its competitors and distinguish itself in the marketplace?

This information can be obtained by scrutinizing the job-search research section (Section 3.12).

Prepare a list of questions you would like answered that will augment the information you have gained through your research. This preparation will help you create a continuous dialogue. For example: Is this a newly created position or a vacancy? If it is a vacancy, who had this position until now? Why is that person being replaced? If it is a newly created position, you may explore the reasons for the new need. You will *manage the impression* the interviewer has of you to the extent that you *ask* these and other *penetrating questions.*

The research should be augmented by informational interviewing with your leads and contacts, including a search person (if involved) and colleagues or mentors who may know the organization. It may take extensive contact interviews before you get to the knowledgeable person through asking others, but the effort will greatly increase your effectiveness during the interview process.

Your next step is to bring to the surface of your conscious attention those skills and experiences that will increase your self-confidence and fluency during this two-way dialogue. Look into yourself and prepare to feel confident by practicing and rehearsing what you wish to say about your skills and background. For these purposes, you need to prepare and rehearse answers to the following three major questions, which are almost always asked in one form or another:

1. *"Tell me about yourself."*

   Prepare a two- or three-minute description of your professional experience, highlighting the points that sell you best to *this employer*. In most cases, begin with your present firm and recent work; your emphasis will depend very sensitively upon what your research has shown that your potential employer is seeking. Since this is usually the beginning of the interview, your answer should be strong and well thought out, creating a positive initial impression. You can add personal factors, such as marriage, family, etc., at the end, but the main focus should be work-related. The *subtext* of this question is, "Why should I hire you?"

2. *"Why do you want to leave your present position?"* (or, *"Why do you want to work here?"*)

   Be positive, optimistic, accurate, and energetic about what you have learned and how you have grown professionally. Never make negative comments about your present employer, but indicate what the position is lacking for you now and specify your present and future goals. If they fit with those of your new organization, you are on your way to being hired. You may be asked why you left your previous position as well, so be prepared with that answer.

3. *"Why should I hire you?"*

   You will probably not be asked this question directly, but it is the ultimate question—the subtext of all interviewer questions. You must address it specifically in preparing for the interview. And you must be persuasive (if possible, compelling) in answering this question. Your prospective employer is looking for a combination of your substantive knowledge and personal traits. Plan for these typical questions with appropriate responses: "Describe the most difficult project you have worked on." "What was the project that you enjoyed the most?" "What are the personal traits to which you attribute your success?" "What are your strengths and weaknesses?"

Think through clearly the reasons why you are the best person for the position. Prepare a number of examples that demonstrate your points and detail your strengths and accomplishments. Once you have mentally prepared yourself thoroughly with this list, try to weave these points into your answers to various questions—*and into your questions* during the two-directional dialogue. Choose those vignettes that seem most appropriate based on what you learned about the position from the interviewer during the meeting.

If these interviews are conducted as breakfast or luncheon meetings, then your preparation is the same, but your points will be presented informally as part of the conversation.

Your Goal

Your Goal: To Get to the Next Step in the Screening Process.

1. *Prepare*
   - Internalize your résumé.
   - Know whom you're going to meet with.
   - Be ready for the most commonly asked question in interviews: "Tell me (something) about yourself."
   - Have your agenda prepared and follow it.

2. *Be Yourself*
   - Keep it on a social, conversational level.
   - Interviewers will see through an affectation—use your own words.
   - If you're uncomfortable—light in your eyes, have to go the restroom, etc.—say so and deal with it.

3. *Be Your Best Self*
   - Remember, "You never get a second chance to make a good first impression."
   - Talk *with*, not *at*, the interviewer. The interview is an exchange of information between people.
   - Give only positive answers; there's nothing to be gained by running down previous or current employers, bosses, institutions, or yourself.
   - Be sure to thank the interviewer for the opportunity—but never thank him or her for the time.

4. *Listen*
   - Have your material so well prepared that you can concentrate on what the job interviewer is saying, and pay attention to needs, tone of voice, preferences, and insights.

- Hear what's being said or asked.
- *Think before you answer.*

5. *Participate*

- You have responsibilities—to inform the interviewer and to be informed.
- Remember, it's just as important to *ask* as to *answer* questions.
- You can help the interviewer (who may be under great stress) make an accurate business decision by revealing those parts of your experience that are germane to the job's requirements.

Note Well:

- Don't accept or reject a job before it's offered.
- Follow up by phone or letter, but follow up.

Because it takes so much in time and effort to gain a job interview—you may invest weeks or months—you must be willing to invest appropriately in the interview preparation. One of our success stories (Donna Ferrandino) invested forty hours in preparation for one interview (Section 3.11). If you view each interview as preparation for the next interview, then a rejection is really another step in the preparation process.

Steps in The Interview Process

Each step in the interview process has a different purpose. The ultimate question to be answered is, *Is there a "fit" or an "overlap" between the employer's needs and your background and personal traits?* Focus on the objective of each meeting as well as the overall question to determine how to prepare. For example:

- On occasion, there may be a preliminary telephone screening interview before you are asked to come in; this is done to save time for both sides.
- A screening or exploratory interview is set up to see if you are someone that the organization should invest more time in interviewing in greater depth. This session, often conducted by a person who interviews frequently, is usually a highly structured process.
- Subsequent interviews focus on the selection process. Those you meet will be managers, or others who do not interview constantly. They often will not know how to conduct the interview. And you will have to appreciate their position. Create a conversation in the ways we have described so that you can present your best attributes convincingly.

- When the employer is seriously interested in you, he or she will ask for references. Follow the pointers about references at the end of this section.

Prepare for these interviews. Videotaping, which career counselors do, is extremely useful. Pay attention to your performance. Polish and rehearse your answers enough to feel self-confident.

When you see how you present yourself in an interview on videotape, you can make an objective analysis of how you are seen by others. This is a major benefit of videotape feedback in preparation and coaching for information, networking, and job interviews. It helps to have such rehearsals or practice sessions immediately prior to the interview. It also helps if your practice coach asks tough, even hostile, questions. This helps you make your mistakes in a practice setting where they do not hurt your job search.

Remember, it is your responsibility to prove that the employer is making the right decision by hiring you. The interviewer is under pressure to choose correctly. If you reduce this stress by building the interviewer's confidence in you as a candidate, then you have greatly increased your own chances of being hired.

Expect These Typical Interview Questions

Go through this list before an interview, answering each question, to gain skill in handling different questions.[36]

1. Tell me about yourself.
2. How would you describe yourself?
3. Why are you leaving _____ ?
4. What were some of the more important problems on your last job?
5. What were some of the things that you particularly liked about your last position?
6. What are your long-range and short-range goals?
7. Why should we hire you?
8. What makes you special?
9. What would you want from this job that you did not have in your last job?
10. Where do you see yourself five years from now?
11. What are your salary expectations?
12. Why would you want to work for us?

13. What is most important for you in a job?

14. What are some of the things that motivate you?

15. What frustrates you the most?

16. What do you feel you got out of college? Graduate school?

17. What areas of study did you enjoy?

18. What is your ideal job?

19. What are your strengths?

20. What are your weaknesses?

21. How are you best managed or supervised so that your work product is of the highest quality?

22. What qualities have you liked/disliked in the senior scientists or managers you have worked for? Why?

23. How do you show your anger and frustration? (How the candidate answers is equally as important as what he or she says.)

24. Discuss the importance of your job vis-à-vis your family and your faith.

25. How do you reward yourself for working hard? How would you spend more free time if you had it? What are your interests outside of work?

26. According to your definition of success, how successful have you been?

27. Have you made any mistakes during your career? If so, what were they? How did you fix them?

28. What is the most adverse situation with which you have had to deal in your personal or professional life? How did you deal with it? What was the outcome?

29. Tell me about the events surrounding firing someone, or severely reprimanding someone.

30. If you were speaking tonight to the American Association for the Advancement of Science (or the Rotary Club), what subject would you select that would enable the audience to see what's special about you as a professional? What topic would you select if it was an organization of potential clients?

31. What was the most difficult ethical decision you have had to make, and what was the outcome?

32. Tell me how you have reacted when you observed a boss propositioning a subordinate.

33. If we hired you next week, what unfinished business would you leave in your current work?

Dialogue Questions

If you have been able to establish a *dialogue* with your interviewer (instead of being *interrogated*), you may wish to intersperse your answers to the above questions with questions like the following:

1. Please describe the ideal candidate for this position.
2. What are the key attributes or skills you are looking for?
3. May I see a detailed (or formal) written description of this position?
4. What do *you* like best about working here? Why?
5. What new services (products) do you anticipate introducing over the next year or so? What new directions might you take?
6. How do you expect the organization to evolve or grow in the next five years? How will this happen?
7. Has this job led to others in the organization?
8. Please tell me about other people who work with you, in your group (division/section).
9. How early (late) can I work here?

How to Answer the Toughest Interview Questions

Honesty, optimism, energy, and enthusiasm are the underlying themes of every successful answer to a tough interview question. (To be a good liar, you have to remember too much, anyway.) If you present yourself and your answers in such a way that the interviewer concludes you have these qualities, you win. (You may not get an offer, but you'll feel good about it.)

But what does this mean in detail? Here are some answers;[37] you can redesign them to fit you.

1. *Why are you changing careers?*

   You can say you want to add to your experience base. You can say that as you got to know yourself better and you saw how you fit into career X better, you realized that your natural affinities tended to . . . or that you'd been steadily gravitating toward, career Y.

2. *What is your ideal job? What do you want to do?*

   You can frame your answer as if it were an employment ad, with a headline over a description of the opening, the employer, and yourself. Prepare the ad in advance so that you can answer it fluently with confidence—and, of course, with the underlying themes mentioned above.

3. *Where do you want to be in five years (ten years, one year, twenty years)?*

If you don't have an answer, you lose. If your answer is incompatible or inconsistent with the opening you are interviewing for at Company Y, you lose. If you say you will be working at Company X in New York, that's too specific. If you give the impression that the opening you are interviewing for is a stepping-stone only, you lose. Here's a pretty good answer. "I'm thirty-four, and I love what I do. My ultimate goal would be to head up a group (division, company), and I hope it can be here. But I know I have to do other things first. The next logical step for me would be the job we are discussing now, and here's why. . . ."

4. *Why did you leave your last job? Why are you unemployed?*

Maybe eight out of ten people leave jobs because of personality clashes with their supervisors or managers. An interviewer might believe this; he or she may have done did the same. But mentioning it can be suicidal. Concentrate on the professional reasons for joining a new employer. "I've learned about W, and now I want to learn about Z, and you (your organization) are a leader in this field." If you were fired and the interviewer knows it, say, "We agreed that the job was not a good fit for me and I am looking to. . . ." Unemployment is not a good state to be in, and it's even worse to let the interviewer know about it. You can say that you decided that you need a breather to reevaluate your career directions, and now you know.

5. *What's the highlight of your career? Your best accomplishment?*

This is a fat pitch; you can hit a home run with proper preparation. Use this to showcase your skills and how your accomplishment benefited your employer, especially if the benefits were quantitative, such as productivity improvement, shorter task time, increased volume or quality of research results.

6. *What are your strengths?*

Limit yourself to three (since you will be asked your weaknesses), and give specific, concrete examples. You could be asked to rank yourself on a scale of one to ten on each, and to explain why some are higher.

7. *What are your weaknesses? What's wrong with you?*

Interviewers are tired of hearing stock answers that try to convert your presumptive weakness into a presumptive strength. "I'm impatient" is a code for hard-charging. Honesty is best here (as everywhere), with damage control: Add how you overcame the weakness. If the interviewer becomes silent, or asks, "And what else?" don't keep volunteering answers. You can try to please by adding new weaknesses until you talk yourself out of a job.

8. *Describe a time you failed.*

The best answer is: "I fell off my horse. I learned my error. I got back up and rode into battle."

9. *Do you get along with your boss? Will you get along well here? Give me an example of how you clashed with your boss, and how you handled it.*

You can explain that you had a disagreement over a professional matter that was settled by airing of the issues. Your style (not you personally) clashed with the boss's style.

10. *Unspoken or unasked questions.*

If you have an apparent disability that may appear to influence your work or job performance, you may not be asked about it. You would do well to bring this up yourself near the end of the interview and lay it to rest: "I was born with this disability, and you may be wondering if I can do the job. Please feel free to ask my supervisors or references about this, but I have never let this diminish my productivity, quality, or growth." Of course, this has to be true for you to say it. If you have limitations that will not influence your performance, say so if they are visible. Remember, what comes from the heart goes to the heart (Talmudic saying).

Questions to Avoid

You probably reveal a great deal about yourself by the caliber of the questions you ask. For example, the following tell the interviewer what you're interested in and should *not* be asked:

1. Time off?
2. Vacations?
3. Sick pay?
4. Personal days?
5. Salary or benefits?
6. My references are . . . (Don't volunteer names until you check with them first; see "Reference Statements About You" following the Job Interview Record.)

Evaluate your own interviews by filling out the following Job Interview Record after each one.

*J*ob Interview Record

TODAY'S DATE: _____

INTERVIEWER: _____
                          Name   Title

COMPANY: _____

PHONE NO: (   ) _____

LENGTH OF INTERVIEW: _____

YOUR IMPRESSIONS OF THE INTERVIEWER: _____

_____

SUMMARY INTERVIEWER'S COMMENTS:

OPENING: _____

_____

MAIN POINTS AND/OR QUESTIONS: _____

_____

JOB DESCRIPTION AND/OR NEEDS: _____

_____

CLOSE AND WHAT WAS CONCLUDED: _____

_____

SUMMARY OF WHAT YOU SAID:

OPENING: _____

_____

MAIN POINTS, QUESTIONS, ANSWERS, YOUR VALUE: _____

_____

CLOSE AND FOLLOW-UP: _____

_____

YOUR PERFORMANCE:

_____ EXCELLENT   _____ GOOD   _____ BLEW IT

SPECIFICALLY:

_____

_____

Reference Statements About You

- A reference statement is a statement about you and your performance abilities.
- When a prospective employer is about to make you a job offer, you may be asked to submit names of people who can attest to your qualifications. These people are called references.
- Select three people (bosses, peers, professional contacts, colleagues) who are familiar with your work and contributions.
- Ask those you select for permission to use their names.
- Most references want to help. They just don't know what points to stress as well as you do.
- To minimize confusion and ensure consistency, you should take the initiative and draft your own reference statement.
- It should be written by you as if you were speaking for the person giving the reference.
- Make your statement concise, clear, positive, and credible.
- Your references may appreciate being relieved of the task, and you have the opportunity to say exactly what you want
- Write your reference statement in outline form so that your references can speak or write from it easily.
- Ask your references for feedback on the statement you give them, so that they are comfortable with the content.
- Bring a list of references, with their phone numbers, to every interview.
- Don't offer references until asked.
- When asked for references, make sure to alert your references to expect an inquiry soon. Tell them who might call, the nature of the position, and why you are interested in the job.
- Thank your references after they've been contacted, and try to get any feedback.
- Be sure to notify your references when your campaign is over, and thank them.

How to Deal with a Job Offer

"Today, we stand at the edge of a deep abyss; tomorrow, we take a giant step forward."   *—A nineteenth-century Brazilian general*

There are two kinds of offers:

A. Initial offer (earned by you, because of your substantive technical skills)

B. Final offer (negotiated by you, on the basis of your negotiating and marketing skills)

Here are some recommendations, based upon our experience negotiating salaries and benefits:

1. You can't compare a final offer with an initial offer or an almost offer. Compare *final offers only*.

2. It's best not to accept an offer on the spot. Express your enthusiasm and interest, and ask for some time to think it over.

3. Remember to talk about *their* needs only—*until* you get an offer! Then talk about *your* needs.

4. Do your homework. Prepare for the negotiations.

5. Examine your "Declaration of Independence."

6. Go over your notes about the organization.

7. Analyze and review *all* the aspects of the offer and job. Use the Total Compensation Summary Checklist (see appendix).

8. Assign decision points (+10 to –10) to each element of the job: (a) type of work, (b) potential for career growth, (c) supervisor, (d) colleagues, (e) equipment, (f) location, (g) reputation, (h) salary, (i) other.

9. Add up the total of these decision points for this job offer. Compare this total with that for any other simultaneous offer, any potential future offer, or your current status.

10. Receipt of a job offer may trigger strong emotions, resulting in a tendency to rationalize and possibly view the job and offer unrealistically.

11. Don't jump at an offer just because the money is great; money isn't everything.

12. Ask yourself, "Am I close to the center of the target I aimed for? Would this position give me a high degree of work satisfaction?"

13. The leverage is in your favor! They made you an offer! They want you!

14. If you don't accept an offer, don't burn your bridges.

Do I Just Accept the Offer or Negotiate?

Benefits of Negotiating:

1. It makes the position more tailored to your needs.

2. It makes you feel better and stronger about yourself.

3. Your starting salary is your base for future increases; therefore, raise it as high as you can.

4. You have a chance to improve your nonsalary benefits package.

5. Integrity negotiating can solidify the favorable impression you have already made.

6. Effective negotiating can establish for both you and your new employer a firmer basis for future respect and understanding.

7. An offer won't be withdrawn because you negotiated. The worst that can happen is that you won't get all that you negotiated for.

The Art of Negotiating

1. You should learn how to do it effectively, tactfully, and diplomatically.

2. Practice until you're comfortable doing it. Do role-play, and tape-record it.

3. It's a process, not an event.

4. You negotiate *only* with equal parties: Masters don't bargain with slaves. Forget negotiating after you're hired.

5. A few thousand dollars more is a lot to you, but not a lot to the company. Keep this in perspective.

6. Practically every job, except entry level, has a salary *range*.

7. If you commit to a specific salary figure or a range before you receive an offer, this weakens your negotiating ability. But be prudent.

8. Negotiate only after you have received an offer.

9. It never hurts to ask for something. Otherwise you might be upset with yourself if you haven't asked before you actually start the new job.

10. The nature and level of the job and the hiring/salary policies of the organization will affect your negotiating.

11. Knowing your *minimum salary figure* and *what you need* to have to be an effective employee is the key to successful negotiating.

Negotiations

Yes, you can negotiate your compensation package, but only after you have received a specific offer.

Suppose the hiring individual asks, "How would you react to an offer of X?" or "Suppose we offered you Y?" Your answer has to be, "Is that an offer?" Since these are hypothetical offers, you are well advised to politely decline to answer.

Suppose the interviewer says, "Everyone who spoke to you was pleased, and we are prepared to offer you Z, pending reference checks. How does that sound?"

This sounds like an offer and may be one, but you should ask to have it confirmed in writing. Silence after this question can be somewhat puzzling, and can be used either to represent genuine conflict or ambiguity or to represent your opening move in negotiation.

You do not have to answer yes or no. In fact, a preferred answer from your point of view is, "I know of a number of openings with similar job descriptions and compensation ranges from A to B." (It is wise to stop speaking at this point and wait, for minutes if necessary, for the interviewer to respond. Your silence is noncommittal and may ratchet up the atmospherics briefly. Silence can be a form of pressure in these circumstances.)

Your goal is to persuade your interviewer that you can bring specific tangible benefits (quantitative if possible) to the position that justifies an offer closer to B than to A. You will have to be very specific: "At my last position, I was able to reorganize the lab/staff/research project in a way that saved my previous employer 12 percent annually, and I can do the same or better for you."

This oversimplified scenario illustrates these elements of negotiation: information, time, and power.

Information that others were pleased with you and your qualifications, and information that you present on the range of salaries offered elsewhere are important ammunition that strengthens your bargaining position.

Time is a factor. If you know that the company has to fill the position within a week to replace someone who has left, *you* have the upper hand. If the company knows that you are unemployed and desperate for a paycheck because you are about to be evicted from your dwelling, *it* has the upper hand. Knowing the other side's timetable is very helpful. Slowing the negotiation process can provide more information and trust.

Power, or rather perceived power, is an important ingredient in negotiating. If you believe that the interviewer is more powerful than you, for any reason, you lose the negotiating advantage. How do you overcome what seems to be an obvious conclusion? Reflect upon the interviewer's situation. This interviewer is as much on the spot as you are, since he or she has to find the appropriately qualified person to fill the slot. The interviewer is under pressure to hire the right or the best person to get the job done. The interviewer needs your help to justify asking his or her superior for more money or benefits to meet the implications of your observed range of salaries (you are implying that you wish to receive a salary at the high end of the range).

If a log jam develops, and you and the offer are too far apart, you can negotiate other forms of nonsalary compensation that may move the negotiation process along—for example; subsidized health benefits, vacation, profit sharing, equity in the form of stock or stock warrants or options, vested contributions to your retirement fund, life insurance, subsidized hospitalization, future educational training opportunities, time off, control over your budget, relocation expenses, a signing bonus, a bonus upon project completion, educational opportunities for your family members, a secretary, or even a performance review in three months instead of six. These are all bargaining chips that you can discuss if the salary numbers are deadlocked. You can add to this list, especially if you have done thorough research and information gathering through contacts or successive generations of contacts (see the Total Compensation Summary Checklist in the appendix).

Win-Win

Harmonizing or reconciling conflicting needs is a possible outcome of a negotiation according to Herb Cohen,[38] if the following conditions are present or created:

1. Build trust and support.
2. Obtain information that your skills and personality fit their organization.
3. Uncover their needs (what are the job specifications?).
4. Use their ideas (speak their language).
5. Develop collaboration (shift from defeating each other to clearing the impasse).
6. Take moderate risks (by building rapport; giving and getting adequate information).
7. Get their cooperation (using their needs).

During the negotiation conversations, body language, information, and choice words can give you clues about how your relationship is evolving. Listening carefully is paramount, especially listening with the "third ear."

These are all learnable skills, but they require the sort of practice we rarely get unless we change jobs or careers often. Just as it makes sense to practice job interviews in venues or on occasions where failure will not hurt you, so too does it make sense to fail or make all your mistakes quickly when you're in a benign environment. A friend, mentor, colleague, or career counselor who can role-play and videotape your negotiation strategy can be extremely valuable.

Decisions

Once you have an offer, you may be pressed to decide immediately. The most common reason is that the employer has other candidates lined up and does not wish to lose them if you decline the offer. One major factor in not getting an offer right away or a decision to hire is the need for employees to consider all candidates (called a "beauty contest"); this may stretch on for weeks or months.

If you plan your job search so that several offers come in at the same time, you are in the catbird seat. You have the luxury of making a decision matrix and comparing the offers with one another. Yogi Berra said, "If you come to a fork in the road, *take it.*" Of course, you may of necessity be driven to a comparison between the lesser of two evils, or "the evil of two lessers."

A decision matrix, in its simplest form, lists all of the attributes or elements of the offers, good and bad, in one column, and offers X, Y, and Z in adjacent columns. Suppose your career priorities are:

1. Potential for growth
2. Stimulating colleagues
3. Location
4. Prestige or status
5. Stature
6. Compensation
7. Potential to learn new skills
8. Transient (position is a bridge or stepping-stone to another job or career)
9. Benefits package
10. Working conditions
11. Equipment and facilities

If you create an evaluation scale (say, -10 to $+10$) with which to rate each offer or career, you can enter your estimate of the numerical value of each factor for each offer in the rows of the matrix.

First, enter the value of each career priority to *you*—your needs, wants, and sum the column for offer X. Repeat for offers Y and Z and compare.

Second, enter the numerical value of each career priority to *your family* (not you), and repeat the process. The purpose is to quantify or objectify some fuzzy factors.

To see a full list of forms of compensations that organizations can offer senior management, please see Total Compensation Summary Checklist in the appendix.

3.16 CAREER TRANSITION UPDATE: WHERE ARE YOU NOW?

I. Return to Section 3.01 and scrutinize "What to Ask Yourself When Developing a Career Plan." Have you answered each of the ten questions? If not, which ones are still unanswered?

_____

_____

_____

_____

_____

II. To review, write a summary of what you have learned about yourself through this process. List your top five values and your strongest and most enjoyable skills. List your strongest interests as well.

Top Values   **Strongest and Most Enjoyable Skills**

_____   _____

_____   _____

_____   _____

_____   _____

_____   _____

_____   _____

Strongest interests: _____

_____

_____

_____

_____

III. List the changes you would like to make in order to satisfy your highest-ranked values *and* to utilize your most enjoyable skills. Will these changes take place in your present job (if appropriate); in science, technology or medicine, or in an alternative career?

_____

_____

_____

_____

_____

IV. What are the conflicts you have about making these changes? Can you identify the risks or sacrifices and obstacles involved?

_____

_____

_____

_____

_____

V. Do you feel clear about your alternatives? ____ Yes   ____ No

If yes, write a statement describing the career areas of different types of jobs you want to explore.

_____

_____

_____

_____

_____

VI. If no, what do you need *now* to help you clarify your career goals?

_____

_____

_____

_____

_____

You have identified a variety of career options with the use of the exercises that addressed your values, skills, interests, and career decision-making patterns. This led you to begin informational interviewing, and then to career options exploration.

Next, you defined your career options. You should have eliminated some options, and chosen others to pursue as career choices or goals. Write the options eliminated below, and why.

1. _____

_____

_____

2. _____

_____

_____

3. _____

_____

_____

4. _____

_____

_____

Write your career goals, career choices, or career directions to pursue. Use one sentence for each goal. Do not try to move forward in more than two career directions simultaneously.

1. _____

_____

_____

2. _____

_____

_____

VII. What are the next three steps you can take to begin your career transition or to clarify your goals?

1. _____

_____

_____

_____

_____

2. _____

_____

_____

_____

_____

_____

3. _____

_____

_____

_____

_____

_____

• •

If you are still unsure of your goals and directions and do not see how you can clarify them, you may wish to consult a career counselor. However, if you are clear on your goals, please proceed to the next section.

Here are some examples of career changers who were able to navigate by using their internal preferences as a form of "radar" to find appropriate fits.

Transition From Political Science To Administration

My own career transition experience is generic. I started out in a specialized field and burrowed deep into its methodology. My dissertation at the University of Chicago was an empirical study of elite behavior in political leadership. Eventually, this led me to broaden my substantive discipline to take on wider subjects: the epidemiology of economic success, and administrative roles.

I noticed that major administrative roles come to people with good "intellectual taste," even if they're not great at the intellectual activity itself. For example, at Chicago, Jim Coleman was a great sociologist. I was good enough to know he was good—to "administer" him, but not to write as well as he did.

As a kid, I wanted to be a missionary or a baseball player, but I didn't give my career much thought. After I got my BA from Southern Methodist University, I thought maybe I'd teach high school. But some people suggested I go to night school and get a master's degree in political science. They recognized something. At Stanford, I held my own; I became a class leader.

Later I became chairman of political science at Chicago. I wanted to be the president of a major university, but I had to learn that it's important to decide what *not* to do with your career. If I had understood this when I was 35, I would have ruled certain jobs out.

When I left Chicago, I was head of the National Opinion Research Council, and I was asked not to leave, since I would be the next dean or provost. I realized I was cutting off a career in academic administration. But I had the chance to be the president of the Social Science Research Council, which broke me free of my empirical positivistic scientific problem solving. I had to learn to deal with the different methodologies and approaches of the humanities and the social sciences. This was my most consequential career transition. I left the campus for an office building in New York, where I stayed from 1979 to 1996, except for a ten-year period from 1985 to 1995, when I was recruited to be senior vice president at the Rockefeller Foundation.

This was a quite deliberate change that took me into fields of science—agriculture, health, environment, population—that I otherwise would have no opportunities to encounter. I was able to see many disciplines without being method-constrained. For people whose career changes include major institutional settings, you can broaden your horizons and agenda, and think of career change as an ongoing intellectual seminar. As a scholar, you have some control over what you do. As an administrator, you are vulnerable to what's on your desk. You have to ask, are you prepared to broaden and thin out? Do you really want this? I serve on many boards, and I am constantly interacting with people in different organizations who educate me in a variety of fields I would have never known.

Now, what about career change is transferable? It sounds like a cliché, but to be a successful changer, you have to step into the unknown. You don't have to do everything well. You have to turn down tempting opportunities because they may lead you away from your central interests. I was offered the presidency of Swarthmore College long ago, but like it or not, money raising would have been my major role. I feel sorry for the presidents of major universities who spend all their time doing this.

Transition From Figure Skating To Developmental Biology

In college and high school I was a figure skater and ice dancer. I competed nationally and internationally for the United States. I started at age 13 and stopped at 22, after seriously competing from 1978 to 1981, when I took a leave from the University of Pennsylvania.

I had been training in Wilmington, Delaware, and concluded that I could not do both college and competition skating well. I rematriculated in 1982 and graduated in 1985 with a B.S. and an M.S. in biomedical engineering. Getting both degrees together was a matter of financial motivation.

I worked on the electrical stimulation of bone growth and repair. I thought engineering would teach me how to think, and I had reasonably good aptitude for science and medicine. I thought this was a better road than premed courses.

I was in the M.D./Ph.D. program at Johns Hopkins from 1985 to 1992. The Medical Science Training Program of NIH supported my tuition and stipend for six years. First you do two years of medical training in medical school, then you complete the Ph.D., and then you finish the M.D. I look back and laugh because I had a strong interest in science and ice skating as well—a bizarre fork in the road. I really wanted to be a scientist, not a physician.

My dissertation was on how enzymes function in white blood cells, fighting bacteria. Medicine attracts people who are disciplined and motivated, but can't make up their minds. It's also wonderful training. My focused personality, both in retrospect and at this time, was responsible for the research skills I use most. I consider myself a basic research scientist in the way I look at a science problem. I feel comfortable collaborating with physicians, and I know hospital environments. I'm not even licensed and I did no residency, however. I felt more comfortable with research problems than with patients.

I decided to follow a standard postdoc route, then set up my own lab. But the Carnegie Institution has a unique staff associate position—instead of a fellowship. I have the opportunity to set up my own lab with myself and a technician for five years, and to try to do something new. Normally, with your Ph.D. thesis you find out if you can do good creative science, and you may pursue that for the rest of your life. I want to be able to say that this research was useful. In a few years I will move in that direction, in an academic environment.

I look at neural patterning, at how the blueprint of the nervous system is laid out and developed in mammals. Mostly, I have been developing new methods to follow the fate of the cells: the early cells that give rise to neurons in the brain, the sheet of cells, the neural plate that rolls up to form a tube and then partitions off into regions of brain, spine, and peripheral systems.

My biggest turning points were the decisions not to skate and to practice scientific research. They were probably motivated by the same things:

a very personal decision to deal with the angst I carry around on a regular basis. I have a need to contribute to a new field. Skating, I tried to find what emotions I could generate from myself and evoke in others. It's the same thing in science. I have to answer, what can I do in that laboratory? When I focus on those goals, I find myself happiest.

I will continue to the next step and go on to build a larger lab in a university setting, expanding upon my current work. But no matter what the level, it's a new challenge. You never know where science will take you. That's what's so alluring.

When ice skating, I had a love/hate relationship with music, dance, and my peer group. Ice skating rules your life. It's not a normal life. You have to love it. With science, it's the same, but it demands a lot. Because it's so demanding, you need to have balance.

I'm someone who, when I'm 80 years old, wants to be able to look back and say that I've done something that's a worthy expression of a life. My most satisfying challenges are ahead: to reproduce good graduate students and to train younger scientists.

I always had a good support structure and system around me—while skating when young, and later in science.

A good protégé is someone who will take a problem from a mentor, try anything, and run with it without needing much advice.

Yes, I do get a high from science when I get a new result. Each day I think, "This is it."

3.17 GOOD CAREER PLANNING HABITS AND HYGIENE

You may wonder how you can integrate all of these exercises—and your new self-knowledge—into a coherent action plan. How do you keep moving ahead and maintain forward momentum? Organization and time management are essential, since career changing/job searching is often a full-time job added on to your existing responsibilities.

The best way to organize yourself and manage your time depends on your style and who you are. There are as many strategies for discovering and searching (Section 3.12) as there are researchers. Similarly, there are at least 450 ways to organize the periodic table of elements that researchers have portrayed in the past century or so. Here are some pointers on how to plan, organize, and execute your career transition.

Impose Action and Structure on Your Search

1. The key to obtaining the job of your choice is *action*. Without it, all the work, insights, resources, and strategies will have been wasted. So, combine your *internal* knowledge, job objective, and *external* knowledge and put them into action for yourself.

2. Be *systematic* and *committed* to your campaign. Keep a journal or diary. Have a filing system for letters, telephone calls, and e-mail messages.

3. Make a plan and stick to it. Your search plan, if systematically followed, will produce the result you want.

4. By pursuing your personal contacts (70 to 80 percent), direct mailing (1 to 5 percent), using agencies/recruiters (5 to 10 percent), and answering ads (5 to 10 percent) you'll ultimately obtain the job offer you're looking for. (Percentages are recommended approximate portions of your total available campaign time to devote to each source.)

5. You should consider the search a *full-time* job and spend *at least* six to eight hours a day five days a week working at it. Our most successful candidates spend up to twelve hours a day, seven days a week, for months at a time.

6. Exponential interviews are the most productive way to find jobs; therefore, don't rely solely on traditional search methods (ads, agencies/recruiters). Spend about three-fourths of your time generating contact or informational meetings and expanding your contacts.

7. Be sure to devote more time to the *critical* tasks (priority A) like cold calling and networking than to the *easy* ones (priority B) like reading want ads. "Dare to look in the dark."

8. Spend about a tenth to a fourth of your time on ads, agencies/search firms, and direct mailing.

9. Put prime daylight time into contact meetings and job interviews. (Try for at least one a day.)

10. Do your writing, reading, and research in the evening and on the weekends.

11. Do not spend too much time on any single activity; shift around and be aware of what activities are working best for you.

12. Do not isolate yourself. Others can help you, and you can assist others too! (Keep a partner—a "buddy," mentor, or counselor—informed on how you're doing.)

13. Since as many as four-fifths of available jobs are filled through contacts and recommendations, exposure can provide your most important leads, so remain as visible as possible. Keep as many people as possible constantly aware of your qualifications, availability, and specific career or job objective. You've got to tell them; they can't read your mind.

14. Be *active* (not passive) in your job search. It is critical to maintain your *health* and *appearance*; regular physical exercise helps energize you.

15. Record all expenses associated with your job search for tax purposes.

16. Monitor yourself (or find others who will help):

    a. Are you using *all* your resources and strategies: contacts, references, librarians, support systems, direct mailing, agencies/recruiters, and advertisements?

    b. Are you presenting yourself *effectively* and with *confidence*?

    c. Are you on *track* or *wasting your time*?

    d. Are you doing priority A or B tasks?

    e. Are you using the telephone effectively?

    f. Use your task sheets, to-do lists, and weekly action plan.

    g. At the end of the week, write your weekly action plan for the upcoming week until you *start* your new job.

17. Preliminary internal actions:

    a. Expand your contact list.

    b. Do adequate research/investigation (library and in person).

    c. Prepare telephone scripts and practice.

    d. Practice focus meetings.

    e. Practice interviewing.

18. Ongoing external actions (in order of importance):

    a. Research (target organizations—list as many as you can) (priority A)

    b. Telephone calls (with contacts and cold calls) (priority A)

    c. Appointments (focus meetings and job interviews) (priority A)

    d. Correspondence (direct mailing and follow-up) (priority B)

    e. Agencies/search firms (establish a relationship with a few) (priority B)

    f. Answering advertisements (priority B)

The secret to a successful job search lies in the systematic and concurrent use of all the above career-transition and job-search strategies. Remember, *looking for a job is more than a full-time job!*

Hard Work, Not Good Luck, Brings Success!

Begin by filling out the Time and Action Planning Form. Any big project—including developing a career- or job-change plan—is doable when it is broken down into defined tasks with deadlines. First, write your career- or job-change goal. Then isolate four or six plan elements that must be set in motion—and completed—by a certain self-imposed realistic deadline. Some examples of plan elements are "write my résumé," "contact Mr. Smith," "research market research positions in three small drug companies," "look at communications and publicity problems of five large software companies," and so on. Keep the elements small so that you can complete them by the dates you have indicated. You will use this form repeatedly, so make copies.

. . . .

*T*ime and Action Planning Form

Career or job-change goal

Plan Element	Realistic Completion Date
_____	_____
_____	_____
_____	_____
_____	_____
_____	_____
_____	_____
_____	_____
_____	_____
_____	_____
_____	_____
_____	_____
_____	_____
_____	_____

Then transfer these elements to the weekly schedule that follows the Time and Action Planning Form. An additional form for recording your job-search activities is also included.

● ●

W*eekly Personal Time Action Chart*

GOAL:

Week 1

(Mon.)   _____ ☐   _____ ☐
          _____ ☐   _____ ☐
          _____ ☐   _____ ☐

(Tue.)   _____ ☐   _____ ☐
          _____ ☐   _____ ☐
          _____ ☐   _____ ☐

(Wed.)   _____ ☐   _____ ☐
          _____ ☐   _____ ☐
          _____ ☐   _____ ☐

(Thurs.) _____ ☐   _____ ☐
          _____ ☐   _____ ☐
          _____ ☐   _____ ☐

(Fri.)   _____ ☐   _____ ☐
          _____ ☐   _____ ☐
          _____ ☐   _____ ☐

(Sat/   _____ ☐   _____ ☐
Sun.)   _____ ☐   _____ ☐
          _____ ☐   _____ ☐

● ●

J*ob Search Activity Form*

Call To: (Date?)	Letter To: (Date?)	Response (Written or Call Date)	Date & Response to Follow-up Call 1	Date & Response to Follow-up Call 2	Interview Set-Up	Other Follow-up Needed

Project Management and Good Career Hygiene

A good scientist or engineer tends to seek optimal solutions, strive for accuracy, deal with things, focus on process, work with immutable laws, specialize to improve, and succeed individually.

However, *a good project manager* tends to seek pragmatic solutions, strive for workability, deal with people, focus on outcomes, work with situational rules, generalize to improve, and succeed through others.[39]

Many of our career narrators have described how they were able to combine both sets of the above tendencies to move forward. Some did this intuitively. Others needed rules and steps to follow.

We have borrowed some methods from the world of project management and scheduling to make the process of career self-management easy to plan and schedule.

Work Planned vs. Work Done: Gantt Chart

The Gantt chart's salient feature is that *work planned* and *work done* are shown in the same space in relation to each other and in relation to time.[40] The discrete plan is displayed as a horizontal bar over a horizontal time axis. Progress against the plan is shown in a parallel hollow bar placed above the same common time axis; but this upper second hollow bar is filled in up to the point ("time now") to which progress has been made against the plan.

The beauty of this scheme (see example below) is that if results are on schedule, then the top bar is shaded up to the "time now" point. If the progress toward specific goals is behind schedule, the shading does not reach the "time now" point. The Gantt chart (1) shows the original plan, (2) shows the present status relative to the plan, and (3) forecasts any necessary changes to the plan.

Those who are changing careers or seeking jobs always ask, "How long will this take?" The answers are: (1) It's hard to know. (2) The more time you invest in your career transition, the sooner you will finish. (3) The "exponent" in your exponential interviewing [$y = A \exp (at)$] will govern how fast your successive generations of contacts and job interviews proliferate, and that will be a strong function of your energy, your optimism, the time invested, your personality, and of course environmental factors. (4) The career management process will be smoother, more organized, and probably faster if you follow a scheme such as the Gantt chart.

To help facilitate this process, we have listed the activities and milestones in your career-transition process. We have several uses for this list. The first is to help you plan and schedule the events. The second is enable you to determine which activities you may reasonably expect to do yourself, assisted only by books, on-line information, friends, advisors, or mentors. There will be activities for which you will need guidance from a professional. For example, if you find you have difficulty in interpreting the results of your self-assessments, you may need a trained career counselor to help you. If you find that you are immobilized by lethargy, fear, anxiety, lack of clarity, or even depression, you should get guidance. These activities are called guided. Not every career transition is purely "self-directed," even if the transitioner says it was.

Events/Task	Jan	Feb	Mar	Apr	May	Jun	Jul	Aug	Sep	Oct	Nov	Dec
1. Self-Assessment		▬▬▬										
	Process Completed											
2. Options Research						▬▬▬▬▬			Process on Schedule			
3. Strategic Self-Marketing						▲						
					Milestone Completed							

Time Now (top arrow pointing down above May/Jun)

Time Now (bottom arrow pointing up below Jun/Jul)

*I*ncremental Career Management Planning Activities and Milestones

	Self-Directed	Guided
1. **Self-assessment** (3.01)		
Career well-being (2.01)		
Decision patterns (3.02)		
Personal priorities (3.03)		
Skills (3.04)		
Taking stock (3.05)		
Nontraditional careers (3.06)		
Your interests (3.07)		
2. **Options research** (3.08)		
Informational interviews (3.09)		
Biography development (3.10)		
Second summary (3.17)		
Exponential interviews (3.11)		
Job-search research (3.12)		
3. **Self-marketing strategies**		
Recruiters/counselors (3.11)		
Letters (3.13)		
Résumé research and development (3.14)		
Job interview preparation (3.15)		
Finding mentors (3.11)		
Project management (3.17)		
Trend tracking (3.08)		

Milestones

Instead of portraying activities or tasks (as in Gantt charts), we can use milestones, which emphasize *events* or *moments in time*. A milestone is usually a significant event that materially contributes to the project's or process's completion.

The milestone symbols differ from the Gantt chart symbols. A hollow triangle represents a significant event that has not been completed, a shaded triangle one that has been. You can use squares or circles to represent conditions such as "ahead of schedule" or "behind schedule," and so on. We have shown a chart that combines both Gantt and milestone symbols for a variety of career activities.

The short version of the career-transition process (1.01) is simply (1) assessment (who are you?), (2) options research (explore alternatives), and (3) strategic self-marketing (how to get where you'd like to be). Each of these activities can be represented by a horizontal bar, partially shaded as your progress warrants. Subactivities within each of these general activities may be shown as well.

A stage in your career transition may be an event, such as completion of your self-assessment (your Career Well-Being Inventory, your Skills Inventory) or a certain number of telephone calls, job interviews, or exponential interviews. You may also use milestone symbols.

Earned Optimism

Knowing that during a complex and lengthy process such as a career transition, you will face the probability of failures (targets decline to be interviewed, rejection after job interviews) is reason enough to begin to plan with some pessimism.

But if you can sidestep these failures, or take them in stride, you can transform your initial essential pessimism into not only *learned* optimism (see "What's Good About Pessimism? What's Bad About Optimism? in Section 3.02) but *earned* optimism. Planning is the process of converting justifiable pessimism into learned optimism.[41]

Others who have been through a career transition have discovered that they encounter many rejections before they eventually succeed. Optimists welcome the noes because that's one less no to deal with, and one no closer to yes.

Depression and Career Hygiene

The overlap between those who are undertaking a career transition and those suffering situational or clinical depression is large. Career-change candidates or clients are surprised when they learn that others experience similar symptoms (sustained lethargy, inactivity, sleeplessness, pessimism, inability to concentrate extending over months or years). See the Depression Inventory below for a quick self-test.

It is true that clinical depression, which 24 percent of women and 15 percent of men suffer from[41], is often either undiagnosed or misdiagnosed. "Some people mistakenly assume that being sad most of the time is an aspect of their personality or a normal response to a troubling situation. Others realized they suffer from depression but do not seek help out of fear of being stigmatized at work or at home," according to a panel of experts reported in the *Journal of the American Medical Association.*[42]

Primary physicians often fail to recognize symptoms of depression in their patients, and even if they do recognize these symptoms, they may dismiss them as hypochondria or give too low a dose of medication for too short a period.

The selective serotonin reuptake inhibitors (like Prozac, Zoloft, Paxil, and others) increase the brain's levels of serotonin, a neurotransmitter that influences mood. When administered under expert care, these drugs are safer than their predecessors. The clinically depressed career candidate should consider specialist treatment if long-term depression interferes with the career transition. (It usually does.)

D*epression Inventory*

Circle the number for each statement that best describes how you felt or behaved *during the past week:*	Rarely or None of the Time (Less Than 1 Day)	Some or a Little of the Time (1– 2 Days)	Occasion- ally or a Moderate Amount of Time (3– 4 Days)	Most or All of the Time (5– 7 Days)
1. I was bothered by things that usually don't bother me.	0	1	2	3
2. I did not feel like eating; my appetite was poor.	0	1	2	3
3. I felt that I could not shake off the blues, even with help from my family or friends.	0	1	2	3
4. I felt that I was just as good as other people.	3	2	1	0
5. I had trouble keeping my mind on what I was doing.	0	1	2	3
6. I felt depressed.	0	1	2	3
7. I felt that everything I did was an effort.	0	1	2	3
8. I felt hopeful about the future.	3	2	1	0
9. I thought my life had been a failure.	0	1	2	3
10. I felt fearful.	0	1	2	3
11. My sleep was restless.	0	1	2	3
12. I was happy.	3	2	1	0
13. I talked less than usual.	0	1	2	3
14. I felt lonely.	0	1	2	3
15. People were unfriendly.	0	1	2	3
16. I enjoyed life.	3	2	1	0
17. I had crying spells.	0	1	2	3
18. I felt sad.	0	1	2	3
19. I felt that people disliked me.	0	1	2	3
20. I could not get going.	0	1	2	3

HOW TO SCORE YOURSELF

Add up the numbers you have circled. Your total score has a possible range of 0 to 60, and this single score "is used as an estimate of the degree of depressive symptomology. Scores of 16 or more are considered 'cases' of depression." (M. M. Weisman, et al., *American Journal of Epidemiology* 106, no. 3 (1977): 203–213; L. S. Randolff, *Applied Psychological Measurement* 1, no. 3 (1977): 385–401.)

••

The Folded Map

If you are using a road map on a long trip through unfamiliar territory, you fold the map so that you see a small section that contains only the area you need at the moment. Once this area is traversed, you refold the map to reveal the next region you will traverse. You continue this unfolding and folding to keep the viewing area consistent with your physical location.

Imagine that the map is the career-transition planning process, including activities and milestones.

If the time scale on your Gantt plus milestone chart is days or weeks, then your planning focus is "near term." If the time scale on your Gantt plus milestone chart is weeks or months, then your planning focus is "intermediate term." If the time scale on your Gantt plus milestone chart is months or years, then your planning focus is "long term." (We have heard of people who actually make career plans that extend five, ten, or more years. Some advisors even suggest that we plan ahead twenty years.) The folded map metaphor implies that we employ high-resolution planning near term, and therefore we can overlook the intermediate- and long-term planning temporarily.[42] But this is risky strategy, and this "fixed focus" on the near term must be updated periodically for risk and control assessment in the longer term, or with a "wide-angle" focus. If your short-term goal is to "leave the academic world" and your long-term goal is to "manage a software company," then both time horizons must be looked at both in detail (telephoto mode) and in general (wide angle mode).

T̲he Folded Map

Galbreath lists 130 reasons why complex project management and schedules fail.[38] Many of the these apply to career management planning:

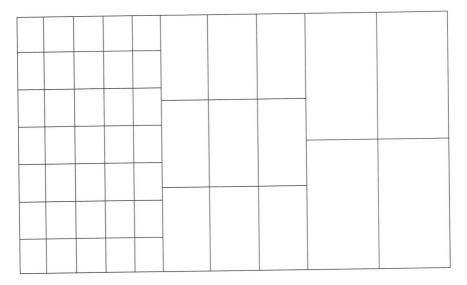

1. *Fast tracking.* Overlapping certain activities that are better performed sequentially or consecutively. For example, finish the assessment module *before* you move on to the options exploration; finish information gathering in a new career path *before* you write your biography or résumé for that direction.

2. *Moving targets.* Pervasive social and technological change can outrun your career plans. For example, the automobile made buggy whips obsolete, and some fields of software development exponentiate so rapidly you cannot stay abreast unless you work at it full time; most computer courses are woefully behind companies' leading-edge developments.

3. *What worked last time.* A motto to apply to this defect is, "There was no last time."

4. *Short and sweet.* The larger you make this project, the more susceptible to risk it becomes. Normal, healthy individuals succumb to old age, and career-transition projects can collapse under their own weight of detailed planning.

5. *Matrix gridlocks.* If you have divided loyalties distributed among several different objectives and methods, you can fail to keep up your forward momentum.

6. *Transient contrivance.* If you know that you will be working at your career transition for ten to twenty months (we're not saying you will), you will plan differently than if your transition will last ten to twenty weeks.

7. *Warm bodies.* People are not commodities, nor are they interchangeable parts in some giant organism called "my network" or "my colleagues."

8. *Risk-free.* There are no guarantees in your career transition; no one owes you anything; you cannot predict when you will succeed.

9. *Paralyzed by risk.* If you thought about the probability of getting hit by a car when you cross the street (maybe it's one chance in a billion), you would not cross the street; but you have to get to the other side, so cross.

10. *Unbounded optimism.* The Pollyanna perception, that making a career transition is a snap, may not be an appropriate belief for you, although it might have been for Leonardo or Ben Franklin.

11. *Forget perfection.* If it's not perfect, do it anyway—whether it's a career transition plan or a new career direction (it can be a stepping-stone to the next job or career).

12. *Paper tiger.* If your plans are made but not followed, they are useless.

13. *Information infatuation.* If the information is deified and made an end in itself, it will impede your goal, not support it. If your computer information vehicle is more troublesome than your destination, you won't get there. If you focus entirely on accuracy, you will miss usefulness.

14. *Ignoring human factors.* On college campuses, architects have been known to arrange sidewalks in straight lines, orthogonal, over inefficient routes; but students find short-distance routes because they're human, with abiding creaturehood behavior. But people skills demand that we do follow rules of courtesy, gratitude, and emotional intelligence.

15. *Not invented here.* You can learn methods and techniques from others, and from books, and invent a few of your own to reach your career goals.

16. *Self-flagellation.* A career transition is difficult enough without whipping ourselves, which can be painful and immobilizing. Avoid rigid deadlines, which when missed can be cause for unreasonable self-criticism.

17. *Them!* You can light a candle, or curse the darkness. You can blame mentors or supervisors, or move ahead with your life. Enmity is an enemy, and war is hell.

Among Galbreath's rules for success in managing complex, long-term projects are:

1. Learn failure, don't practice it.
2. Know what your next steps are.
3. Aim for reasonable targets.
4. Expand your options.
5. Change perspectives.
6. Focus on results, not process.
7. Leverage your successes.
8. Accept some failure.
9. Build credible images (of your steps and yourself).
10. Keep your bearings and your baselines.

T*he Positive Energy Pledge*

The following assertions are urged by Howard Figler and other career counselors upon every candidate undergoing a career metamorphosis.

1. I promise to complain, curse, and "kvetch" about the ugliness of job hunting—then to smile and move forward on my career transition with energy and optimism.

2. I pledge to try to solve the employers' problems—not my own.

3. I will be the hero of my own journey—my Odyssey from home to help to challenge to prize.

4. I will try to smile at everybody I meet, because everyone is in a struggle.

5. I pledge that I will not allow myself to become a prisoner of my résumé, because "my résumé is not yet as good as I am."

6. I understand that somebody, somewhere will want my talents, no matter how unusual or odd they may be. "My symphony is yet to be written."

7. I promise to choose my work based upon my ideals, no matter what the cynics say.

8. I accept that I must create a "system" for finding and getting rejections, because after I have been rejected enough times, I will be accepted. (Diagram of a typical job search: no, no, no, no, no, no, no, no, no, no, no, no, no, YES, no, no, no, no, YES.)

9. I must remember that "imperfect movement is better than perfect paralysis," and that (as Woody Allen says) about 80 percent of life is simply showing up (preferably on time!).

Q*uestions I Must Answer*

A. What would I sell if I had to earn a living as a salesperson?

B. What is the product or service that people really need—that I can provide?

C. What are the best things I have ever done, and where or how can I get the chance to do them again?

D. If I had all the talent I wanted, if the labor market was hospitable, and if money was not a problem, what kind of work would I do?

E. If I was counseling or advising myself, what would I say to myself?

Your "Declaration of Independence" (A Simple Optional Exercise, But It Works!)

How to Improve Your Job-Search Performance Daily by Creating Your Own Personal Script and Audio-Tape

PURPOSES:

1. To increase your *motivation* to find a job in your field

2. To enhance your *self-confidence*

3. To build your *optimism, energy,* and *self-confidence*

4. To improve your *job-search efficiency,* especially in your command of:

   a. Self-assessment

   b. Library research

   c. Informational (contact) interviewing

   d. Exponential interviewing

   e. Job interviewing

5. To *accelerate your success*

• •

• •

How to Make Your Script

Write your answers to the following questions in detail. If you have trouble answering these questions clearly, ask your partner, your mentor, or a friend to ask you these questions, and write down your anwers.

I. *What are your long-range and short-term career goals?*

    A. Be very specific. *Example:* "Long range (2–3 years), I wish to teach and do pure research in my field at Harvard or Princeton; short-term (3–4 months), I wish to teach at a local community college."

    B. State the cost to you. *Example:* "I will spend seven hours a day, seven days a week, doing the necessary career-transition activities specified in my project scheduling plan and my "theory of career victory."

II. *What are the necessary steps you must take?*

    A. Rank-order the steps according to their priority. *Example:* "*First,* I will spend two hours to inventory my skills. *Second,* I will go to the library two days per week, obtaining five leads per hour to professional contacts in my field. *Third,* I will write seven broadcast letters per day, as I continue to build forward momentum. *Fourth,* as my confidence increases, I will begin making eight telephone calls per week for informational interviews . . ." (and so on).

   B. What is "perfect execution"—who does this process very well? *Example:* "My mentor got a new job in 3.5 months by using these career-change job-search methods energetically. I will strive to do the same."

III. *What are your past successes, achievements, accomplishments?*

   A. These may be from your work, personal or social life, marriage, etc. *Example:* "My doctoral dissertation was a theoretical prediction that was confirmed by experimental measurements three years later." *Example:* "I saved $3 million in one year with my patented method of removing radioactivity from the water system in Chernobyl."

   B. What does it feel like to have these successes? *Example:* I am proud that I saved my previous employer so much money with my patent. *Example:* My friendships are a great source of continuing pleasure.

Write out your answers in clear, simple declarations or assertions. Ask a friend, a colleague, or someone you respect to read your answers into an audiotape recorder. If you prefer, you may record it yourself. Listen to the tape every day in the early morning when you wake up, in the evening right before you fall asleep, and whenever you have free time. Many people who do this may find it embarrassing or simple-minded at first, but once you get used to the power of auto-suggestion (or "self-hypnosis") and you see the benefits, it becomes a practical habit. It works. Try it! You are in effect, inoculating yourself with antibodies against discouragement, or self-administering "earned optimism" or "Vitamin O."

• •

• •

*B*enefits of *"Vitamin O"*

"The mind is its own place, and in itself can make a Heaven of Hell, a Hell of Heaven"—John Milton

Your brain's software can be reprogrammed to encourage and energize you to plan your work and work you plan. You can reformulate any negative messages that you send yourself and replace them with positive messages. (Visualize e-mail messages from friends.)

I. *Categories of Positive Mental Messages*

• Habit changing (blaming others, not setting your priorities, complaining, "kvetching" etc.)

• Attitude building (self-esteem, overcoming personal limitations, self-confidence)

• General motivation (getting optimistic or "up" when you are discouraged or "down")

• Situation (when confronted with a challenge, problem, or difficulty, etc.)

II. *Rules to Develop Positive Mental Messages*

• Use the present tense. Be extremely specific. Be positive.

III. *How to Utilize Positive Mental Messages*

- Silently repeat the messages to yourself. Repeat the messages out loud. Have a conversation with yourself. Write the message. Tape the message. (E-mail the message to yourself.)
- Keep a job-search diary; keep daily track of your contacts, your conversations, and your mental and emotional states.

Example statements:

- "I take responsibility for everything about me—my behavior, my thoughts, everything." "I am in control of the vast resources of my own mind."
- "I alone am responsible for what I do and what I tell myself about me. No one else can share this responsibility with me." "I enjoy being responsible."
- "I am trustworthy." "I can be counted upon." "I am the master of my destiny."
- "I take care of myself physically." "I like being in good physical condition and feeling good." "I do not smoke." "My lungs are strong and healthy." "I can breath deeply and fully." "I have no habits that are harmful to me."
- "I can achieve any goal I set for myself." "I see in my mind a clear picture of myself having already accomplished my goal. I see it often. I create it. I remember it by listening to my tape, by reading my script, by talking about it with myself, my friends, my relatives, my colleagues, my buddies."
- "I am organized. I do not waste time. I am always on time for any meetings." "I am in complete control of what I think, what I do."

*H*ow Hard Are You Looking for a Job?

Here's a self-test to keep you on track. You can score yourself every week and track your progress.

IN THE LAST WEEK, HAVE YOU . . .

1. Spent at least ten hours at a library searching for leads and professional contacts?
2. Found at least twenty contacts?
3. Sent at least ten letters to those who seem appropriate?
4. Made at least ten phone calls to new contacts (strangers)?
5. Thought of one new geographic area to look at (Connecticut, Wisconsin, California)?
6. Looked at directories to see what organizations exist in that area that might hire you?
7. Gone to one meeting of a group (civic, professional, trade association, church, synagogue) to meet new contacts (strangers!) face-to-face?

8. Contacted one new person you have already met recently, in order to get more new contacts?

9. Called one person on your list that you have not previously contacted?

10. Contacted two people you spoke to more than one month ago, to see if they have any new ideas?

11. Looked at newspaper or magazine or journal ads in your field that are six months old, called three firms with such ads, and presented yourself to the person one level above the advertised position to see if the position may soon be vacant?

12. Spoken to your personal friends, colleagues, fellow seminar participants, etc., to find out the latest marketplace conditions in your specialty?

13. Shared professional contacts with your fellow seminar participants?

"Strong" and "Weak" Situations

Your personality powers your career transition. About 40 percent of the variance in the herring catch among Iceland's 200 or more fishing boats depends upon the captain's personality. About 15 to 25 percent of the profitability of hundreds of large companies was accounted for by the personality of their chief executives.[43] Apparently, there are "strong" situations in which organizational cues enforce an expected way of behaving: Think of a time in your career when others' expectations encouraged a status quo. But there are also "weak" situations in which your personality can trump the status quo: Think of positive mental messages you send yourself.

High and Low "Self-Monitors"

You can characterize yourself as a high "self-monitor" or a low "self-monitor." In corporations, high self-monitors pick up on organizational cues and deliver the expected behavior, like chameleons. They get the most promotions and raises, and can be outspoken when that is deemed acceptable. By contrast, low self-monitors stick with their own instincts, even when this makes them unpopular, and where shutting up is the preferred behavior, they have a rough time.

Hindsight and Foresight

It turns out that some of us tend to emphasize looking backward, with long retrospective time spans. And some of us tend to emphasize looking ahead, to invest our thinking in long prospective time-spans. Certain personality traits tend to be associated with each kind of tendency: toward hindsight, toward foresight, or toward a mixture of both. The traits that are associated with each tendency were extracted from interviews with individuals of each persuasion.

....

Mini-Test for Hindsight/Foresight

Here is a self-inventory test to help measure your hindsight/foresight capabilities. Sixteen (of ninety) test items are listed below. A person high on foresight would tend to agree with eight of them; a person high on hindsight would agree with the other eight. Try it! First see if you agree or disagree with each of the items. Then see if you can guess which are hindsight items and which are foresight.

Check One	*Agree*	*Disagree*
1. In order to merit the respect of others, people should show the desire to better themselves.		
2. I tend to suppress anger if it might damage a friendly relationship.		
3. I feel I am a very worthwhile person.		
4. A newspaper usually has to make events seem more sensational in order to build circulation.		
5. People are lonely because they don't try to be friendly.		
6. Once in a while I like to poke fun at some people.		
7. People are basically different in their makeup, interests, and personalities.		
8. It's hard to get ahead without cutting corners here and there.		
9. With change taking place so rapidly, it seems as though anything could happen.		
10. I very much enjoy competition.		
11. Even if you give me a few facts about a person, I still won't have a good idea of whether or not I like the person.		
12. Most of the time I have good luck.		
13. Clever or sarcastic people often make me feel uncomfortable.		

14. War is inherent in human nature.

15. First impressions are very important.

16. I spend a fair amount of time deciding what clothes to wear.

If You Agree with Statements	*If You Agree with Statements*
1 3 5 6 8 10 12 14	2 4 7 9 11 13 15 16
tendency is toward high	tendency is toward high
foresight	hindsight

If You Agree With Four Statements in each category, it probably indicates an average mix of hindsight and foresight.

Hindsight Tends to Associate With	**Foresight Tends to Associate With**
Long retrospective time spans	Long prospective time spans
Creativity	Logical and orderly thinking
Spontaneity	Empathy and involvement
Narcissism	Flexible controls
Variety of response	Depth of response
Openness to experience	Emotional integration
Sensitivity	Achievement and self-realization
Strong superego	Strong ego and defenses
Imaginativeness	Belief in one's own maturity
Harmonious and anger-free relationships	Relatively happy and anxiety-free
Intropunitive reactions	Constructive endeavors
Immaturity and anxiety	Masculinity
Low Aggressiveness	

Retrospective Fantasy Tends To	*Prospective Fantasy Tends To*
Master past frustrations	Rehearse future actions
Serve as inner compensation	Prepare for growth and development
Punish transgressions	Implicate major goals
Confuse casual relationships	Make compromises with reality

How to score your results?

Add up the number of your "yes" answers: 10 to 13 is very good; 6 to 9 is OK. Anything lower: you need a "dose" of optimism, energy, self-confidence. Reread (or rewrite) your "Declaration of Independence" script. Play your tape.

••

A Balanced Life: "Happiness" Defined for Scientists

Bertrand Russell, in a splendid, slender, barely known volume called *The Conquest of Happiness,*[44] remarks how it is "the wise who have seen through all the enthusiasms of earlier times." He quotes Ecclesiastes: "For in much wisdom is grief . . . increased knowledge increases sorrow."

He suggests, on the contrary, that the life of scientists possesses all of the conditions of happiness, and that the following conditions define "happiness":

- An activity that utilizes your abilities to the fullest

- Achievement of results that appear important to you and to the general public (even if not understood)

- An ability to allow your interests to be as wide as possible

- A willingness to let your reactions to things and persons that interest you be as friendly as possible

- An investment in zest, affection, family, work, and effort

We call this, as do our career-change champions, "a balanced life."

NOTES

1. Two scientists who did cancer research on rats together meet at a conference years later, after one has moved to another lab to do cancer research on chickens. The rat-cancer researcher asks, "What can you learn about rats from chickens?"
2. Adapted from Martin Seligman, New York, Pocket Books: *Learned Optimism,* 1993.
3. www.harbornet.com/biz/office/sct001.html, www.toa-services.net/sct001.html
4. www.harbornet.com/biz/office/sct001.html, www.toa-services.net/sct001.html
5. www.harbornet.com/biz/office/sct001.html, www.toa-services.net/sct001.html
6. Michael Novak, *Business as a Calling* (New York, N.Y.: Free Press, 1996).
7. Timothy Butler and James Waldroop, *Discovering Your Career in Business.* (Reading, Mass.: Addison Wesley, 1997).
8. Fred Owens, Roger Uhler, Carmine A. Marasco, *Careers for Chemists: A World Outside the Lab* (Washington, DC: American Chemical Society, 1997).
9. A tradesman says to a professional, "I dreamed the number seven for seven nights straight, so I bet on the number seven times seven or forty-three and I won the lottery." The professional says, "But seven times seven is forty-nine." The tradesman: "You educated people will never learn how to make money."
10. Published by VGM Career Horizons, Lincolnwood, IL.

11. Petras et al., *Jobs '97: The Essential Job Hunting Guide* (New York: Simon & Schuster, 1995).

12. Harry S. Dent, *The Great Jobs Ahead* , (New York: Hyperion, 1995).

13. Gerald Celente, *Trend-Tracking* (New York: John Wiley & Sons, 1990).

14. Christian and Timbers Inc., 1997, personal communication.

15. Christian and Timbers Inc., 1997, personal communication.

16. Andrew Grove, *Only The Paranoid Survive* (New York: Currency Doubleday, 1996).

17. *New York Times*, September 11, 1996, p. D1, and *Small Business Administration,* Dun & Bradstreet, 1995

18. Stephanie Mehta, "A Number of Venture Capital Firms Tap Trainees For Major Projects," *Wall Street Journal*, January 21, 1997, p. B1.

19. His e-mail address is srosenc@ix.netcom.com.

20. Mark Granoveteer, "The Strength of Weak Ties," *American Journal of Sociology*. 78, no. 6 (1973) 1360–1380

21. Suggested by career consultant David Rottman.

22. Howard Gardner, *Frames of Mind.* New York: Basic Books, 1973.

23. Daniel Goleman, *Emotional Intelligence*, (New York: Bantam Books, 1995.

24. Bonnie Oglensky, *Looking for Mr. Goodmentor. A Study of the Emotional Dynamics and Character of Mentor-Protégé Relationships.* Proposal for dissertation research, City University of New York Graduate Center, April 1995.

25. Kathy Kran, *Mentoring at Work.* Lanhan, MD, University of America Press, 1985.

26. Kathy Kran, op. cit.

27. Granovetter, "The Strength of Weak Ties."

28. Nancy Zeldis, private communication.

29. Richard Bolles, *What Color Is Your Parachute?* (Berkeley, Calif.: Ten Speed Press, 1996, pp. 382–399. Editions are updated annually.

30. Elizabeth MacDonald, "Is There a Party Animal Lurking Beneath All Those Spreadsheets?" *Wall Street Journal*, January 2, 1997, p. B1.

31. "Investors Seem Attracted to Firms with Happy Employees," *Wall Street Journal*, March 18, 1997, p. B1.

32. Bridget O'Brian and Gabriella Stern, "Contact Sport," *Wall Street Journal*, March 19, 1997, p. A1.

33. Gale Research, Detroit, Mich.; (800) 521-0707.

34. Gale Research, Detroit, Mich; (800)521-0707; 3 volumes.

35. Robert Root-Bernstein, *Discovering* (Cambridge, Mass.: Harvard University Press, 1989).

36. Ron Fry, *101 Great Answers to the Toughest Interview Questions* (Franklin Lakes, N.J.: Career Press, 1996).

37. Joan Rigdon, *Job Interviews, National Business Employment Weekly*, April 23, 1995, p. 42.

38. Herb Cohen, *You Can Negotiate Anything.* (New York: Bantam Books, 1987).

39. Robert D. Galbreath, *Winning at Project Management* (New York: John Wiley & Sons, 1986).

40. Quentin W. Flemming, John W. Brown, and Gary C. Humphreys, *Project and Productive Scheduling* (Chicago: Probas Publishing Co., 1987).

41. Susan Gilbert, "Lag Seen in Aid for Depression," *New York Times*, January 22. 1992, p. C9.

42. January 21, 1997, by Dr. Martin Keller, professor of psychiatry at Brown University and a panel member.

43. W. Jenkins Holman, Jr., "Wanted: One Ever-Changing Ego; Values Unimportant" *Wall Street Journal*, September 10, 1996, p. A23.

44. Bertram Russell, *The Conquest of Happiness* (London: George Allen and Unwin, 1930).

APPENDIX

....

CAREER SEARCH SELECTION CRITERIA

You can make contact with information sources and employers through the channels we have mentioned in Sections 3.09 and 3.11:

1. Through your own web of sources and successive generation of contacts
2. On-line, using directories, chat groups, bulletin boards, and individuals
3. Through exponential interviews, face-to-face or by telephone, snail mail, e-mail
4. Through a career library
5. By asking someone else to collect targets for you from databases

Specify Criteria

If you can specify what your search criteria are, you can ask for help. You must be able to select one or more of the following search criteria:

A. Industry group or subgroups
B. Location group or subgroups

C. Employer size (maximum or minimum number of employees, annual budget, or annual billings)
D. Title or job description of your contact or target

Please check off on the following lists those items that match your search criteria. Use this in your research for contacts, information interviews, and job openings. Your response rate will vary greatly depending upon your purpose and target. For writing to contacts, we have seen a range (depending on the letter's content) of from 20 to 80 percent, assuming that you do not enclose a résumé. For information interview requests, somewhat smaller response rates are likely. For a "cold" approach to a stranger, letters with a résumé included will generate under a 1 percent response rate generally; the rate will be higher if a biography replaces the résumé.

We Search

Scientific Career Transitions will execute your search if you send us your detailed criteria (Scientific Career Transitions, 1776 Broadway, Suite 1806, New York, NY 10019-2002, E; srosenc@ix.netcom.com; no telephone calls please). Although we are a nonprofit organization, we charge a fee, the amount to be determined by the size of your mailing and other help you may need in framing your letters and your strategy or "theory of victory."

*S*earch Selection Criteria

I. Select the INDUSTRY groups or subgroups you wish to search.

ADVERTISING/PR
___ In-House Ad Agencies
___ PR Firms
___ Advertising Agencies
___ Media Services Firms
___ Sales Promotion Firms

ASSOCIATIONS
___ Cultural Organizations
___ Social Organizations
___ Social Welfare Organizations

___ Health & Medical Organizations
___ Public Affairs Organization
___ Fraternal, Nationality & Ethnic Organization
___ Religious Organizations
___ Patriotic Organizations
___ Hobby & Avocational Organizations
___ Athletic & Sports Organizations
___ Labor Unions Assoc
___ Chamber of Commerce

___ Greek, Non-Greek Societies,
Associations

COLLEGES/UNIVERSITIES

___ 2-year Institutions

___ 4-year Institutions

___ Upper-Level Institutions

___ Comprehensive Institutions

___ 5-Year Institutions

___ Universities

CONSTRUCTION

___ General Contractors

___ Heavy Construction

___ General Nonresidential Construction

___ Highway Construction

___ Plumbing & Heating

___ Electrical Work

___ Concrete Work

CONSULTANTS

___ Agriculture/Forest/Landscaping

___ Architecture/Construction/Interior
Design

___ Art/Graphics/Communication

___ Business/Finance

___ Computer
Technology/Telecommunications

___ Educational/Personal Development

___ Engineering/Science/Technology

___ Environment/Geology/Land Use

___ Health/Medical/Safety

___ Human Resource Development

___ Management

___ Manufacturing/Transportation

___ Marketing and Sales

___ Politics/Social Issues

EDUCATION/K–12

___ Catholic Schools

___ Private Schools

___ Public Schools

ENTERTAINMENT

___ Motion Picture Production

___ Theatrical Producers

___ Orchestras, Bands, Actors

EXECUTIVE SEARCH

___ Search Firms—All

___ Contingency Search Firms

___ Retainer—Major

___ Retainer—All

FINANCIAL INSTITUTIONS

___ Banks

___ Credit Unions

___ Savings Banks

FINANCIAL SERVICES

___ Mortgage Bankers

___ Security/Commodity Brokers

___ Holding/Investment Off.

HEALTH CARE (OP)

___ Ambulatory Surgery

___ Diagnostic Imaging

___ Home Health Care

___ Hospices

HMO/PPO

___ Health Maintenance Organizations

___ Point of Service

___ Preferred Provider Organizations

___ Biological & Environmental Science

___ Business & Economics

___ Computers & Math

___ Education

___ Engineering & Technology

___ Government & Public Affairs

___ Humanities/Religion

___ Labor & Industrial

___ Law

___ Medical/Health Science

___ Multidisciplinary Programs

___ Physical/Earth Science

___ Regional/Area Studies

___ Research Coordinating

RESTAURANTS

___ Restaurant Chain Headquarters

___ Hotel/Motel Restaurant
Headquarters

RETAIL/WHOLESALE

___ Retail

___ Retail Store Sites

___ Wholesale

SPORTS

___ Agents

___ Major College Sports

___ Promotion/Marketing Agencies

___ Executive Search Firms

___ Sports Facilities

___ Sporting Goods–Retail

___ Sports Attorney, Non-agent

___ Sports Manufacturers

___ Manufacturers' Representatives

___ Media

___ Sports Organizations/Gov Bods

___ Professional Services Providers

___ Market Research Firms

___ Corporate Sports Sponsors

___ Sports Teams

TECHNOLOGY

___ Automation

___ Biotechnology

___ Chemicals

___ Computer Hardware

___ Defense

___ Energy

___ Environmental

___ Manufacturing Equipment

___ Advanced Materials

___ Medical

___ Pharmaceuticals

___ Photonics

___ Software

___ Subassembly/Components

___ Test & Measurement

___ Telecommunications Equipment

___ Transportation Equipment

___ Holding Companies

TELEPHONE

___ Cellular Telephone Services

___ Telephone Companies

TRANSPORTATION

___ Railroad Transportion

___ Local/Suburban Transportation

___ Motor Transportation

___ Water Transportation

___ Air Transportation

UTILITIES

Electric Companies

___ Gas Companies

___ Water Conservation

___ Sanitary Services

VAR'S

___ (Value-Added Resellers)

VENTURE CAPITAL

___ Aerospace

___ Agriculture

___ Banking

___ Biotechnology

___ Chemicals

___ Communications

___ Computer Products

___ Construction

___ Consumer Products/Services

___ Education Products/Services

___ Electronic Equipment

___ Energy-Related Products/Services

___ Entertainment

___ Environmental Products/Services

___ Equipment

___ Food

___ Financial Services

___ General

___ Health-Related Products/Services

___ High-Technology Industries

___ Hospitality/Hotel

___ Industrial Products

___ Instruments

___ Insurance

___ Low-Technology Industries

___ Manufacturing Industries

___ Marketing/Direct Marketing

___ Specialty Materials

___ Mining

___ Natrual Resources

___ Oil & Gas

___ Pharmaceutical/Drugs

___ Plastics

___ Publishing

___ Research & Development

___ Real Estate

___ Retail

___ Services

___ Software

___ Supplier to Parent

___ Transportation

___ Utilities

___ Waste Products/Services

___ Wholesale Distribution

II. **Select the LOCATION groups or subgroups you wish to search from the following list (each state is broken down into cities and metropolitan areas, and the larger cities are further broken down by commuting patterns). A distance from Zip code function is also available.**

ALASKA

GREAT LAKES

___ Illinois

___ Indiana

___ Michigan

___ Minnesota

___ Ohio

___ Wisconsin

HAWAII

MIDDLE ATLANTIC

___ Delaware

___ Maryland

___ Pennsylvania

___ Virginia

___ West Virginia

___ Washington, D.C.

MOUNTAIN PLAINS

___ Colorado

___ Iowa

___ Kansas

___ Missouri

___ Montana

___ Nebraska

___ North Dakota

___ South Dakota

___ Utah

___ Wyoming

NEW ENGLAND

___ Connecticut

___ Maine

___ Massachusetts

___ New Hampshire

___ Rhode Island

___ Vermont

NORTH ATLANTIC

___ New Jersey

___ New York

NORTHWEST

___ Idaho

___ Oregon

___ Washington

PUERTO RICO

SOUTHWEST

___ Arkansas

___ Louisiana

___ New Mexico

___ Oklahoma

___ Texas

SOUTHEAST

___ Alabama

___ Florida

___ Georgia

___ Kentucky

___ Mississippi

___ North Carolina

___ South Carolina

___ Tennessee

WEST

___ Arizona

___ California

___ Nevada

III. Select the PROFILE criteria to target industry-specific company size.

ADVERTISING/PR

___ Minimum/Maximum Employees

___ Minimum/Maximum Annual Billings

ASSOCIATIONS

___ Minimum/Maximum Staff

___ Minimum/Maximum Annual Budget

COLLEGE/UNIVERSITIES

___ Minimum/Maximum Enrollment

EXECUTIVE SEARCH

___ Minimum/Maximum Level Handled

FINANCIAL INSTITUTIONS

___ Minimum/Maximum Branches

___ Minimum/Maximum Assets

HMOs/PPOs

___ Minimum/Maximum Enrollees

HOSPITALS

___ Minimum/Maximum Number of Beds

K–12

___ Minimum/Maximum Enrollment

NURSING HOMES

___ Minimum/Maximum Beds

RESTAURANTS

___ Minimum/Maximum Number of Units

RETAIL/WHOLESALE

___ Minimum/Maximum Number of Units

___ Minimum/Maximum Annual Sales

VENTURE CAPITAL

___ Minimum/Maximum Capital Managed

The following industries are either ___ Minimum/Maximum Employees and/or ___ Minimum/Maximum Annual Sales:

CONSTRUCTION

CONSULTANTS

ENTERTAINMENT

HOSPITALITY

MANUFACTURING

OIL & GAS

PUBLIC SAFETY

RECREATION

TECHNOLOGY

TELEPHONE

TRANSPORTATION

UTILITIES

VARS

Industries where PROFILE is not applicable: FINANCIAL SERVICES, HEALTH CARE, HOSPITAL MANAGEMENT, INSURANCE, REAL ESTATE, SPORTS.

IV. Select CONTACT names from a list of industry-specific department heads. (A generic list is provided below for reference.)

___ PRESIDENT

___ CHIEF EXECUTIVE OFFICER

___ EXECUTIVE VICE PRESIDENT

___ VICE PRESIDENT

___ CHIEF FINANCIAL OFFICER

___ CHIEF OPERATING OFFICER

___ SENIOR SALES EXECUTIVE

___ SENIOR MARKETING EXECUTIVE

___ SENIOR PERSONNEL EXECUTIVE

___ SENIOR ADMINISTRATION

___ SENIOR INFORMATION SYSTEMS

___ PUBLIC RELATIONS DIRECTOR

___ DIRECTOR/MANAGER RESEARCH

___ DIRECTOR/MANAGER R&D

___ DIRECTOR/MANAGER ENGINEERING/TECHNOLOGY

___ DIRECTOR/MANAGER DEVELOPMENT

Total Compensation Summary Checklist

	Amount	Offered Yes	No	Comments	Needs	Wants
Direct/Regular Income:						
Basic salary						
Sign-on bonus						
Commissions						
Bonuses, corporate/ Christmas, etc.						
Profit sharing						
Stock options						
Matching funds						
Investment programs						
Salary Review 3, 6, 9, 12 months						

		Offered				
	Amount	Yes	No	Comments	Needs	Wants
Deferred compensation (401K)						
Cost of living increases						
Incentive pay						
Indirect/Other Benefits:						
Position						
Title						
Line/staff relationships						
Functions						
Responsibility/authority						
Support (personnel budget)						
Facilities, equipment, etc.						
Pension plans (vesting provision)						
Pension credit from previous employers						
Vacations, holidays (number of weeks)						
Extra vacations (beyond normal)						
Expense account (reimbursements)						
Company car						
Accelerated performance review						
Sick leave and pay						
Free parking						
Cafeteria/executive dining room privileges						
Use of corporate property (vacation, phone, boat)						
Low-interest loans						

	Amount	Offered Yes	No	Comments	Needs	Wants
Country club or other memberships						
Consumer product discounts						
Professional association memberships (release time)						
"Personal days"						
Company credit card						
Health:						
Hospital						
Dental						
Major medical						
Life insurance (self, family, accident)						
Travel insurance						
Disability						
Annual physical exam						
Moving/Housing:						
Packing, moving, unpacking						
Payment for house-hunting trips						
Lodging between homes						
Additional shipping costs (cars, R.V.s, boats, etc.)						
Purchase of home						
Mortgage funds (bridging loans, etc.) rate differential						
Real estate brokerage fee						
Prepayment penalty						
Closing costs						
Special allowance for home fixtures and appliances						

		Offered				
	Amount	*Yes*	*No*	*Comments*	*Needs*	*Wants*
Separation:						
Employment contract (senior management)						
Pension/retirement						
Deferred compensation						
Severance pay (salary continuance)						
Outplacement						
Health-care insurance continuance						
Insurance conversion privileges						
Use of office, secretary, charge cards, phone						
Noncompetition terms						
Other:						
Estate or financial planning assistance						
Tax assistance						
CPA service						
Legal assistance						
Tuition refunds (education)						
Employee assistance programs						
Dependent scholarships						

REFERENCE/RESEARCH MATERIALS

Catalogs

Small Business Bookstore—A minicatalog. A series of books from *Entrepreneur* magazine (e.g., *Small Business Advisor, Starting an Import/Export Business*). Catalog available from Wiley Small Business Bookstore; 1-800-456-9515.

Kennedy Consultants' Bookstore—*The Overnight Consultant; Applied Strategic Planning: The Consultant's Kit; Marketing and Matchmaking Services for Management Consultants;* and many more. Kennedy Publications, Templeton Road, Fitzwilliam, NH 03447; 1-800-531-0007.

Kennedy Publications Job & Career Library. Includes seventy-one items. Covers self-assessment, career advice, job search, starting out, career research sources, electronic search, search firms, international jobs, networking, résumés, cover letters, interviewing, and negotiations (see "Newsletters").

Hoover's Regional Business Guides, The Reference Press, Inc., 6448 Highway 290 East, Suite E-104, Austin, TX 78723; 1-800-486-8666.

Hoover's Catalog—business books, career resources, CD-ROMs and disks, global company guides, on-line resources (see above).

Small Business Development Catalog—Be Your Own Boss. From *Entrepreneur* magazine. A catalog of over 200 Start-up guides, books and software to help you succeed in a business of your own. Entrepreneur Magazine Group, P.O. Box 1625, DesPlaines, IL 60017-1625; 1-800-421-2300.

How-To

Dive Right In—The Sharks Won't Bite: The Entrepreneurial Woman's Guide to Success, by Jane Wesmann. $19.95. Dearborn Financial Publications: Dearborn Trade.

Balancing Work and Family, by Ken Lizotte and Barbara Litwak. Offers clear-headed advice to help working parents regain control of their lives. An AMACOM Worksmart guide. Covers practical issues like time management and scheduling, parenting issues, how to's for better communication. Filled with exercises, real-life stories, and quizzes to help you identify what eats time and what you would like to find time for. $10.95.

AMACOM, Division of American Management Association, 1601 Broadway, New York, NY 10020; (212) 903-8087.

Working with Difficult People, by William Lundin and Kathleen Lundin. A small book from which everyone can benefit. Chapters include: "Mean and Angry," "Suspicious," "Pessimists," "Cynics," "Cold and Distant," "How Do I Love Me?," "Extreme Competitiveness," "Over-Controlling," "It Takes Two to Make a Toadie." Lessons and case studies with handling solutions. $10.95. AMACOM (see above).

Six Months Off: How to Plan, Negotiate, and Take the Break You Need Without Burning Bridges or Going Broke, by Hope Dlugozinaa, James Scott, and David Sharp. Covers many bases, including financing, negotiating, identifying sabbatical opportunities, jump-starting a career, and engineering a smooth landing upon return to work. Owl: Henry Holt & Co., 115 W. 18th St., New York, NY, 10011.

Job Shift—How to Prosper in a Workplace Without Jobs, by William Bridges. A seminal work. Very accurately describes the new realities of employer/employee relationships. $13.00. Addison-Wesley Publishing, 170 Fifth Avenue, New York, NY 10010; (212) 463-7881.

Finding Work Without Losing Heart—Bouncing Back from Mid-Career Job Loss, by William J. Byron, S.J. Helps you understand the new realities of today's workplace. It explores how others have taken advantage of their core beliefs in their search for meaningful work. Managers who face difficult decisions will find this insightful but pragmatic work invaluable. $12.95. Adams Publishing, 260 Center Street, Holbrook, MA 02343; 1-800-872-5627.

The Portable Executive: Building Your Own Job Security—From Corporate Dependence to Self-Direction, by John A. Thompson and Catherine A. Henningsen. "The only job security left today is the ability of an individual to recognize and develop their portable job skills and be able to market them" says the co-founder of IMCOR, the nation's pioneering and leading supplier of interim managers. Includes making the transformation from corporate dependence to self-direction, seizing the many advantages and opportunities offered by the new shift, recognizing differences between low-risk and high-risk opportunities, and developing a pricing system for almost any new type of portable business. $12.00. Call Laurie Colchamiro, Fireside Books, Simon & Schuster, 1230 Avenue of the Americas, New York, NY 10020; (212) 698-7279.

National Business Employment Weekly Guide to Self-Employment, by David Lord. (1) Begins by illustrating the reasons we have come full circle from being independent to having "jobs" to a return to independent employment. (2) Covers how to examine if a self-directed career is for you. (3) Choosing a path. (4) Starting a business. (5) Buying a business. (6) Operating a franchise. (7) Consulting. (8) More ways to work. (9) Getting started. Each section is packed with examples and sound thinking learned from those who have been there. Not only is the content of extreme value, but the text includes the NBEW list of best franchises, where to find interim (professional temporary) firms, full details for acquiring resources referenced in the text (and there are many), including books, publications, guides, and a bevy of on-line resources on associations, franchising, consulting, freelance temping and contract staffing, home-based business, marketing and technology, health and time management, and finances. $12.95. Jessica Church, John Wiley & Sons, 605 Third Avenue, New York, NY 10158; (212) 850-6336.

Virtual Office Survival Handbook—What Telecommuters and Entrepreneurs Need to Succeed in Today's Nontraditional Workplace, by Alice Breden. Includes creating your virtual office, overcoming the challenge of working alone, separating personal and business life, preserving your professional image, and maintaining visibility. Excellent if you want to work full or part time at home. $16.95. John Wiley & Sons, 605 Third Avenue, New York, NY 10158.

Telecommute! Go to Work Without Leaving Home, by Lisa Shaw. Filled with real-world examples, it informs potential telecommuters of the best and worst jobs for telecommuting, how to approach your supervisor, setting up your office, balancing home and work life, ways to relieve isolation, the future of telecommuting, and who is telecommuting now. $14.95. John Wiley & Sons, 605 Third Avenue, New York, NY 10158; 1-800-225-5945

How to Incorporate in CA, NJ, FL, NY, IL, NC, MA, PA, MI, TX. Each state is a separate volume, with those listed being the issues currently available from the publisher. Contain basic information on starting and operating a business beginning with choosing the right opportunity, how and why to incorporate, federal rules and regulations. Each has fully comprehensive state-specific information, whether your state recognizes the S corporation, licenses, excise taxes, buying an existing business, hundreds of money-saving tax strategies. $16.95. Adams Publishing, 260 Center Street, Holbrook, MA 02343; 1-800-872-5627.

Entrepreneur Magazine's Starting a Home-Based Business. This a comprehensive guide to help you transform your home, know the pros and cons, recruit personnel, etc. Content includes creating a business identity, obtaining start-up financing, tackling legal issues, licenses and permits, conducting market research for the best product for you, what to ask before buying into a franchise or business opportunity, and purchasing equipment and supplies. John Wiley & Sons, 605 Third Avenue, New York, NY 10158; (212) 850-6336.

Getting Publicity, The Very Best Book for Your Small Business, by Tana Fletcher and Julia Rockler. This "how-to" explains how to make the most of every opportunity, from free coverage to distribution of press releases. Content includes: What is the media looking for? Is it possible to plan an effective campaign without spending a lot of time and money? What constitutes an effective press release? How does one hold a press conference? What's the best way to get on talk shows? How can one master the media interview and the art of public speaking? $14.95. J. J. Harvey, Publicist, Self-Council Press, 1704 N. State Street, Bellingham, WA 98225; (604) 986-3336.

Finding Government Information on the Internet: A How-to-Do-It Manual. The most comprehensive overview of government information on the Internet. After introductory information, the rest of the book focuses on describing and analyzing individual services by fields of interests, such as science and technology, legal, legislative and regulatory, business, social science, and the humanities. There are also chapters on state and local sources and international sites. $39.95. Neal-Schuman Publishers Inc., 23 Leonard Sreet, New York, NY 10013; (212) 925-8650.

Proving You're Qualified: Strategies for Competent People Without College Degrees, by Charles D. Hayes. The author claims this book will forever change the way people think about credentials and what it means to be qualified, and it will make crystal clear the options and action strategies they need to pursue. Chapters include "Changing the Focus to Outstanding Performance," "Understanding What You Are Up Against," "Understanding Management," "Understanding Credential Methods," "Who Is Really Qualified?," "Leverage, Options & Choices," "Learning to Live with Change," and "Me Inc." $16.95. Autodidactic Press, P.O. Box 872749, Wasilla, AK 99687; 1-800-247-7663.

Selling 101: A Course for Business Owners and Non-sales People, by Michael McGaulley. Addresses the reality that for many displaced employees, the only reasonable option is self-employment, a small business, consulting, or contract work. Selling 101 is the essence of a corporate sales training program in step-by-step task lists. $12.95 + s&h $4.95. Adams Media, 260 Center Sreet. Holbrook, MA 02343; 1-800-USA-JOBS.

Think Before You Speak—A Complete Guide to Strategic Negotiations, by R. Lewicki, et al. This is almost a textbook approach to learning a strategic skill. Chapters include "The Advantage of Strategy," "Assessing Your Position," "Assessing the Other Party," "Context of Power," "Selecting a

Strategy," "Implementing a Competitive Strategy," "Implementing a Collaborative Strategy," "Alternative Strategies," "Understanding and Dealing with Traps and Biases in Negotiation," "Conflict Reduction from Opponent to Collaborator," "When and How to Use Third Parties," "Communication Skills," "Legal and Ethical Issues," "Negotiation Through Teams," "Mastering Strategic Negotiation." $22.95. John Wiley & Sons, 605 Third Avenue, New York, NY 10158; (212) 850-6336.

Job Search

101 Great Answers to the Toughest Job Search Problems, by Ollie Stevenson. $11.99. Career Press, 180 Fifth Ave., P.O. Box 34, Hawthorne, NJ 07507; 1-800-CAREER.

101 Dynamite Questions to Ask at Your Job Interview, by Richard Fein. Learn how important it is to ask the right questions. What employers learn from the questions asked that helps evaluate your candidacy, topics and subjects you should always ask about, five rules for asking effective questions, when you should ask, questions you should never ask, forty questions you need to ask about the job, forty questions you could ask about the company, twenty questions to help assess politics and potential layoffs, how to best close an interview with a key question. $14.95. Impact Publications, 9104 N. Manassas Drive, Manassas Park, VA 22111; (703) 361-7300.

How to Locate Jobs and Land Interviews, 2nd edition, by Albert French. Career Press, 180 Fifth Avenue, P.O. Box 34, Hawthorne, NJ 07507; 1-800-CAREER.

Tom Jackson's Resume Express, Interview Express, Power Letter Express. Most job seekers don't want to spend time learning how to do the search. They just want to get out there and do it. Tom provides all the basics and excellent wisdom in this compact volume. Includes forms and organizing planners. Loaded with activities. 1-800-224-GIFT.

The Interview Kit, by Richard H. Beatty. Adapts classic sales techniques to the interview process, encouraging readers to make it an active experience. How to use every moment from the first impression to the final handshake to the job seeker's advantage. Encourages readers to take charge of the meeting by anticipating the employer's needs and tailoring their presentation. $10.95. John Wiley & Sons, 605 Third Avenue, New York, NY 10158; (212) 281-6201.

The Adams Interview Almanac. Complete job interviews for all fields and industries. 1000 interview questions with great answers; the fifty questions you must be prepared to answer; the fifty most challenging questions you will ever face. In addition to strategic advice on how to land an interview, it features complete job interviews with experts in all field and industries, with great answers and advice. Includes a section on stress interviews, killer interview questions, and advice for career changers and other specific groups. $10.95. Adams Publishing, 260 Center Sreet, Holbrook, MA 02343; 1-800-872-5628.

The Smart Woman's Guide to Interviewing and Salary Negotiations, by Julie Adair King. The author claims you will learn to overcome cultural stereotypes, sell yourself with confidence, find an employer who truly offers equal opportunity to women, negotiate the salary you deserve, and convince your current employer that you deserve a raise. $12.99. Annie Jennings, Career Press, 3 Tice Road, P.O. Box 687, Franklin Lakes, NJ 07417; (908) 281-6201.

Electronic Job Search Revolution, by Joyce Lain Kennedy. Chapters include "The New Job Market," "Résumé Database Services," "Job Computers: Applicant Tracking Systems," "Armchair JoB Hunting—Online Ads and Career Resources," "Amazing New Electronic Employer Databases," "The Computerized Job Interview," and "Bed Knobs, Broomsticks and Job-Seeking Wizardry—High-Tech Tools for Choosing a Career, Landing a Job and Moving Up. $12.95. John Wiley & Sons, 605 Third Avenue, New York, NY 10158.

What Color Is Your Parachute? Richard Bolles. $14.95. Ten Speed Press, P.O. Box 7123, Berkeley, CA 94707. The classic.

How to Get a Job in 90 Days or Less—A Realistic Action Plan for Finding the Right Job Fast, by Matthew J. DeLuca. This is an outplacement manual on its own, with lots of sage and sound advice as well as basic information. There are worksheets, forms, sample letters, and time management methods to keep to the ninety-day plan week by week. $12.95. McGraw-Hill, Inc., 1221 Avenue of the Americas, New York, NY 10020.

Job Search Quiz. A chart on how to rate your job campaign search. $10/hundred & $2 shipping. Garrett Park Press, P.O. Box 190, Garrett Park, MD 20896; (301) 946-2553.

Jobs and Careers with Non-Profit Organizations, by Ronald and Caryl Krannich. Gives the career decision maker and job seeker 700,000 organizations that employ nearly 10 million people. Chapters include "Jobs and the Nonprofit Sector," "Myths . . . ," "Examine Your Non-Profit Capabilities," "Effective Job Search Strategies," "Resources," "Non-Profit Employers . . . ," "The Start-up Directory to Non-Profit Organizations," "Trade and Professional Associations," and "A World of Non-Profits Operating Abroad." $15.95. Impact Publications, 9104 N. Manassas Dr., Manassas Park, VA 22111; (703) 361-7300.

Directories

Gale Guide to Internet Databases. Identifies and describes 2000 domestic and international databases. Entries are arranged alphabetically, with detailed access and retrieval information and the URL. Database content and scope are provided. $95.00. Gale Research, Detroit.

Encyclopedia of Business Information. Gale Research, Detroit.

The Online 100: Online Magazine's Field Guide to the 100 Most Important Online Databases, 1995, by Mick O'Leary. Identifies the most important databases in the most important subjects, rather than the largest or most heavily used. $22.95. Pemberton Press Books, Online Inc., 462 Danbury Rd, Wilton, CT 06897-2126; 1 (800) 248-8466.

International Business & Trade Directories. Lists approximately 5000 directories from all parts of the globe. Entries are alphabetical by one of more than seventy industry groups, subdivided by ten geographical areas. Entries list title, publisher's address, phone, and fax; a one-to three-sentence description; size; price frequency; and distributor. $125. Gray House Publishers.

Directory of Executive Temporary Placement Firms. $24.95. Kennedy Publications, Templeton Road, Fitzwilliam NH 03447; 1-800-531-0007; fax (603) 585-9555. (Also under Newsletters and Catalogs.)

Directory of Executive Recruiters. Contains 7,400 references; 4,400 locations of 3,227 retainer and contingency firms in North America. $44.95. Also available on diskette for $195. Kennedy Publications, Templeton Road, Fitzwilliam, NH 03447; 1-800-531-0007; fax (603) 585-9555.

The Best Directory of Recruiters. Features 16,240 recruiter listings, videoconferencing, Internet, e-mail, telephone, fax, and addresses. U.S. and International. $39.99. Available on disk. Gove Publishing Co., 1105 Lakeview Avenue, Dracut, MA 01826; (508) 957-6000; http://www.BestRecruiters.com.

Plunkett's Info Tech Industry Almanac. Covers the entire scope of the information technology business, from companies that run on-line services to software companies, equipment and computer makers, consulting firms, systems integrators, multimedia and other electronic entertainment and information publishers, and leaders in satellite communications, fiber optic communications, and telecommunications. The author has combined the most successful, fastest-growing companies into the InfoTech 500 and presented a thorough analysis of these companies and their industries. $125 + $5 shipping. Plunkett's publications also include *The Almanac of American Employers, Plunkett's Health Care Industry Almanac*, and the *Corporate Jobs Outlook* bimonthly newsletter. Plunkett's Research, Ltd., P.O. Box Drawer 8270, Galveston, TX 77553; (409) 765-8571.

Hoover's Guide to Computer Companies. Covers 1,135 top companies in the computer industry worldwide, including producers and distributors of hardware, software, communications, peripherals, and on-line services. Contains two-page profiles of 77 leading firms, 173 one-page profiles, and directory listing of 885 others. Concludes with two indices and includes a Windows electronic version on disk. $34.95. The Reference Press, Inc., 6448 Highway 290 E., Suite E-104, Austin, TX 78723; (512) 454-7778.

World Chamber of Commerce Directory. Includes U.S. chambers of commerce, economic development organizations (American and Canadian), and foreign tourist information bureaus. Listings include city name in alphabetical order, name of chamber, executive director, complete address and phone with fax, population, number of members. $35.00. P.O. Box 1029, Loveland, CO 80539; (970) 63-3231.

Thomas Register of American Manufacturers. A 30-volume directory that lists virtually every industrial product or service offered in North America, along with who makes it and how to get it. $240. 20 volumes of products and services, 2 volumes of company profiles. Five Penn Plaza, New York, NY 10001; 1-800-699-9822 x 444. (Now available free on the Internet.)

Vankirk's Venture Capital Directory. Tracks and profiles 2,000 venture capital, buy-out, and other private equity investment firms worldwide. Useful for CEO and high-level executive candidates and those starting or buying a business. Recently bought by Asset Alternatives, Inc., 7 Lehigh Rd, Wellesley, MA 02181; (617) 235-1110.

CorpTech Directory. Lists e-mail and home page addresses. The best resource for technical employers and careers, containing 45,000 updated high-technology company profiles. Free information kit at 1-800-333-8036. Free industry analysis on home page of over 300 reports can be accessed at http://www.corptech.com. Corporate Technology Information Svcs., Inc. 12 Alfred St., #200, Woburn, MA 01801. (Included in Career Search Database.)

Standard & Poors Register of Corporations, Directors and Executives. Print $650, CD-ROM $995. Standard & Poors, 65 Broadway, New York, NY 10006; 1-800-221-5277 x 4052.

CD-ROMs—Research

Encyclopedia of Associations—National Organizations of the US. Gale Research, P.O. Box 33477, Detroit, MI 48232-5477; 1-800-877-4253. (Also in print.)

CD-ROMs in Print. See Gale Research (above).

American Business Information. 70 million households phone directory. $595.

Infon Venture Capital (Bellevue, WA). Lists more than 500 firms and 2000 venture capitalists. Contains information about investment strategies along with career and educational background of each company's employees.

Business Phone. Top tool for the investment. Look up an SIC code, then use this CD to access the companies (lists 15 million) and get the name, address, phone, and description. Can search, sort, and export data. $29.95. Pro-CD, Inc., 222 Rosewood Drive, Danvers, MA 01923; Http://www.procd.com.

Phone Disc—Business Pro. Find any business in the United States with this 5-CD set. Reverse indexing allows you to search by name, business, business type, address, and phone number and export to a variety of label formats. You receive first update free. $49.95. Egghead Software, http:/www.egghead.com.

Phone Disc Powerfinder Pro. Has superior search capabilities. Over 112 million residential and commercial listings, sorts by individual or business name, address, SIC code, Zip code. The nine-digit Zip code feature saves money on direct mailings. First update free. $139.95 (see above).

Phone Search USA. Access to over 80 million residential and business listings. Search by name, phone number, or SIC. Filter search by state/city/zip. Unlimited listing export to databases, word processors, or spreadsheets. $139.95 (see above).

Standard & Poor's Register. The premier guide to American business is combined with the speed and power of CD-ROM. Provides instant access to a wealth of information on America's leading corporations. Over 55,000 company profiles, including names and titles of more than 400,000 corporate executives and brief biographies of 70,000 top officials. Choose a variety of search criteria, generate custom lists and print copies. Lee H. Richards Poor's Register: Standard & Poors, 25 Broadway, New York, NY 10024; 1-800-221-5277.

American Business Information Directories. American Manufacturers Directory. 531,000 manufacturers nationwide. Locate any firm with more than 20 employees by name, SIC code, employee size, and other fields. Information includes name, address, phone, business description, and size. Download 2500 company profiles. More profiles may be purchased. Hardcover 2-volume set and the CD-ROM for $595. *American Big Business Directory* lists 160,000 public and private companies in the United States with more than 100+ employees. The CD lists 431,000 key executives. View, print, or download 2,500 full company profiles. Hardcopy book and CD $595/set. Guides for individual states are also available. ABI 1-800-555-6124, 5711 So. 86th Circle, PO Box 27347, Omaha, NE 68127

CD-ROM—How-To and Job Search

WinWay Resume. Disk or CD-ROM. Runs on Windows 95 and 3.1, and the package comes with a CD-ROM and disk version. This software allows job seekers to connect directly to the Internet. Features automatic résumé and letter writing, contact management, interview simulation, and salary negotiation. Extra features include integrated Internet access—at a click you hook into WinWays Web site, where career experts have identified the best places to look for jobs, post résumés, and obtain career development advice. The site includes hyperlinks to hot job sites. Integrated e-mail automatically converts résumés and cover letters into ASCII or RTF format and then sends them to the potential employer's e-mail address using Microsoft Exchange. Over 12,000 job descriptions. In-depth database outlines the tasks and responsibilities associated with each job title. Allows users to customize résumés/letters and highlight strengths that qualify them. Microsoft Internet Explorer is included free, so users without a current Internet connection can access the Internet and take advantage of on-line career opportunities. It does it all, and you can understand all the steps and features easily. $39.95. The WinWay Corporation, 5431 Auburn Blvd, Suite 398. Sacramento, CA 95841-2801.; 1-800-4-WINWAY; http://www.winway.com.

Executive Advisor. A new interactive do-it-yourself systems for executives seeking a career transition (changing job or career). The program leads and motivates users through eight key steps in the job-search process while engaging them in a series of interactive queries to elicit information for a self-assessment, assisting in résumé design, coaching users on networking and interview techniques, and instructing them on effective negotiation strategies. Mouse driven, it takes approximately eight hours to complete the program. Packaged with workbook. The program provides for 1 hour phone contact with a consultant. $500–$600. Career Interactive 1-800-44-SEARCH.

Adams Job Bank. This is a unique software package for the consumer. So much is included for the price. There are hiring contacts for more than 17,000 companies, listing 20,000 names of hiring executives. Full information for making résumés and cover letters on which one can base one's own. Résumés cover various levels and meet needs of all audiences. Provides listing of agencies and search firms. Also included are more than 100 sample interviews in full-motion video and sound, containing the tough interview questions and the best answers for them. The package includes access to the Adams Online Internet service (listings of current job openings from companies across the country). $40.00. Adams Publishing, 260 Center Street, Holbrook, MA 02343; (617) 767-8100, 800-872-3628.

Adams Job Interview Pro. Multimedia product CD-ROM for Windows/Mac. Watch, listen, and Respond to tough interview questions. Over 300 video clips, 200 audio clips, 300 interview questions, and 3 full interviews show interactions between interviewees and job candidates, 11 short tutorials help master the fine points of interviewing. $21.58. Adams Publishing, 260 Center Street, Holbrook, MA 02343; (617) 767-8100; 800-872-5628.

Daniel Lauber's The Job Finder's Tool-kit. This CD-ROM directs users to on-line job and résumé databases on the Internet. Thousands of directories are described for trade and professional organizations. Contains source lists of hundreds of job hot lines. Lists periodicals where insiders find job postings. Descriptions of thousands of directories of companies, government agencies, and nonprofits that will lead to employment targets. Lists scores of overseas sources where these positions will be found. Help and resources for interviewing, salary negotiations, and résumé and letter advice. $49.95. Planning Communications, 7215 Oak Ave, River Forest, IL 60305; 1-800-829-5220.

Software

Damn Good Ready to Go Resumes. Package contains three disks of résumé templates for Microsoft Word, Macintosh, and WordPerfect for PCs. The 125-page manual includes instructions, hard copy of all the templates, over two dozen sample résumés, a crash course in résumé writing, and a résumé clinic. Each disk contains 287 sharp design layouts: chronological, functional, combination, and accomplishment. $29.95. Ten Speed Press, P.O. Box 7123, Berkeley, CA 94707; 1-800-841-2665.

Designing the Perfect Résumé. Barron's. Chapters cover different aspects of a résumé, showing how to word and design your information to reflect your unique abilities, personality, and occupation. Use your personal computer to create a professional-looking résumé that stands out from the crowd. Includes a comprehensive thirteen-page index of title and wording ideas, offers advice on designing letterheads, cover letters, and making imaginative use of paper and paper color. Emphasizes résumé appearance, including the effective use of fonts, graphic elements, and layout techniques. Provides hundreds of sample résumés created using WordPerfect software. $12.95. Barron's Educational Series, Inc., 250 Wireless Blvd., Happauge, NY 11788; (516) 434-3311 x 208.

Search Select. The electronic version of the *Directory of Executive Recruiters.* Kennedy Publications. See "Newsletters" or "Books/Directories."

Internet Research

Thomas Publishing Places Register of American Manufacturers on World Wide Web. Thomas Publishing Co. is providing free access to an Internet version of *Thomas Register of American Manufacturers,* accessible at http://www.Thomas register.com.

CorpTech on the WWW. http://www.corptech.com offers lots of good stuff for job seekers. Access a free company directory, including all public and most of the largest private companies. Each is linked to new stories and other data; 350 free employment trends reports, updated monthly, by state, region, industry and major product group.

Internet How To

How to Register a Trademark Online. Corporate Creations at http://www.corpcreations.com./cc/ offers forms and can help you through the process electronically. You can e-mail the service with questions and read answers to frequently asked questions. Federal and state fees for trademark application and even business incorporation are modest. Incorporation in Delaware costs $119, and a four-hour trademark search costs $515.

Internet Job Search

Biomedical Market Newsletter, Inc. has released Medical Industry Executive Search Firms & Recruiters, profiling 650 medical search firms. Published quarterly, in print and on disk. Web home page is http://www.bio-medical-market-news.com/bmn.

CareerWeb. This site's mission is to be the leading global one-stop career recruitment service on the Internet. CareerWeb offers advanced technology and remarkable features. It effectively profiles companies to potential job candidates (many links to the companies' home pages for additional information), lists available positions, and prescreens applicants to ensure that companies get only the "best in class" candidates. There is also a CareerWeb library, Career Fitness Test. http://www.cwcb.com

National Association of Female Executive (NAFE). http://www.nafe.com.

CareerPath.com. http://www.careerpath.com allows simultaneous search of job listings from the *Boston Globe,* the *Los Angeles Times,* the *New York Times,* the *San Jose Mercury News,* and the *Washington Post.* As many as 37,000 jobs listed.

The Womans' Center for Employment. http://amsquare.com/america/wcenter/center.html reviews books and articles for women, including employment, industry trends, and the 100 best companies for women.

Job Listings

Newsletters

Consultants News by Kennedy Publications. Kennedy Publications, Templeton Rd, Fitzwilliam, NH 03447; (603) 585-6544 1-800-531-0007.

Executive Recruiter News. Contains articles of interest to those assisting persons to find professional jobs. $187/yr. (See above.)

MIT Enterprise Forum. Cambridge, MA and local chapters in selected cities.

Netshare Job Lead Reports is published twice monthly for the following functions: human resources, management, marketing and sales, finance, and information systems. Half the leads have base salaries of over $100,000. The cost is $110 for 3 months and $175 for 6 months.

Netshare Senior Management Job Lead Report. The key determination of a senior management lead is the reporting relationship—must report to board of directors or inner circle of senior management team. $125 for 3 months and $195 for 6 months. 1-800-241-5642; www.netshare@netshare.com.

Recareering Newsletter. Geared to managers and others who are seeking new career paths. Helps career changers focus their energies and tap a wealth of resources. 12 issues for $59. 655 Rockland Road, Suite 7, Lake Bluffs, IL 60044; (708) 735-1981.

National Association for Female Executive (NAFE). Monthly newsletter. 1-800-321-EXEC, x 200.

Videotapes

Business Networking Made Easy. Candid, live-action answers to the questions of how to ask and what to say at business gatherings, pinpointing break-away and ice-breaking conversation. $29.95. Prescott Group. Distributed by 411 Video Information, P.O. Box 1223, Pebble Beach, CA 93953; (408) 622-9441.

Finding a Job on the Internet. Viewers learn how to post résumés, navigate to and through job search directories, and find bulletin boards on the Internet. Job-Net is an easy-to-use, timely production that contains lively discussions about job-search techniques found on the information superhighway. $79.95. Cambridge Educational, 370 Seventh Avenue, New York, NY 10001; (212) 564-1495 or 1-800-468-4227

Extraordinary Answers to Common Interview Questions. Outlines key principles of effective interviewing and then applies those principles to numerous questions most likely to be asked. $79.95. (See above.)

Audio Tapes

Conversation Power. The first step in becoming a more powerful person. This is a 6-cassette tape program with two recorded learning session per tape. Helpful for candidates, teaching conversation and negotiation skills for interviewing, in coaching programs, and for management development. $39.95. Nightingale Conant, 7300 N. Lehigh Ave., Niles, IL 60714; 1-800-525-9000.

Periodicals

National Business Employment Weekly. 12 weeks for $52.00, and choose one of their guides—Résumés, Interviewing, or Networking—free. NBEW, Dow Jones & Co., P.O. Box 435, Chicopee, MA 01021-9982.

Fast Company. Promoted as the fast-paced, fearless, and fascinating new business magazine that's all about change: How to manage it, how to survive it, and how to initiate some of your own. $29.95 for 12 issues. Fast Company, P.O. Box 52760, Boulder, CO 80322.

SELECTED BOOKS TO HELP YOU EXPLORE YOUR CAREER OPTIONS

Bellman, Geoffrey. *The Consultant's Calling*. San Francisco: Jossey-Bass, Inc., 1990.

Bird, Carolyn. *Second Careers: New Ways to Work After 50*. Boston: Little, Brown & Co., 1992.

Cohen, Lilly, and Dennis Young. *Careers for Dreamers and Doers: A Guide to Management Careers in the Non-Profit Sector*. New York: The Foundation Center, 1989.

Eberts, Marjorie, and Margaret Gisler. *Careers for Culture Lovers and Other Artsy Types*. Lincolnwood, Ill.: NTC Publishing Group, 1992.

Eberts, Marjorie, and Margaret Gisler. *Careers for Bookworms and Other Literary Types*. Lincolnwood, Ill.: NTC Publishing Group, 1992.

Fein, Cheri. *Getting into Money A Career Guide*. New York: Ballantine Books, 1988.

Field, Shelley. *Career Opportunities in the Music Industry*. New York: Facts on File, 1990.

Field, Shelley. *Career Opportunities in the Sports Industry*. New York: Facts on File, 1990.

Field, Shelley. *Career Opportunities in the Theater and Performing Arts*. New York: Facts on File, 1990.

Germer, Jerry. *Country Careers*. New York: John Wiley & Sons, 1993.

Guiley, Rosemary. *Career Opportunities for Writers*. New York: Facts on File, 1990.

Ito, Dee. *Careers in Visual Arts* New York:. McGraw-Hill, 1993. (Includes art direction, film and video, fine arts, graphic design, and photography.)

Jones, Rochell. *The Big Switch: New Careers, New Lives After 35*. New York: McGraw-Hill, 1980.

Kocher, Eric. *International Jobs—Where They Are and How to Get Them*. Reading, Mass.: Addison-Wesley Publishing Co., 1993.

Krannich, Ronald L., and Caryl Rae Krannich. *The Complete Guide to Public Employment*. Manassas, Va.: Impact Publications, 1990.

Lant, Jeffrey. *Consultant's Kit: Establishing and Operating Your Successful Consulting Business*. Cambridge, Mass.: JLA Publications, 1996. (Order from Whole Earth Catalogue, (303) 447-1087.)

Maze, Marilyn. *The Enhanced Guide for Occupational Exploration*, Revised 2nd edition. Indianapolis: JIST Works.

McAdam, Terry W. *The First Complete Guide to Careers in the Nonprofit Sector: Doing Well by Doing Good*. New York: Viking Penguin, 1991. (Paperback)

Mogel, Leonard. *Making It in the Media Professions*. New York: Collier Books, Macmillan Publishing Co., 1993.

Mogel, Leonard. *Making It in Public Relations*. New York: Collier Books, Macmillian Publishing Co., 1993.

Peterson's *Job Opportunities in Internships, Hidden Job Market, Graduate Education* are part of a series of career books. 800-225-0261, 609-243-9111, www.petersons.com. Princeton, NJ, 1997.

Reed, Maxine K., and Robert M. Reed. *Career Opportunities in Television, Cable, and Video*. New York: Facts on File, 1990.

Rubin, Karen. *Flying High in Travel: A Complete Guide to Careers in the Travel Industry*. New York: John Wiley & Sons, 1992.

Taylor, John. *How to Get a Job in Sports*. New York: Collier Books, MacMillan Publishing Co., 1992.

Hoover's Guide to Computer Companies, 2nd ed.Austin, Tex.: Hoover's Business Press, 1996. CD-ROMs on company profiles, electronic master list of major U.S. companies (also regionally), emerging companies, world business, media companies.

Career Advisor Series, Visible Ink Press. Detroit: Gale Research, 1994. You can calibrate the quality and level by looking at one of these in a field you already know; authoritative "spokespersons" who have worked in a field write about it. Volumes on physical sciences, chemistry, engineering, geosciences, paleontology, etc.

"Careers in . . ." Series for bachelor's-level information about careers in advertising, business, computers, environment,international business, journalism, law, marketing, etc. Lincolnwood, Ill.: VGM Career Horizons, 1995.

Major Job Search Research Sources

1. *Business Periodicals Index*. Cumulative subject index of articles appearing in over 170, magazines including trade publications and popular financial periodicals.
2. *Business Index*. Covers 650 publications. This source is more up to date than the *Business Periodicals Index* and is an excellent choice if available.

3. *Reader's Guide to Periodical Literature.* Cumulative index of articles on general subjects in about 130 *popular* magazines.

4. *Directory of Directories.* Lists thousands of business and industrial directories, scientific and professional rosters, and other guides and lists of all kinds. (Please see entry 23.)

5. *Guide to American Directories.* Lists 6,000 directories in virtually all career fields; over 300 major professional, industrial, and mercantile categories arranged by subject, with alphabetical listing at the end.

6. *Dun & Bradstreet Million Dollar Directories.* Excellent source to find names, addresses, phone numbers, officers, annual sales, and number of employees of companies with net worth of $500,000 or more (5 volumes).

7. *Standard & Poor's Register of Corporations, Directors, & Executives.* Contains over 45,000 companies, the majority of which are private, by divisions, with biographies of 72,000 officers, it is similar to Million Dollar Directories, and so it would be useful to use both.

8. *Moody's Industrial Guide.* Describes some 5,000 companies and subsidiaries. Moody's also produces manuals (7) on Banks & Finance, Transportation, Public Utilities, etc. Includes history of the company and its operations, plants, products, and officers.

9. *Standard & Poor's Corporation Records.* Similar to Moody's manuals, but in addition, it has a news section daily. It is a good source for up-to-date information on public companies.

10. *Polk's Bank Directory.* Primary reference listing banks and other financial institutions by address, with geographic indexing, and names and titles of officers.

11. *Thomas' Register of American Manufacturers.* An alphabetical and geographic listing by product and company of over 100,000 manufacturers. Useful in locating manufacturers, both large and small, of many specific products (12 volumes).

12. *F&S Index of Corporations and Industries.* Index to articles appearing in over 750 publications, arranged by company name and Standard Industrial Classification (SIC) code. Best source for locating a summary of news articles on a company or industry. Look at an alphabetized list of SIC codes and select those categories of greatest interest to you. Note the SIC code numbers, then use those numbers to find news articles in that category on company or industry targets.

13. *McCrae's State Industrial Directories.* One for each state. Lists manufacturers alphabetically, geographically, and by SIC code.

14. *Directory of Corporate Affiliations.* Good source to identify subsidiaries . Lists over 4,000 major U.S. corporations, divisions, subsidiaries, and affiliates. Geographic index lists information by city and state.

15. *Encyclopedia of Associations.* Guide to over 16,000 national professional societies, interest groups, and trade associations in almost every field.

16. *Ward's Business Directory.* Ranks over 50,000 public and private companies by sales and industry so that you can see which firms dominate a particular industry.

17. *Consultants and Consulting Organizations Directory.* Excellent source to find names, addresses, phone numbers, officers, annual sales, and number of employees of consulting companies with net worth of $50,000 or more (5 volumes).

18. *Best's Insurance Reports.* Primary reference on insurance companies.

19. *Dun & Bradstreet Business Information Reports.* Most in-depth and comprehensive source of information about private companies.

20. *Annual Reports and Form 10Ks.* Issued by all publicly held corporations. Just phone a company you are interested in and it will send these items. 10Ks provide financial data and brief biographies of principals and their salaries.

21. *Science Citation Index.* Available in libraries. Allows you as a scientist or high-level engineer who has published many articles in refereed journals to find the names of others who have cited your work in the scientific or technical literature. These names then become "contacts" or targets for informational or exponential interviewing and for job interviewing, since they know your work. Useful if you are continuing in the field cited.

22. *Research Centers Directory.* 14th Edition, 1990. A guide to over 11,700 university-related and other nonprofit research organizations, with continuing research programs in agriculture, astronomy or space sciences, behavioral and social science, biological science and ecology, business and economics, computers and mathematics, education, engineering and technology, government and public affairs, humanities and religion, labor and industrial relations, law, medical services, physical and earth sciences, and regional and area studies. Lists address, telephone number, names of directors, research activities and fields, organizational notes, and publications.

23. *Directories in Print.* (formerly the *Directory of Directories*), 7th Edition, 1990. A guide to 10,000 business and industrial directories, professional and scientific rosters, directory databases, and other lists and

guides published in the United States, with subject and title and keyword indexes. Lists name, address, telephone number of the directory publisher, description of director, and price.

24. *Directory of the Association of Orthodox Jewish Scientists.* Over 1,400 Orthodox Jewish scientists engaged in natural, behavioral, and health sciences in the United States and Canada. Gives name, affiliation, home address and phone, business name, address and phone, highest degree earned, and science specialties. (Available to members only.)

25. *Who's Who in Technology.* Over 36,500 engineers, scientists, inventors, and researchers in seven volumes: electronics and computer science; mechanical engineering and materials science; chemistry and plastics; civil engineering; energy and earth science; physics and optics; and biotechnology. Name, title, affiliation, address, personal, education and career data, publications, inventions, field, expertise. Arranged by field, then discipline.

26. *American Men and Women of Science.* Over 125,000 U.S. and Canadian scientists active in the physical, biological, mathematical, computer science, and engineering fields. Name, address, personal and career data, research interest, memberships.

27. *Corporate Technology Directory.* Over 40,000 high-technology firms operating in the United States, including manufacturers of computer hardware and software, photonics, robotics, artificial intelligence, biotechnology, advanced materials, and other high-tech products. Company name, address, phone, key personnel, description of business, sales, number of employees, SIC code. Emphasizes smaller and mid-size companies.

28. *Directory of Research and Technology.* Over 11,275 research facilities, public and private. Organization name, address, phone, key personnel divisions, R&D facilities or activities, research emphasis, number of research staff with discipline.

29. *Research and Development Directory.* Firms that received R&D contracts from the federal government during the preceding fiscal year.

30. *Research and Development Telephone Directory.* Over 4,000 manufacturers, distributors, and suppliers of products and equipment to industrial research facilities.

31. *Research Services Directory.* Over 4,170 commercial laboratories, consultants, firms, data collection and analysis centers, individuals, and facilities in the private sector that conduct contract research in all areas of business, government, humanities, social sciences, and science and technology. Firm name, address, phone, name of chief executive, name and title of contact, staff size, revenues, principal services, clients, and fields of research.

32. *Scientific and Technical Organizations and Agencies Directory.* Over 15,000 national and international organizations and agencies concerned with the physical sciences, engineering, and technology, including associations, computer information services, consulting firms, educational institutions, federal government agencies, libraries and information centers, patent sources, research and development centers, science-technology centers, state academies of science, and government agencies: all fields.

33. *Society of Research Administrators, Membership Directory.* Over 2,200 persons interested in the management of research of all types in all fields. Name, office address and phone, highest degree, area of occupational specialization. Exercise caution here. Reread Sections 3.05, 3.09, 3.10, and 3.12.

Key Periodicals and Other References

Barron's

Business Week

Crain's Business (regional editions)

Conference Board Record

Dun's Review

Forbes

Fortune

Inc.

Money

National Business Employment Weekly (index in first January issue)

Nation's Business

The *New York Times* (with separate index)

The *Wall Street Journal* (with separate index)

Occupational Outlook Handbook

Value Line Investment Survey

Venture

Chamber of Commerce Publications

Telephone Yellow Pages

Trade magazines related to your new field(s)

Authors of articles (newspapers and magazines)

Directory of Toll-Free Telephone Numbers

You can call many large companies toll free if they have a special "800" number—usually for encouraging their customers to place orders to purchase their products or services. Sometimes you can call these numbers and ask to be connected to the person you are trying to reach, who may not be in the sales or marketing department. In many cases, however, there is a "firewall" between sales and other departments or divisions. It's worth a try. If you do not have the Toll-Free Directory, dial 1-800-555-1212, which is the free information operator for toll-free telephone numbers.

CD-ROM Products in Science and Technology

Applied Science and Technology Index. This database, searchable on CD-ROM, indexes 335 periodicals covering engineering, chemistry, applied mathematics, physics, computer science, data processing, and energy-related disciplines, among other subjects. It covers articles from October 1983 to the present. The index can be searched manually for information prior to that date. Most of the articles found in this database are available in the Science and Technology Research Center.

General Science Index. This database, searchable on CD-ROM, indexes 111 periodicals covering astronomy, biology, environment, conservation, health, microbiology, and oceanography, among other subjects. Articles from May 1984 to the present are included.

Business Periodicals Index. The *Business Periodicals Index* (1982–Present) covers articles relating to the chemical industry, petroleum and gas industries, pulp and paper industries, and transportation, among many other subjects.

Science Citation Index. The *Science Citation Index* is a multidisciplinary index to the literature of science, technology, medicine, and related disciplines, including but not limited to agriculture and food technology, astronomy and astrophysics, biochemistry, biology, chemistry, computer science, earth science, electronics, engineering, environmental science, mathematics, medicine, meteorology, and physics. The CD-ROM edition covers 1986 to the present and may be searched by authors, title words, author addresses, cited works, cited authors, and journal titles. *It may not be searched by subject terms.*

Computer Library. The *Computer Library* covers over 100 major computer industry periodicals in the areas of hardware, software, electronic engineering, and communications. The bibliographic information, indexing terms, and summaries nay be searched and displayed for all entries. Each disc covers one year.

Compendex. Compendex is a computer-readable version of *Engineering Index.* It provides abstracts and full bibliographic citations for literature encompassing all fields of engineering. Journal articles, technical reports, monographs, and conference proceedings are included in the database. Yearly disks are available. Either a DIALOG Command Mode for experienced searchers or an Easy Menu Mode may be used.

ICP Software Directory. This database is a directory of industry-specific application software, applications development software, cross-industry application software, and systems software. It includes products for micros, minis, and mainframes. The database may be searched by product name, category, hardware supported, source language, and keyword.

American Business Disk. The *American Business Disk* was compiled from the Yellow Pages of over 4,800 telephone directories covering the entire United States. Companies may be searched by name or SIC code and may be limited by city, state, or Zip code.

Career Search for Windows. Career Search, a database wholesaler, is an expensive subscription service that provides the candidate with access to a database of some 450,000 (as of January 1997) potential employers nationwide. The information comes from many specialized database publishers. Outplacement firms and large corporations are prime purchasers. [Scientific Career Transitions can do a custom search for you on request.]

USE AND MISUSE OF THE INTERNET FOR CAREER TRANSITIONS

Refer to the list of pros, cons, and how-tos in Section 3.12, "Job Search Research." Before going on-line with your search, you should be highly focused. By one estimate, there are some 12,000 Web sites on the subject of job search, employment, or career development. So it's simple, once you enter the massive labyrinth of information and data available online, to be deflected from your course. Instead of a massive list of sites, we present a workable starter list (Tom Denham, Career Development Center, Union College, Schenectady, NY).

A Primer on Basics of an Internet Search

This primer covers the basics of an Internet career search, containing a sample of useful sites. If you need more specific sites, try using some of the search engines listed. The Internet is not a replacement for the more effective job-search strategies mentioned in Sections 3.01 to 3.13. However, it can give you an edge in uncovering more leads and information about employers in this competitive job market A few of our career-change narrators did find leads on-line.

What Is the World Wide Web?

The WWW is just one part of the electronic information exchange known as the Internet. It is called the Web because of its structure. The information is not laid out in neat outline with a beginning and an end. You can "link" to related information in many directions. The type and variety of information on the Web ranges from the practical to the absurd.

How Do I Get to the WWW?

You need a computer, a piece of software known as a browser, a modem to connect your computer to the Internet, and appropriate wiring. Netscape Navigator and Microsoft Explorer are popular current graphical browsers. You do not need an account on any specific computer service to use the Web. Scientific Career Transitions has a website and homepage on-line at http://www.harbornet.com/biz/office/sct001.html, and at http://www.toa-services.net/sct001.html

Navigating with Netscape

There are three different ways to access Web pages:

1. Click on highlighted text or pictures and be automatically transferred to that page.
2. Enter an "address" of a Web page (under Open).
3. Use an existing "bookmark" to take you directly to a site.

Of the buttons at the top of the screen,

Netscape Logo: Displays shooting stars as a connection is made and information is transferred. (Microsoft Explorer baar different displays.)

Progress bar, at bottom right of screen: Displays the percentage of document layout being loaded.

Stop: To halt any page transfer in progress, click here.

Back/Forward/Home: Will move you back to the previous page, or to the next page.

Go: Netscape maintains a history of pages visited (since current log-on) and lists them in the "Go" menu.

Searching

For assistance in finding a particular area or subject on the Web, select either "Internet Search" or "Internet Directory" from the Directory menu or use any other "search engine."

Search: Enter any relevant word or phrase.

Directory: Presents a list of areas (e.g., art, literature, etc.) where more information can be obtained.

Printing: For hard copies, click the Print button.

Quit: End session by selecting Quit from File menu.

Bookmarks

A bookmark provides fast and easy access to favorite Web pages. While perusing pages, you may select Add Bookmark from the Bookmarks menu and the title and location will be stored for you. Selecting the title from the menu will bring that page directly to your screen. You can modify/arrange bookmarks from the menu item View Bookmarks.

Web Addresses (URLs)

Every page on the Web has a unique address, known as a URL (Uniform Resource Locator). If you don't know the URL, you can click on highlighted text to get there. If you know the address for a Web page:

1. From the File menu, select Open Location.
2. Type the address and click the Open button.

Sample Web Sites

(Those with an asterisk are especially helpful. This is by no means a complete list.)

General Search Engines

Yahoo: http://www.yahoo.com

WebCrawler: http://webcrawler.com

Assessment

Kiersey Temperament Sorter: http://sunsite.unc.edu/jembin/mb.pl

Occupational Index by Name: http://www.etc.bc.ca/provdocs/jobfutures/TitleIndex.html

Occupational Outlook Handbook: http://stats.bls.gov/ocohome.htm

Self-Assessment Exercises: http://www.cba.bgsu.edu/class/webclass/nagye/career/

For Undergraduates or Predocs: What Can I Do with a Major In . . .

gopher://gopher.wustl.edu:70/11/WU_Links/Career_Center/majchoose/major/

General Job-Search Web Sites

4Work: http://www.4work.com

*America's Job Bank: http://www.ajb.dni.us/

AmericaNet: http://www.americanet.com/classified

Career Magazine: http://www.careermag.com

*Career Mosaic: http://www.careermosaic.com

CareerNet: http://www.careers.org

*Career Path: http://www.careerpath.com

*Career Resource Home Page: http://www.rpi.edu/dept/cdc/homepage.html

CareerWeb: http://cweb.com

*Catapult: http://www.wm.edu/csrv/career/stualum/index.html

Commercial Sites Index: http://www.directory.net

Employment Edge: http://www.sensemedia.net/employment.edge

EPage Internet Classifieds:
http://epage.com/

E-Span: Interactive Employment Network (IEN): http://www.espan.com

Help Wanted: http://helpwanted.com

Investors Edge: http://irnet.com

*JobCenter: http://www.jobcenter.com

JobList: http://asae.org/jobs/

JOBS Page: http://ageninfo.tamu.edu/jobs.html

*Job Trak: http://www.jobtrak.com

*JobWeb: http://www.jobweb.org

Meta-list of Job Search Resources and Services: http://www.job-hunt.org

*On-Line Career Center: http://www.occ.com

Recruitment Resources:
http://www.ezweb.com/recruit/reference.html

*The Riley Guide: http://www.jobtrak.com/jobguide/

*Union College's CDC Jobs Link: http://apollo.union.edu/career/CDC/CDC.
html

Employer Research

Career Fairs 1: http://www.jobweb.org/cfairsr.htm

*Directory of Over 15,000 Companies: http://www.directory.net/

Employer Directory: http://www.jobweb.org/cgi-dos/eindex.cmd

*Hoover's On-Line: http://www.hoovers.com

International Business Directory: http://www.gnofn.org/whs1/business/Wel-
come.html

*Monster Board: http://www.monster.com

NationJob: http://www.nationjob.com/allcomps

*Thomas Registry of Manufacturers: http://www.thomasregister.com:8000/

US News Online—Career Section: http://www.agtnet.com/usnews/fair/

Graduate & Professional School Sites

Graduate and Professional School Guides: http://www.wm.edu/crsv/ca-
reer/stualum/guidschl.html

Kaplan: http://www.kaplan.com

Peterson's: http://www.petersons.com

Princeton Review: http://www.review.com

Internships

Intern-NET: http://www.vicon.net/~internnet/

Internship Listings Nationwide: http://www.virginia.edu/~career/intern.html

Web Sites by Career Field

Advertising & Public Relations

American Academy of Advertising: http://www.utexas.edu/ftp/coc/adv/AAA/index.html

Arts & Arts Administration

American Council for the Arts: http://www.artsusa.org

American Institute of Architects: http://www.aia.org

ArtSource: http://www.uky.edu/Artsource/artsourcehome.html

World Wide Art Resources: http://wwar.com

Business

BizWeb: http://www.bizweb.com/

Business Job Finder: http://www.cob.ohio-state.edu/dept/fin/osujobs.htm

National Business Employment Weekly: http://www.nbew.com/

Training and Development: http://www.tcm.com/trdev/jobs/

Communications & Media

Corporation for Public Broadcasting JobLine: http://www.cpb.org/jobline/index.html

Electronic Newsstand Homepage: http://gopher.enews.com/

Instructional Technology: http://education.indiana.edu/ist/students/jobs/joblink.html

Journalism-Related Job Openings: http://eb.journ.latech.edu/jobs/jobs_home.html

TV Jobs: http://tvnet.kspace.com/jobs/

Consulting

Andersen Consulting: http://www.ac.com

Jobs in Consulting: http://www.cob.ohio-state.edu/dept/fin/jobs/consult.htm

Education

Chronicle of Higher Education: http://chronicle.merit.edu

Education Jobs Page: http://www.nationjob.com/education

Engineering & Computer Science

Institute of Electrical & Electronics Engineers: http://enginee.ieee.org/usab/DOCUMENTS/EMPLOYMENT/employment.menu.html

National Engineering Search: http://www.nesnet.com/nesnet/

TechCareers: http://www.techweb.com/careers/careers.html

Environment

EnviroLink: http://envirolink.org/orgs/

Environmental Careers Organization: http://www.eco.org/

Outdoor/Environmental Career Guide: http://www.princeton.edu/~rcurtis/careeroe.html

Finance

100 Careers on Wall Street: http://www.globalvillager.com/villager/WSC.html

Careers in Investment Banking: http://www.cob.ohio-state.edu/~fin/jobs/ib.htm

Government & Public Policy

Federal Web Locator: http://www.law.vill.edu/Fed-Agency/fedwebloc.html

FedWorld: http://www.fedworld.gov/

Health & Human Services

Good Works: http://www.essential.org/goodworks/

HospitalWeb: http://neuro-www.mgh.harvard.edu/hospitalweb.nclk

MedSearch: http://www.medsearch.com

International

Guide to Working Overseas: http://www.magi.com/~issi/

Overseas Job Express: http://www.overseasjobs.com/

Asia

Asia Career Web: http://www.rici.com/acw

Asia-Net: http://www.asia-net.com

Personal Southeast Asian Career Connection: http://spider.ucs.indiana.edu/~intlcent/aspire

Australia

Australian Employment Opportunities: http://www.employment.com.au

Europe

Employment Network (People Bank UK): http:www.peoplebank.co.uk

EuroJobs (all of Europe): http://www.demon.co.uk/EuroJobs/

European Job Links: http://cip.physik.uni-wuerzburg.de/jobs.html

Russian and Eastern European Opportunities: http://www.indiana.edu/~reeiweb/indemp.html

North America

Canadian Workweb: http://www.cacee.com/workweb

Law

Deparment of Justice: gopher://justice2.usdoj.gov:70/11/careers

Law Employment Center: http://www.lawjobs.com/

Legal Classifieds: http://www.ljx.com/public/classy/top.html

Research & Science

American Institute of Physics: http://www.aip.org

BioJobs: http://www.infi.net/~ecw/jobs/ecobio.txt

Psych Web: http://www.gasou.edu/psychweb

Physics Around the World: Jobs, Postdocs & Summer: http://tph.tuwien.ac.at/physics-services/physics_other.html

Science Jobnet: http://www.edoc.com/sgnc/Lineads.html

SPIE Web Employment: http://www.spie.org/web/employment

Sales & Marketing: http://www.marketingjobs.com

Sports & Recreation

Club Med: http://www.clubmed.com

Cool Works: http://www.coolworks.com/showme/

HospitalityNet: http://www.hospitalitynet.nl/home.htm

National Sports Jobs Weekly: http://www.sportsjobs.com/

On-Line Sports Career Center: http://www.onlinesports.com/pages/CareerCenter.html

Minority Resources

JobWeb: http://www.jobweb.org/minorities.htm

Resources for Minorites on the Internet: http://www.vjf.com/pub/docs/jobsearch.html

Web Sites by Geographic Region

Boston Job Bank: http://www.bostonjobs.com/

City Net: http://www.city.net/

Job Resources by U.S. Region: http://www.wm.edu/csrv/career/stualum/jregion.html

New York Capital Region Employment Network: http://www.global2000.net/cren

New York State Department of Labor: http://www.labor.state.ny.us/

Relocation Salary Calculator: http://www.homefair.com/homefair/cmr/salcalc.html

RentNet: http://www.rent.net

Internet Discussion Groups

Career Development Network
    E-mail:CARDEVNETREQUEST@WORLD.STD.COM
Capsnet (Cooperative Education and Internships)
    E-mail:LISTSERV@UA1VM.UA.EDU

Publicly Accessible Mailing Lists

http://www.neosoft.com/internet/paml

An Actual On-line Search by a Real Scientist Undergoing a Real Career Transition

Background of the sample on-line search: I have a Ph.D. in experimental condensed matter physics. My dissertation was on the properties of magnetic materials. I am looking for a computer-related job in the Washington, DC area. The date is April 8, 1997.

Search Synopsis:

1. I conducted a search for general career information by connecting to Infoseek, and search for the words "career" and "job." I chose In-

foseek because it is my favorite engine; any other engine would work as well.

2. Infoseek returned a set of pages with links to over a million pages with the words "career" or "job" in them. Near the top of the page is a link labeled "Careers". I selected it and discovered that it leads to pages with links to 3,542 career resources.

3. I selected the link labeled "Career Exploration Links." It took me to the Career and Educational Guidance page at the University of California at Berkeley. The page contains links for occupational information on the following fields: agriculture; architecture; arts & letters; biological sciences; business; computer science; education & social work; engineering; environmental; government; health; industry, trades, & services; international; law; media; nonprofit; physical sciences; and social sciences & humanities.

4. I chose the link for computer science, which took me to a page with various computer career–related links. Two if them looked promising: "Careers in Computers and Engineering" (an on-line article) and "Computer Scientists and System Analysts" (from the 1996–97 edition of the *Occupational Outlook Handbook*). I selected the link to the article and read it. I then went back to the page of computer-related links and selected the other interesting link and read the page from the *Occupational Outlook Handbook*.

5. Armed with information about careers in the field of computers, I decided to look for jobs, so I went back to the Infoseek "Careers" page and selected the link to "CareerMosaic" listed as a "[f]ull service career site for job seekers and employers."

6. Once in CareerMosaic, I selected the link to the J.O.B.S., where I searched for jobs in Washington, D.C., related to the words "Computer" and "Network." The query resulted in seventy matches, which are listed on a page as links. I saw four job titles from KPMG Peat Marwick LLP, AGB, and William M. Mercer that looked promising, so I checked them out. After reading the job descriptions, I was attracted to the jobs from KPMG Peat Marwick, LLP.

7. I then repeated my search for jobs related to "Computer" and "Network" in Virginia and Maryland, with similar results.

8. Since I was interested in a job being offered by KPMG Peat Marwick, LLP, but knew nothing about the company, I checked to see if the company was listed on the CareerMosaic"Employers K-O" page. It was listed as a link to "KPMG." When I selected the link to

KPMG, it took me to the company's home page, which gave me some background on the company. From there I selected a link to a page that listed some recent business activities of the company. These I compared with my own interests and qualifications so that I could begin to sculpt a biography or a résumé.

9. If I wished to gather more information about the company, I would frame a one-page biography and send it to appropriate individuals at KPMG that I identified from the firm's corporate annual report, Standard & Poor's, Corptech Directory, or additional online searches. I would ask for an informational interview and seek to engage a technical professional at this company (or preferably others like it).

10. Subsequently, if I wished to apply for a job at KPMG, I would frame and polish a résumé based upon what I had learned from each of the steps above, especially the informational interviews. I would include in the résumé those experiences and skills that I had learned that KPMG (or its competitors) want.

11. I stopped the on-line search at this point because I felt that I knew enough about the jobs being offered and the company so that when ready, I could write a very good biography, résumé, and cover letter.

Infoseek is a registered trademark of Infoseek Corporation. CareerMosaic is a registered trademark of Bernard Hodes Advertising, Inc.

INDEX

Dedication

My mother, Aileen Phillips, was a source of great energy and optimism. My father, Sol Paul, exemplified practical wisdom and entrepreneurial talent. From both, I learned the value of communications . . . the written and spoken word.

I dedicate this book to their memory.

Celia Paul
New York, August 1997

"Your father has been the sunshine of my life", my mother told me as she was dying. Both Emma and Mike brought sunshine to many lives, as well as compassion, grit, and humor. My children, Daniel and Lisa, like Mark Twain between the ages of fifteen to twenty five, are "surprised at how much the old man has learned in just ten short years". My grandchildren, Jascha and Tanya, the result of wonderful upbringing, are living legacies. My wife, who after twelve years of marriage still treats me as if I were her equal, is the sunshine of my life. I am part of all of them—and so is this book.

Stephen Rosen
New York, August 1997

....

ACKNOWLEDGMENTS

....

This is the best definition of intelligence we know: the ability to make other people feel good.

The Alfred P. Sloan Foundation, in its letter announcing the grant to our nonprofit organization (Science & Technology Advisory Board) that made this book possible, wrote: "There is a great deal of anguish out there among young scientists who find themselves, after up to ten years of graduate study, facing an extraordinary chilly job market for their highly-honed skills. We believe that many of them will find the perspectives and insights in your proposed book to be of great value to their career choices . . . [and it] . . . will be an important contribution to a field that is currently fallow."

Our heartfelt thanks to Ralph Gomory, Michael Teitelbaum, Frank Mayadas, and their colleagues at Sloan for their crucial support, healthy skepticism, and confidence in this project when most needed. We strived to make the book's features and benefits worthy of their trust, and to improve the lives of our readers.

Some time ago, we suggested to the publisher of *DOS for Dummies*, *Sex For Dummies*, etc. that it publish a series of books for intelligent people (such as *Careers for Smarties*, *Jobs For Einsteins*, etc.). We were told: "The market is too small. Not enough intellectuals buy self-help books. Someone tried it once and lost money."

This book, written for educated people, was initiated and commissioned by Dr. Frank Cynar, acquisitions editor at Academic Press, who was also trained as a scientist. His good nature, perseverance, diplomacy, and eagerness to keep us and the project on target was invaluable. The enthusiasm of the team at Academic Press, Bob Donegan, Chuck Glaser, Heidi Kiki Forsythe, and Chrysanne Lowe, was contagious.

"When young, I admired clever people; now that I am old, I admire kind people." These words of Rabbi Abraham Joshua Heschel capture our admiration for the many other scientists, engineers, physicians, entrepreneurs, and technical professionals, both kind and clever, who consented to be interviewed—some sixty in all. Those whom we can thank by name are Kevin Aylesworth, Joseph Atick, David Bachrach, Vernon Ehlers, Peter Eisenberg, Peter Fiske, David Fox, Donna Ferrandino, Robert Frosch, Boyd Hunter, Lech Kalembka, Randy Krauss, Tom Lehrer, Walter Massey, Justin McCarthy, Nathan Myrhvold, David Nash, Ken Rind, David Z. Robinson, Maxine Rockoff, Robert Scott Root-Bernstein, Jack Stewart, Byron Wachsman, Harding Willinger, and a host of émigré scientists, including Vladimir Minden, Victor Mishkevich, Mark Yankelevich, Alla Raykin, and Moses Fayngold.

Many friends and colleagues made special efforts to read and critique all or part of the manuscript. Among these are Kevin Aylesworth, Warren Bennis, Don Berets, Eli Ginzberg, William Golden, Rena Grossman, Roald Hoffmann, Bob Levinson, Elliot Mordkowitz, Bonnie Oglensky, Barbara Paladino, Alan Pickman, David and Nan Robinson, David Rottman, and Dan White. Thank you for saving us from excess.

Louis Grossi is the best assistant any authors could hope for: his keen memory and excellent judgment saved the day many times. Thanks to Victoria McGovern for help in interviewing young professionals.

We gratefully acknowledge permission to quote or use materials from the following: Deborah Arron (*What Can You Do with a Law Degree?*); Randy Krauss (*The Physiologist* 39, Nov. 5, 1996); Edward R. Tufte (*The Visual Display of Quantitative Information*), Louis Weber (*How Thing Work*), Thomas Lupo (Standard & Poor's); Martin E. P. Seligman (*What You Can Change and What You Can't*); Charles Teeter (Anderson Consulting); The National Museum and the Royal Library, National Library of Sweden, Stockholm; The Victoria and Albert Museum, London; the Workers' Museum, Copenhagen; Science Museum, London; Ronnell's Antikvariat, Stockholm; Cordon Art-Baarn-Holland for the M. C. Escher Foundation; Roger Friedman (Antiquarian Books); and Statens Museum for Kunst, Copenhagen.

About the Authors

Stephen Rosen

Trained in theoretical physics, with a specialty in high-energy astrophysics and cosmic radiation, Dr. Rosen's research articles have appeared in *Nature, Physical Review, Il Nuovo Cimento*, and other science journals. He has held joint appointments at the Institut d'Astrophysiques in Paris, the Centre d'Etude Nucleaire de Saclay, and was a Senior Professional Staff member in science policy at the Hudson Institute. He is the author of three books: *Future Facts* (1974), *Weathering* (1979), and *Cosmic Ray Origin Theories* (1968).

In 1990, he founded Scientific Career Transitions, a non-profit program that pioneered the development of systematic methods, internet access, and specialized techniques for guiding high-functioning professionals (including east European refugee scientists) to successful resolutions of their career dilemmas. Supported in part by foundations, including the Alfred P. Sloan Foundation, several thousand participants have benefitted from the program.

Articles by or about the program have appeared in *The Wall Street Journal, Science, The Scientist, The New York Times, The Sciences, National Business Employment Weekly, BioTechnology*, on the Internet and the World Wide Web. He has spoken on career development at MIT's annual Alumni Homecoming, the annual meetings for the American Association for the Advancement of Science, and the International Association of Career Management Professionals.

Celia Paul

Celia Paul is the founder and president of the career management firm Celia Paul Associates, which specializes in career mobility planning for high-level professionals, particularly attorneys, MBAs, financial executives, and physicians. Since its inception in 1980, the firm has guided over two thousand credentialed men and women to satisfying careers.

Author of articles in professional and general publications, Celia Paul is cited as an expert on career transitions for doctors in the AMA book *Leaving the Bedside*, and serves as a referral source to the AMA Physician Career Resource Service. Her work with professional clients has been prominently featured in, among others: *Medical Economics* (1990), *The New York Times* (1989), *Physician Executive* (1995), *American Medical Association News* (1994), and *The Wall Street Journal* (1995).

She is a regular speaker at Harvard and Duquesne Law Schools, the New York State Medical Association, the New York Bar Association, Women's Bar Association, the New York County Bar, and produces group workshops, for among others, Chemical Bank and Chase Manhattan.

Evaluate this Book!

Dear Reader:

We are eager to have your comments to help in planning the next edition of "Career Renewal", and other possible career books for professionals. Please snail-mail, photocopy and fax, or e-mail to us, the following information, as it appears below, or informally. We welcome your reactions, feedback, and suggestions.

Our coordinates: Stephen Rosen or Celia Paul, Scientific Career Transitions or Celia Paul Associates, 1776 Broadway, Suite 1806, New York, NY 10019-2002, Tel: 212-397-1021; Fax: 212-397-1022; E: srosenc@ix.netcom.com or cpaul001@counsel.com Thanks.

Your view of "Career Renewal"

	4 Great	3 Good	2 OK	1 Needs Work
Usefulness of Book's Content				
Section 1				
Section 2				
Section 3				
Appendix 4				
Level of Detail, Specificity				
Section 1				
Section 2				
Section 3				
Appendix 4				
Visuals/Graphics/Art				

What was most valuable to you about this book? _____

_____

What was least valuable? _____

_____

What would you like to see in future editions? _____

_____

What specialized career book(s) would you welcome? _____

_____

How did you hear about "Career Renewal"? _____

Do you have a career transition or transformation story of interest to our readers? ____

(If we use it with your permission, you'll receive a free copy of our next edition.)

Other comments? _____

_____